JOHNNY
CASH

AND THE PARADOX
OF AMERICAN
IDENTITY

Profiles in Popular Music
Glenn Gass and Jeffrey Magee, editors

JOHNNY CASH

AND THE PARADOX
OF AMERICAN
IDENTITY

LEIGH H. EDWARDS

Indiana University Press

Bloomington • Indianapolis

This book is a
publication of

Indiana
University
Press
601 North
Morton Street
Bloomington, IN
47404-3797 USA

http://iupress.indiana.edu

Telephone orders
800-842-6796

Fax orders
812-855-7931

Orders by e-mail
iuporder@indiana.edu

The paper used in this
publication meets the minimum
requirements of American National
Standard for Information Sciences—
Permanence of Paper for Printed
Library Materials, ANSI Z
39.48-1984.

Manufactured in the
United States of America

Library of Congress
Cataloging-in-Publication Data

Edwards, Leigh H., date
Johnny Cash and the paradox of
American identity / Leigh H. Edwards.
p. cm.
Includes bibliographical references and index.
ISBN 978-0-253-35292-7 (cloth : alk. paper) — ISBN
978-0-253-22061-5 (pbk. : alk. paper)
1. Cash, Johnny—Criticism and interpretation.
2. Country music—History and criticism.
3. Country musicians—United States.
I. Title.
ML420.C265E48 2009
781.642092—dc22
2008033364

1 2 3 4 5 14 13 12 11 10 09

for my family

Contents

Acknowledgments

During the course of writing this book, I had the pleasure of conferring with fellow travelers who believe, like me, in the power and importance of popular culture and popular music. First and foremost, many thanks, of course, to all the good people at Indiana University Press, especially Jane Behnken. When I made my pilgrimage to the Country Music Foundation archives at the Country Music Hall of Fame and Museum, the historian John Rumble was incredibly gracious, helping me track down a wealth of Johnny Cash materials.

Fellow panelists and conference-goers were receptive and enlightening in their feedback as I presented this research at academic conferences over several years. I wish to thank, in particular, the popular music scholars who were kind enough to speak on the Johnny Cash panel I organized for the American Studies Association in 2004: Cecelia Tichi, David Sanjek, and Barry Shank. At the International Association for the Study of Popular Music, U.S. Branch events, Cynthia Fuchs was especially incisive in her feedback, as she has been as my editor at *PopMatters* (the online journal of cultural criticism), where she has allowed me to write numerous articles about Cash and country music. I have also presented from this research at the Popular Culture Association, the Popular Culture/American Culture Association in the South, the Southern American Studies Association and Living Blues Symposium, the Conference on Literature and Film, the American Men's Studies Association, and the Film and History League of the American Historical Association conferences.

I was honored to have parts of my introduction, and chapter 1, appear as an article in the edited collection *Literary Cash: Writings Inspired by the Legendary Johnny Cash* (Batchelor, 2006). I was inspired by the enthusiasm of editor Bob Batchelor for the collection, and by the wonderful academic essays, literary essays, and short stories contributed by a lively group of writers. They, like me, believe that Johnny Cash has something to tell us about American culture.

I am very appreciative of the early training I received in American studies and cultural studies from my Ph.D. committee in English at the University of Pennsylvania: Betsy Erkkila (now at Northwestern University), Nancy Bentley, Christopher Looby (now at the University of California, Los Angeles), and Eric Cheyfitz (now at Cornell University), as well as from others at Penn, such as Peter Stallybrass, Herman Beavers, and Jim English. I am also grateful for my undergraduate training in English at Duke University, where I benefited from being an editorial assistant at *American Literature* under Cathy Davidson and studying with Toril Moi, Annabel Patterson, Tom Ferraro, and Deborah Pope. Although this book is entirely separate from the dissertation I wrote on American literature, my literary studies training gave me the foundation to prepare for my subsequent work.

I wish to thank my colleagues in the English department at Florida State University (FSU), especially Andrew Epstein and Darryl Dickson-Carr (now at Southern Methodist University), who have been truly exemplary colleagues. A special thanks to Denise Von Glahn and Michael Broyles, music colleagues at FSU, who have been extremely supportive of this research from the beginning and who have been very generous in their feedback. Many thanks also to a number of FSU colleagues who have offered their continued support, including my English colleagues Kathi Yancey, Nancy Warren, Meegan Kennedy, Jerrilyn Mc-Gregory, David Kirby, Barbara Hamby, Mark Winegardner, Robert Olen Butler, Rip Lhamon, Fred Standley, Ann Mikkelsen (now at Vanderbilt University), Chris Shinn, Amit Rai, fellow rockabilly fans Ned Stuckey-French, Elizabeth Stuckey-French, and Tim Parrish, fellow bluegrass fans David Vann and David Johnson, and colleagues from across the university, especially Jennifer Proffitt, Vall Richard, and Bev Bower. My students in my popular culture classes at FSU have been quite enthusiastic about this book, which gave me added motivation.

I must thank my bluegrass guitar teacher, Mickey Abraham, and fellow lesson buddy Nancy Flores. Also much appreciation to friends who gamely went to concerts with me, featuring everyone from Rosanne Cash to Kris Kristofferson to Dolly Parton, or who happily talked with me about the music and my project, especially Tatianna Flores, James Mitchell, Renee Bergland, Katie Conrad,

Vickie E. Lake, Maria Fernandez, Monica Hurdal, Kim Hinckley, Karen Barnett, Lori DiGuglielmo, and my cousin Allison Carothers and her daughters Brittney Carothers Harvey and JuliaAnne Carothers Harvey.

A special thanks to my dear Chris Goff, Brian Ammons, and Patricia Thomas for their steadfast support and feedback along the way. Writing this book was like coming home for me in some ways, digging into a Southern regional culture, thinking through my own family's experience. As soon as I did return home, I knew I would write a book like this one. As an eighth-generation Floridian from Tallahassee, I had the pleasure of asking my father, Steve Edwards, to explain what he remembered about Southern rural music growing up in Quincy, Florida, and to tell me about his brother, Ryan Edwards, playing piano on an old Jimmy Dean record. Also, my deep thanks and love to my mother, Helen Carothers Edwards, and my sister, Ashley Carothers Edwards, for their support, encouragement, and willingness to listen to still more Johnny Cash or June Carter Cash songs. I also wish to honor my extended family, including those who have gone before us, from my grandfather, Milton Washington Carothers, who passed on a love of education and who makes me, following my father, the third generation of my immediate family to be a professor at FSU, to the youngest ones coming along now. They include Milton Washington Carothers, Julia Stover Carothers, Charles Graham Carothers, NancyAnne Carothers, Charles Graham Carothers Jr., Allison Carothers and her family, Melissa Anne Carothers Moon and her family, Milton Stover Carothers, Sarah Jane Carothers, Milton Washington Carothers II, Irene Ryan, Harley Ryan, Theresa Gray and the Ethel Edwards Loper family, and the Pat Edwards and the Ryan Edwards families. I give thanks for all the roots and branches.

JOHNNY CASH

AND THE PARADOX
OF AMERICAN
IDENTITY

INTRODUCTION
Cash as Contradiction

Johnny Cash's death in September 2003 prompted an intense emotional response from a vast number of artists and fan communities worldwide. Such a large-scale emotional investment in a popular artist calls for an inquiry into Cash's cultural impact and legacy, and how his image, body of work, and public reception reflect larger issues in American popular culture.[1] Although there is healthy scholarly interest in Cash, there are few academic studies of the man thus far, and there is a clear need to analyze the entire scope of his media image and career. Most discussions focus on one aspect of his work or appear in more general works on country music, where he is not the sole focus.[2] The majority of the publications on Cash have been popular biographies and collections of music journalism.[3] Moving beyond retrospectives, this is an analysis of cultural meaning and social construction that places him in the context of cultural theory and the history of American thought.[4] Cash's public image and work illuminate important social questions, including the status of authenticity in popular music and the social construction of identity categories such as race and masculinity in popular culture.

From rockabilly rebel to country music's elder statesman, Johnny Cash embodied paradoxical or contradictory images. There was no one single Cash. He was always multiple, changing, inconsistent. He was the drugged rock star trashing hotel rooms and the devout Christian touring with Billy Graham. He was the Man in Black, a progressive voice for the disenfranchised, but also the Southern patriarch performing at Nixon's White House. He was the outlaw hillbilly thug, and he was the establishment. His most famous image has him snarling and flipping off the camera at his 1969 San Quentin concert, where he almost sparked a prison riot. Yet another has him pointing reproachfully to a tattered American flag on his album cover for *Ragged Old Flag* (1974), which features an anti–flag burning title song.

My inquiry into Cash's iconography, then, begins with—indeed repeats—a simple observation: popular culture images of him consistently, and even obsessively, refer to him as a contradiction. For the most famous example, we need look no further than Kris Kristofferson's tribute song, "The Pilgrim; Chapter 33" (dedicated to Cash and Kristofferson's other musical heroes). There, Cash the man becomes a mythological figure, appearing as the troublemaker, stoned musician, and preacher-prophet. Merging fact and fiction, Cash becomes the lonely, empathetic, fallen pilgrim searching for redemption. Kristofferson's lyrics point to the dual roles Cash played—both the sacred and the profane. He is both prophet and "pusher," and he is a "walkin' contradiction" who is "partly truth and partly fiction." Significantly, his searching entails failure as he takes "ev'ry wrong direction on his lonely way back home."[5] This depiction is typical, in that it fetishizes Cash for being a paradox. I wish to explore an important question: What is the allure of this image of Cash as a walking contradiction, and what is its cultural work?

I argue that Cash's corpus and image illuminate key foundational contradictions in the history of American thought, particularly through his fraught constructions of a Southern white working-class masculinity. Cash's persona brings disparate or even opposed ideologies into close, symbiotic relationship with one another. This artist's iconic image in fact depends on his ability to stage the idea of irresolvable ambivalence—to illuminate how that model of cultural ambivalence, what we might call a "both/and" idea, is an important paradigm for U.S. popular music and for American identity. Cash embodied the tensions in the American character without resolving them. And, in so doing, he encouraged listeners to engage with our most fundamental national paradoxes, from the violence of a free democracy founded on slavery to the whipsaw between individual rights and national identity. Cash once said to an audience, "I thank God for freedoms we've got in this country. I cherish them and treasure them—even the right to burn the flag." As some booed, he went on, "We also got the right to bear arms, and if you burn my flag, I'll shoot you. But I'll shoot you with a lot of love, like a good American."[6] At times, Cash sounded like both sides of the Toby Keith–Dixie Chicks debate over the role of patriotism and social protest in popular music. But what he does is to see the irony in, and push adamantly against, false logic and false opposition, in this case involving the vagaries of "natural rights," where one person's idea of individual freedom can restrict another's. His comment is not simply perverse; it also limns American tautologies.

Cash illuminates key issues at the crossroads of American studies and popular music studies because he is an exemplary case study for popular music's projections of authenticity and country music's formulations of race, gender, and a Southern working-class culture.[7] Cash builds his version of authenticity through equivocating models of Southern white working-class masculinity, thus elucidating changing paradigms of authenticity. Moreover, his conceptual rubric of irresolvable contradictions becomes part of his projection of authenticity. Through this dynamic, he represents major social tensions in their intricacy, framing them as troubling, true, and distinctively American. His work helps explicate popular music's role in society because what the music does here is engage emotionally with such ideological issues. Cash also offers models for thinking about how popular culture can question traditional categorical binaries (tradition versus social change, establishment versus anti-authoritarian, conservative versus progressive, patriot versus traitor, morally righteous versus fallen, pure versus impure). His work exposes the problems with such rigid categories, whether political or musical.

In this book, the trope of contradiction is analyzed for how it permeates the social construction of Cash. Historicized textual analysis is combined with a discussion of relevant theoretical issues in popular music, American, and media studies. Drawing on the interdisciplinary approaches of those fields, my concern is with interrogating how this popular culture both shapes and reflects U.S. ideologies. The methodology involves literary studies techniques of textual analysis and close reading, as well as the discipline's historicist approaches that focus on text and context, placing the analysis of a text in relation to relevant historical contexts (whether social history or cultural history). As Barbara Ching has argued, literary criticism and cultural theory are particularly useful disciplines for discussing country music because of the genre's heavy focus on lyrics and characterizations.[8] My goal is to offer what Clifford Geertz would term a "thick description" of the functions and cultural contexts of these texts.[9] Although the field of popular music studies is discussed, this is not a work of musicology or ethnomusicology, although an analysis of the music itself is integrated wherever possible. The central concern is Cash's media image and the ideologies in his work, which are addressed through a combination of approaches used in literary studies and American studies.

My synthesis of several methodological approaches has much in common with recent scholarship on country music and in popular music studies, a deeply multidisciplinary field that supports a number of different techniques of inquiry. Charles Wolfe has pointed out that, although the first generation of scholarship about country music (dating from Bill C. Malone's still foundational history, *Country Music U.S.A.* [1968]) emerged from history, literature, and folklore, a new generation of scholarship since the 1990s brings the increasingly important interdisciplinary academic specialties of gender studies and media studies to bear on the genre.[10] Joining an emerging, critical conversation about gender in country music, this book also references larger conversations about the evolution of masculinity in the U.S. and draws on the work of masculinities researchers such as R. W. Connell and Michael Kimmel. As detailed in later chapters, Cash's texts often examine the strategies that his working-class heroes use for adapting to or resisting dominant cultural ideals of masculinity.

The objects of study include Cash's own self-presentation, including his two autobiographies and his lyrics, music, liner notes, interviews, and the marketing of his iconographic Man in Black image. Also addressed is how others have depicted him in biographies, in first wife Vivian Cash's posthumous publication of his letters to her, in documentaries and music journalism, in the producer Rick Rubin's marketing of him for the American Recordings label, as well as in the *Walk the Line* biopic and his fan club materials in the archives at the Country Music Foundation in Nashville.[11] Because his autobiographical and biographical narratives have received such wide circulation, they are a part of his public image. I include extensive discussion of Cash's signature songs (from "I Walk the Line" to "Folsom Prison Blues") and his performances and visual texts. I address his most notable music videos in particular, including Mark Romanek's award-winning video for the song "Hurt" (2002) and the identity politics it references in Cash's oeuvre concerning white–American Indian race relations. I also examine the video for "Delia's Gone" (1994), which sparked an intense controversy over gender politics and folk traditions such as murder ballads.[12]

My discussion of Cash includes an analysis of all these elements, from his projections of identity to his musical output, the fact and the fiction, the biography and the mythology, because they all contribute to creating Cash's cultural image. Joli Jensen, in her analysis of Patsy Cline's iconography, notes that such star figures are polysemic—there is no "true" or "real" version of the artist, only complex layers of representation.[13] Similarly, in his discussion of using musical codes for analyzing the meanings and effects of popular music, the musicologist David Brackett describes how the popular musicians are themselves polyvalent signs. In one aspect of his analysis, Brackett catalogues "the *topoi* central to the collection of recordings, images, and biographical details known as 'Hank Williams.'"[14] Brackett goes on to show how myths about Williams influence the affect produced by his recordings and the connotations of memory and history, including genre expectations, that individuals bring to the experience of listening to him.

Although Cash's model of "both/and"—in which he presents opposed ideas and leaves them unresolved or insists on the validity of both sides of a binary—is not a radical critique of dominant U.S. culture, it is not simply a model of liberal pluralism either, because it does not take dissension and turn it into consensus (as the critic Sacvan Bercovitch has famously noted of American liberalism).[15] Rather, Cash's oeuvre incorporates a struggle over meaning as part of his identity construction, and as a model for authenticity, because it insists on presenting the incongruities themselves and eschews easy resolution. His texts participate in and illuminate the dominant culture's anxieties, but they remain stubborn and disjunctive. As such, his work illuminates some of the precise ways in which popular culture is a site of negotiation and struggle and not simply a playground for escapism or for only corporate agendas. Here, I side with critics using a neo-Gramscian approach to argue that, although the culture industries produce commercial culture—and thus market forces control popular culture—they do not completely control the range of meanings that consumers might derive from that culture, however limited the audience's agency is.[16] As George Lipsitz helpfully describes, popular music texts are commodities and at the same time also complex collective expressions and spaces for creating identity, sites where audiences can create meaningful connections to the past.[17] In the literary studies model that I employ, I frame how Cash's work reflects and helps shape larger cultural ideas and norms, and although I do note how he has been marketed and how he presents his persona in his autobiographies, I am not arguing about authorial intention or auteurism. My focus, instead, is on these texts and their multiple significations.

Though I concentrate primarily on text and context, I do note the importance of questions of production and consumption. The media studies critic Julie D'Acci notes the interrelation of four principal spheres involved in making cultural meaning: production, text, consumption, and socio-historical context.[18] In a model more specifically adapted to case studies of country music stars, Jensen, in her discussion of Patsy Cline, argues that the popular image of any artist is the result of the interplay of forces of production (the media), consumption (the audience), and the aesthetic (the work itself).[19] Similarly, popular music studies in general have looked at how individual listening communities shape and circulate mythologies about musicians as part of their process of creating meaning and identity in relation to popular music.[20] A full account of production and reception dynamics in Cash's case is beyond the scope of this book, and I do not attempt to provide his full reception history. However, I do attend to some key issues involving the political economy of the Nashville country music industry (as part of the popular music industry controlled by five major multinational corporations) and Cash's specific record labels such as Columbia Records, now owned by parent company Sony BMG, which controls more than a quarter of the current market share for popular music albums.[21] I discuss general issues of media and audience reception, examining, for example, the group that protested the use of Cash's image at the 2004 Republican National Convention in New York. I analyze the protesters' interpretation of "Johnny Cash" as a text and the purposes he served for them. I side theoretically with the "active consumption" approaches advocated by the critics Simon Frith and John Storey (as opposed to Theodor Adorno's classic account of popular music as a standardized form that promotes passivity in listeners).[22] In this case of reception, I suggest that what Stuart Hall calls the "emotional realism" of popular music does not encourage listeners into passive consumption but rather into active contemplation of the vexed ideas that make up the American character.[23]

The protest at the Republican National Convention provides a particularly spectacular example of opposing responses to Cash's political complexity. Convention organizers held a reception, sponsored by the American Gas Association, honoring Lamar Alexander and Cash at Sotheby's to coincide with the Cash memorabilia auction there after his death (the auction, necessitated by estate taxes, earned more than four million dollars, triple what was expected). Student Erin Siegal organized a protest, replete with six hundred fans wearing black, pompadours, and guitars, all insisting that Cash's populist message could not be co-opted by the Republican Party.[24] What does "Johnny Cash" symbolize, why would both the Left and the Right want to claim him, and why does he need defending? As the story made national news and Republican organizers defended their right to celebrate Cash, Cash's family responded to the controversy only by saying that he did not have an official party affiliation.[25] Crucial here, and explored further in later chapters, is that Cash's cultural image allows enough equivocation for both sides to believe that they can claim him. While other country stars have also been charged with employing opportunistic politics (the journalist Chris Willman has, for example, termed both Cash and Merle Haggard "omnipoliticians")[26] or have drawn audiences to diverse messages, Cash's dynamic of contradiction is distinctive, more integral to his media image, and more wide-reaching.

There is obvious manipulation involved in the notion that Cash can play to both sides of the aisle. Cash and his record companies have used his conflicted persona to rake in millions. However, Cash's engagement with contradiction also exceeds the logic of the market, because it resonates beyond its status as a commodity practice. He draws out the absurdities inherent in U.S. paradoxes, as evidenced in his flag comment. If he is "authentic" because he embodies competing tendencies, then Johnny Cash does the cultural work of putting long-running sociopolitical incongruities in U.S. culture on the table, displaying ideological problems without resolving them. Cash can both enact the generative energy of cultural mixing as well as the sense of ambivalence and complication that some of his boundary crossings provoke.

In the chapters that follow, as I trace Cash's trope of contradiction through different historical moments and thematic nodes, I detail how it becomes linked to American identity and to basic issues in the history of American thought. In telling examples of how journalists and fellow artists often characterize Cash by using U.S. national symbols, Kristofferson christened Cash "Abe Lincoln" with a "dark, wild streak," and the music journalist Brian Mansfield has compared him to Walt Whitman in order to make sense of him as a large, democratic, national figure who can contain multitudes.[27] Music journalist Anthony DeCurtis described Cash's enduring appeal: "When you think about classic American heroes, you often think about a kind of loner brooding figure with inner demons but still somebody who takes on great social, cultural and artistic burdens and redeems both himself and the people who believe in him, and Johnny Cash just fits that bill perfectly."[28] These linkages are appropriate for an artist who released a wealth of American-themed material that envisions a conflicted culture. Among his hundreds of albums released, he made flag-waving tributes to the nation, such as *America: A 200-Year Salute in Story and Song* (1972) (which features him reading Lincoln's Gettysburg Address) and *From Sea to Shining Sea* (1967). Yet he also recorded major, iconographic protest albums, most famously *Man in Black* (1971), where the title song established him as the black-draped protest figure speaking on behalf of the poor, the disenfranchised, prisoners, Vietnam protesters, and victims of war. Similarly he released social justice protest pieces such as the proletarian concept album *Blood, Sweat and Tears* (1963), and the pro–American Indian rights *Bitter Tears: Ballads of the American Indian* (1964).

As I trace such multiple levels of Cash's image, I argue that his legacy is most importantly about his ability to slip out of boxes or categories, to make us look at discordances without papering over them, to express radical ambiguity that insists on painful complexity.

Contradiction and Country Music

To provide a critical framework for my analysis in the following chapters, I use cultural theory here to specify what the issue of contradiction involves, demonstrating how it manifests itself in the country music genre and how Cash offers a distinctive example. Providing support for my subsequent discussions, I offer an overview of Cash's biography and his career arc for how they illuminate this trope of contradiction and patterns in Southern working-class masculinity.

Johnny Cash is obviously not unique in addressing contradictions in American thought through popular music. Scholars have observed the relevance of paradox in popular music, most notably in two of Cash's peer artists: Elvis Presley and Bob Dylan. Greil Marcus, in his landmark study, detailed how key rock 'n' roll artists like Elvis articulate the equivocations of American democracy, between separation and community, rebellion and conformity, and how they consequently fight over the mythology that is American identity.[29] Timothy Parrish has argued that artists such as Elvis reveal the ongoing influence of American pragmatism by embodying American paradoxes of self-creation.[30] The cultural theorist Barry Shank has argued eloquently for how Bob Dylan in the 1960s embodies the countervailing search for both autonomy and authenticity in American culture. But as Shank notes, each artist is specific in how he or she engages with American problems in distinct socio-historical contexts, yielding insights particular to their work,[31] and my analysis addresses this distinctiveness and particularity for Cash.

Ideas of contradiction and cultural ambivalence are significant issues in American thought, whether stemming from capitalism and class struggle or the legacy of race slavery and the dispossession of the American Indians from their land. Popular culture both shapes and reflects understandings of these problems; because it is a primary cultural space for mediating on these issues, it has a significant role in discursive battles over meaning. Stuart Hall argues that popular culture is a site where "collective social understandings are created" and texts are involved in a competitive "politics of signification" to normalize their worldviews for audiences.[32] Hall's cultural studies model (growing out of Marxist-derived definitions of ideology) is helpful for understanding this issue of contradiction, as it asserts that cultural texts and practices offer competing ideological significations of the world that engage in conflict and negotiation. A clear example is when a dominant group tries to make its interests seem universal—for instance, through the normalizing of bourgeois domesticity or white supremacy at various points in U.S. history—attempting to make the incongruities caused by power imbalances of class or other hierarchies such as gender or race appear natural.

Country music is a particularly apt site for the analysis of such competing ideological visions of the world, as it is a dominant popular music genre (it has long been the top radio format in America)[33] and insistently voices tensions in American society. Cecelia Tichi has called for more American studies and cultural studies of country music precisely because its "folk poetry" plays a role in the formation of American thought.[34] The genre has a strong connection to the endurance of folk practices, and it is deeply invested in thematic binaries that express the tensions in Southern working-class life. The critics Richard Peterson, George Lewis, and Bill Malone have traced the dualisms in the value systems expressed in the genre, linking them to sources in Southern working-class history. They note that the genre is compelling because those dualisms exhibit the friction between oppositions such as the rural past and the urban present, home versus rambling, and freedom versus restraint.[35] Along these lines, Peterson has demonstrated that Hank Williams, in his lyrics and live-hard, die-young life, exemplifies the conflicting, recurring country music themes: "the stark contrasts of hard work and dissipation, family loyalty and alienation, home and the open road, profound love and bitter hatred, good and evil."[36] Lewis argues that the genre's broad thematic conflicts between self and society arise from massive social changes that include, most notably, the twentieth-century labor migrations of poor Southerners to cities in the 1920s, to California in the Great Depression, to northern factories in the late 1930s and 1940s, to service abroad in World War II in large numbers, and continual migration around the country after that time. Even as they spread their cultural practices across the country in their travels over the course of the twentieth century, these Southerners experienced a sense of cultural dislocation or culture shock encapsulated in the nostalgia and yearning expressed in the music.

Like jazz and the blues, country music developed from earlier Southern folk cultures and defined itself through emerging media forms as it began gaining circulation on radio and through record sales in the 1920s. "Hillbilly music" was drawn from the folk music of the Appalachian Mountains and the rural South, a mix of music carried over by Irish and European immigrants and vernacular music brought by African slaves—a syncretism of Old and New World, of African and European-derived influences. The founding moment of commercial country music occurred when Ralph Peer recorded hillbilly acts in Bristol, Virginia, in 1927 for distribution on the Victor recording label (to be marketed to poor Southern whites). He brought to a mass audience folk or "hillbilly" music (a term sometimes seen as derogatory), what by the 1940s would be less controversially dubbed "country" music. One breakout act from the Bristol Sessions was the Carter Family, comprised of A. P. Carter, his wife Sara, and his sister-in-law Maybelle Carter (who was married to his brother, Ezra "Eck" Carter). The founding family of country music, their recordings and arrangements of traditional songs shaped the genre. Wedding Maybelle's daughter June, Cash not only married into this dynasty but also kept their legacy alive. After the original roster disbanded in 1943, Maybelle's later version of the Carter Family (consisting of her and her daughters, Helen, Anita, and June, sometimes billed as Mother Maybelle and the Carter Sisters) continued to tour on Cash's road show beginning in the 1960s.

The country genre makes insistent claims for authenticity, demanding of its performers some proof of credibility (sometimes earned through affiliation with rural life, demonstrable hard-luck life experiences, or dedication to the Nashville music community). Scholars have pointed out that country music's construction of authenticity involves a perceived tension between artistic purity versus the market, organic rawness versus commercial polish, anti-modern nostalgia for rural agrarianism versus modernity and the commercialization of the mass media marketplace.[37] Such narratives of authenticity are constructed ones, stories different cultural actors (from singers and songwriters to record producers and radio programmers) wish to tell about a popular music genre at a particular sociohistorical moment. This market-versus-purity dualism in country music as a mass art form is particularly cogent, because the genre's roots are in folk culture but it has always been commercial from the start of mass circulation in the 1920s (and even in earlier, nineteenth-century contexts).[38]

Country music is thus a particularly helpful case study for larger debates about popular culture, because it often nostalgically celebrates an "authentic" folk culture as part of a premodern rural past. This dynamic involves a fantasy of something somehow outside modernity, staged in the very mass media form that helps perpetuate the conditions of modernity that listeners seem alienated by in their search for the folk and the pure. Similarly George Lipsitz notes how post–World War II commercialized leisure, as expressed through mass culture, tends to meditate on the very loss it is furthering.[39] Barbara Ching and Joli Jensen have urged for the need to analyze the problematic processes whereby individuals try to script premodern nostalgia onto this popular-cultural form—what Jensen calls "purity by proxy," whereby "other people and forms manifest and maintain virtue

for us" in the genre's "downhome versus uptown" tension or in fantasies of a supposedly "simpler" time.[40] These two critics argue for the importance of reading
complexity rather than simplicity in the genre.

Even though country music has expanded beyond a Southern white working-
class audience and milieu, that subculture remains central to the genre. I agree
with Malone, who insists on connecting the two, because that subculture generated the music from shared folk cultures in the region, although always with a
mix of white and black folk cultures.[41] Audiences for country music have always
been broader than a Southern rural working class, as scholars such as Wolfe have
established. Efforts to track listeners have found that they are diverse and make
varied uses of the music. Some evidence indicates, however, that there remains
a large working-class component to audiences across the nation, with a high per-
centage in urban areas, the result of Southerners migrating from rural to urban
areas from the 1920s on.[42] A famous study by DiMaggio, Peterson, and Escoe in
the 1970s found that core country music listeners are largely "urban living, white
adults with rural roots who are established in home, family, and job, and yet who
are content with none of these."[43] I agree with Malone that many other groups
consume their fantasy of a Southern white rural working class through the music,
often, again, as a projected nostalgia for a folk culture that somehow represents
a premodern or "simpler" time before industrialization, urbanization, and the
alienation associated with modernity.[44]

Even in the process of consumption, therefore, the Southern white working-
class subculture remains crucial to the genre. As both folk poetry and a mass media form, country music expresses what Raymond Williams terms the "structure
of feeling," or the shared values of a particular group.[45] It can, for example, speak
to the tensions that a Southern rural working-class subculture experienced as it
migrated to cities in great numbers after World War II, or as it grappled with a
suburban middle-class boom in the 1950s. The late 1940s–early 1950s honky-tonk
music of Ernest Tubb or Hank Williams was disruptive to postwar domesticity,
just as the mid- to late-1950s rockabillies like Elvis and Cash were seen as a threat
to suburban middle-class society. Meanwhile, the smooth "countrypolitan" Nashville Sound of Jim Reeves or Eddy Arnold, seized upon in response to the inroads
of rock 'n' roll, instead tried to embrace the modern nuclear family ideal.[46]

My examination of Cash pertains most directly to Southern white working-
class masculinity. Cash's discussion of this manhood has much in common with
long-running thematic traditions in country music. W. J. Cash famously identified
one of the central pressures in Southern working-class life as the battle between
piety and hedonism in the "divided" Southerner, or the "man in the center," who

struggles between his Saturday night carousing and his Sunday morning holiness.[47] Correspondingly, Lewis points out that thematic conflicts for masculinity in country music involve freedom and independence versus the cultural pressure for men to marry and support a family instead of chasing "honky-tonk angels."[48]

Cash offers more than another link in a long chain of cultural tradition; his texts build on familiar cultural tensions but also present a more multifaceted exploration of these issues because they question gender constructions. Cash establishes a heroic working-class masculinity and then explores the uncertainties in that identity. As a case study, Cash can help explicate the careful performance of gender or the arbitrary construction of working-class identity through popular music in different historical contexts.

Malone argues that Cash was the first "bad boy" of country music because Cash identified so strongly with a rambler trope through his outlaw image, particularly in his prison albums.[49] The rambler, the most common figure embodying domesticity versus freedom in the genre, is the man who defies social conventions or lives apart from society.[50] Malone traces a populist admiration for the outlaw (long present in the rural music that eventually became commercial hillbilly music), in which the outlaw could express resistance to restrictive class lines and social mores. He could articulate a working-class fantasy of liberty from the constrictions of work and a nostalgia for the individualism of a rural life lost with the advent of sharecropping after the Civil War and the movement from farms to cities in the early twentieth century. The rambler is a hard-living trickster who jumps trains and often drinks heavily and carouses with women at every station, refusing to be bound by the ties of stable domesticity or family. The convict, portrayed as a sympathetic figure who is falsely accused or who was simply trying to help his family in the face of poverty, is another variation on the rambler theme. The rambler has a long history in country music, popularized by Jimmie Rodgers in the 1920s, Hank Williams in the late 1940s and early 1950s, and by the Outlaw movement headed by Willie Nelson and Waylon Jennings in the 1970s. Williams offers one of the strongest comparisons to Cash, given how the former emphasized a rambling-versus-home dichotomy in his music. In contrast, Cash's binaries remain in play whereas Williams often collapsed his; in his religious questioning, Williams, unlike Cash, was profoundly worried that there was no religious salvation. The two singers also had drastically different voices; Williams's high-pitched, plaintive singing encapsulated the "high lonesome" sound, projecting masculinity differently than did Cash with his deep voice.

Although other singers have explored these strains inherent in Southern working-class life (from Williams to Merle Haggard), Cash is distinctive for the depth of engagement he has with these themes in his work, the thoroughness with which he explores both sides of opposing forces—without collapsing familiar binaries such as rambling versus home into an easy resolution—and in the degree to which he incorporates that tension into his own media image. As a songwriter, in the more than two hundred songs he penned, Cash imagines a version of heroic Southern working-class masculinity, and yet he also questions that gender role construction, devoting a great deal of attention to the uncertainties, ambivalences, and vulnerabilities of that manhood. His protagonist is often a "common-folk" man who works hard to provide for his wife and their children, takes pride in his labor, and affirms his own sense of worth in the face of frustrations over his class status or struggles to support his family in the midst of an unjust world. At the same time that Cash's protagonists are devoted to home and family, they are also drawn to the rambling life. They never resolve the friction between the acceptance of domesticity and a rebellious rejection of social norms, a desire to live at the margins of society, free from social constraints. The male character is drawn to home, mother, religion, and the bonds of family. Yet he also yearns to jump trains, revel in licentious love affairs, and rebelliously act out his proletarian and masculine frustrations. For every rambler or working hobo whom Cash admires for his mobility and freedom (for example, in the songs "Come and Ride This Train," "Locomotive Man," and "Ridin' on the Cotton Belt"), he has tunes about men who express their deep desire to return home from their rambling ("Hey, Porter"). Yet his songs do more than examine both sides of the rambling-versus-family dichotomy. For instance, Cash's songs about female ramblers, a much less common trope in the genre, question gender role conventions, as I discuss more fully in chapters 2 and 3.[51]

Distinctive here is Cash's signature embodiment of saint and sinner, family man and rambler, establishment patriot and outlaw rebel. His manipulation of these opposing images is striking for its longevity and circulation, as he deploys these themes throughout his long career to global popularity. But, again, most distinctive and important about his opposing images is that he does not resolve them. He leaves the diametric poles in productive tension, exploring each side of the opposition and adding a deep sense of complexity and commitment to both sides.

Furthermore, Cash often uses these opposing tensions—and his insistence on holding onto both sides of the binary—as grounds for social critique. Here I disagree with Malone, who asserts that Cash, like the country music genre as a whole, tends to offer only personal, individualistic resolutions to labor tensions.[52] Malone uses Cash's version of the song "Oney" as an example. In that song a shop floor worker pledges that as soon as he retires he will take revenge on his abusive foreman by attacking him physically. Malone argues that this is emblematic of a larger dynamic in country music in which artists rarely question the political or social structure leading to travails in working-class life and instead focus on individual sympathy for working people and a promotion of conservative moral values.[53] He sees country music's potential for class criticism blunted by being deflected into fantasy resolutions: "The problems addressed by country music song lyrics are real, but their proposed resolutions often take the form of fantasy—nostalgia, machismo, escapism, religion, and romantic love."[54] He contrasts such "individualistic responses" with calls to coordinated action, such as the Populist movement of the 1890s or the union drives in the 1930s. For Malone, then, the treatment of tensions in working-class life in this music commonly involves a fantasy resolution, one that might return to emphasizing the love of mother and home or that settles the issues by recourse to the conservative moral values discourse, especially the idea that the patriarchal household and men's status there can offer rewards that will counterbalance class anger. Michael Kimmel sees a similar dynamic in the "angry man" country music of the 1990s and 2000s (for example, that of Toby Keith), involving a retreat to individualism (and the escapism of sex, cars, and beer) rather than any kind of structural social critique.[55]

I argue, instead, that Cash departs significantly from the model drawn by Malone. Although some of his song lyrics do imagine fantasy solutions to the troubles of working-class life that would fall into the categories of escapist romance narratives or that detach from secular problems by emphasizing a promise of religious salvation, Cash more commonly links sympathy with working-class men to structural social critiques. Cash's prison songs exemplify this dynamic, a topic explored in greater detail in later chapters. In those songs he draws on his work in prison reform advocacy (such as his efforts to win parole for convicts or his testimony at the 1972 U.S. Senate hearings on prison reform, where he advocated for employment programs). Sometimes by dramatizing real-life cases, his songs urge listeners to agitate for prison reform and accuse politicians and prison officials of corruption in regard to abusive prison conditions. Similarly, he makes insistent political critiques in his many songs that explicitly castigate the U.S. government over ongoing American Indian policies. He connects his social justice advocacy to his conception of an outlaw, heroic masculinity.

Johnny Cash is an apt case study for these gender questions because he is one of the most iconic figures in the country music genre in terms of his projections of masculine ideals, and yet his performance of gender is more complex than that of any other male superstars. Cash raises questions about identity categories. As I discuss more fully in chapters 2 and 3, Cash, for some, by marrying into the Carter family, embodied masculine authority as the patriarch of country music's "First Family." The Musician Bono of U2, who recorded with Cash, declaimed: "We're all sissies in comparison to Johnny Cash."[56] Yet, for others, his work sometimes questioned traditional gender role identities and socialization. Teresa Ortega has claimed Cash as a lesbian icon, because he allows fans to identify with "troubled and suffering masculinity."[57]

These countervailing interpretations of Cash, I argue, result from the irresolvable contradictions in his texts. Thematically, a number of his songs speak to the tenuousness of gender as a social category, precisely by raising contradictions on this topic and leaving them in play. For example, in one of Cash's most famous songs about gender, "A Boy Named Sue" (1969), Shel Silverstein's lyrics describe a speaker who wants to seek out and kill the father who left the family and left him with the girl's moniker, "Sue." But once found, the father informs Sue that the name has been a pedagogical lesson in how to be tough in a man's world, since it would be bound to force the son to fight. Although the song is played for humor, it simultaneously marks gender as a socialized behavior and observes the difficulties individual men can face in navigating gender norms and the directive to act masculine in response to societal pressure. By simply bearing a name conventionally associated with girls, the boy, the song imagines, will be the target of continual attacks by those eager to police the strict boundaries of a gender binary (for fear the boy named Sue is troubling gender borders). Yet, if gender categories were so natural, inherent, and readily evident (a biological essence rather than a social construction), a social marker like a name would not spark such violent responses. The song thus speaks to the arbitrariness of gender socialization and gender role ideals.

Indeed, many of Cash's signature songs focus on core moments of paradox, especially regarding gender role ideals. "I Walk the Line" assures the speaker's faithfulness because "I keep the ends out for the tie that binds," but the lyrics also suggest the inevitability of failure as he sings "For you I know I'd even try to turn the tide," a romantic gesture but a hopeless endeavor. In his version of the murder ballad "Delia's Gone," the speaker kills "his woman" but then feels remorse as she haunts him when he sings of his vision of murder and love, violence and marital union, as flip sides of the same coin: "If I hadn't have shot poor Delia, / I'd have had her for my wife." Although such domestic violence in murder ballads has long been a tradition, Cash amplifies the aggression with lines describing Delia as the "kind of evil make me want to grab my submachine."

This kind of thematic, troubled masculinity is appropriate coming from an artist who started out in rockabilly, that mid-1950s urban fusion of "white" hillbilly music and "black" rhythm and blues, which was promoted by the producer Sam Phillips at his Memphis Sun Studios and spawned rock 'n' roll and the first rock stars. Mary Bufwack and Robert Oermann have shown how rockabilly stars violated gender taboos, taking on feminized behaviors such as hip-shaking, sob-raking performances. Michael Bertrand has shown how "culturally schizophrenic" Hillbilly Cats crossed both racial and gender taboos. In his study of Elvis, Bertrand details how the rockabilly integration of "white" hillbilly music and "black" rhythm and blues in the 1950s and 1960s South symbolized racial integration and was seen as dangerous in the context of desegregation and the Civil Rights movement. Also incendiary was how the rockabilly stars identified with outsider aspects of black masculinity, drawing on affinities between black and white Southern working-class cultures.[58] This troubled and troubling racial identification and appropriation emerges from the kind of love and theft that Eric Lott reads in earlier blackface minstrelsy.[59] In an artist such as Cash, who later spoke explicitly to social movements targeting racial inequity, the multifaceted sympathies and appropriations that comprise his racialized gender performances place his performance of stable identity categories under question.

Life Narratives and Historical Contexts

Cash's long career allows for an exploration of how its ups and downs comment on and reflect the evolution of Southern white working-class history. The basic outline of his career begins with his early Sun Records rockabilly years with Sam Phillips (1955–58), then moves to a long stint with Columbia (1958–86), covering the 1960s and his concept albums, his flirtation with the urban folk revival, his wildly popular prison recordings in the late 1960s, his early 1970s superstardom and network television show (1969–71), and finally Nashville's abandonment of him as a solo artist in the 1980s when Columbia dropped him from their label. The 1980s and 1990s witnessed his participation in supergroup The Highwaymen (with Willie Nelson, Waylon Jennings, and Kris Kristofferson), Mercury's half-hearted attempt to revive his solo career (1986–92), and his career resurgence with American Recordings (1993 until his death in 2003, with posthumous releases still appearing). Although he became an establishment figure at various times in the Nashville industry, he was also always an outsider critical of industry practices and sympathetic to various insurgent or reform movements, including his rockabilly start in the 1950s, the urban folk revival of the 1960s, the Outlaw movement in the

1970s, later neotraditionalist resurgences like that in the 1980s, and the flowering of alternative country and Americana roots music in the 1990s.

Filling out these basic outlines, Cash's well-publicized biographical and autobiographical narratives reflect some typical patterns of work and migration for Southern men of his generation. As his biographer Michael Streissguth notes, Cash's early travels were typical of his peers.[60] Like so many Southern men coming of age in the postwar period, he moved north to seek work in industries such as auto factories or left home for military service.

The details of his life story are well known. Although his personal account in his two autobiographies, *Man in Black* (1975) and *Cash: The Autobiography* (1997), is definitive, more recent biographies such as Streissguth's have disentangled historical events from the mythologies that Cash created about himself. Biographers and music journalists often posit his narrative as a Horatio Alger–like, rags-to-riches story—a man grows up poor picking cotton in Arkansas, then fights through the hardships of the music business, drugs, marital woes, personal tragedies, and hobbling health problems, and ultimately casts an imposing shadow in popular music for five decades. Born in 1932 in Kingsland, Arkansas, Cash grew up the son of sharecroppers, one of seven children in Dyess, Arkansas, a Depression-era New Deal cooperative agricultural colony where the government gave farmers land until they could raise crops and repay the debt. Cash later joked that he "grew up under socialism" or "communalism."[61] As he worked the cotton fields with his family, they sang constantly, and Cash's mother called his voice "the gift" from God.[62] Cash obsessively listened to a rich mix of music on the radio, including gospel, spirituals, blues, and hillbilly music by the Carter Family, among others.

After graduating from high school in 1950, he traveled to western Arkansas to work briefly as a field hand, and then went to Pontiac, Michigan with friends from home to work in a General Motors plant. After less than a month there, he enlisted in the U.S. Air Force and spent four years as a radio operator (intercepting and recording Cold War–era transmissions) on a base in Germany. He returned home in 1954 and moved to Memphis, where he worked in appliance sales while trying to find entry into the music business. When Cash returned to the states, he married his first wife, Vivian Liberto, whom he had met in San Antonio while there for basic training before deployment to Germany. With her, he had four daughters, including musician Rosanne, the eldest, followed by Kathy, Cindy, and Tara. After securing his place with Phillips at Sun, Cash and his makeshift band, the Tennessee Two (originally comprised of Cash on rhythm acoustic guitar joined by moonlighting mechanics Luther Perkins on electric lead guitar and

Marshall Grant on standing bass), embarked on tours with Elvis, June Carter, and others of their ilk. Within eleven months, Cash made it onto the Grand Ole Opry (notoriously, years later, he would be asked not to return as a guest artist when he smashed the stage floor lights in a drug-fueled rage during one performance in 1965).

He left his early fame with Phillips in 1958 for a lucrative contract and the chance to record gospel as well as concept albums at Columbia. But he also fell into a ten-year drug haze of amphetamines and barbiturates, which he had begun taking to deal with the pressures of touring and fame. He moved his family to Southern California, but his long absences while on the road and numerous infidelities strained his marriage, which fell apart (they divorced in 1968, but Cash's practice of infidelity continued during his marriage to June Carter). Meanwhile, he earned a reputation as an unreliable performer. Strung out on drugs, Cash's voice was frequently hoarse from dehydration, and he would cancel concerts often enough to make promoters wary. He had commercial and critical successes, but, as countless biographical narratives have it, he spent most of the 1960s struggling with drugs, God, and his adulterous love for June Carter (a painful love immortalized by Cash's hit, "Ring of Fire" [1963], penned by June Carter and Merle Kilgore).

Cash staged a comeback in the late 1960s with his prison albums, after he completed one of his ongoing drug recoveries. While Cash's two autobiographies both admit his ongoing struggle with drugs and periodic relapses, they also both emphasize his dramatic moment of conversion in 1967 when he detoxed after a suicide attempt. Cash often attributed his turnaround to a renewed commitment to God, but many biographical accounts credit June Carter's influence (as evident in the *Walk the Line* biopic). In striking contrast, Streissguth, along with Cash's band mate Marshall Grant, argue that although Cash's most intense years of drug use occurred between 1958 and 1967 (when Cash was taking hundreds of pills a day), except for a six-year period beginning in 1970 (after his son's birth), Cash was abusing drugs heavily throughout his adult life until his death. Grant argues: "There wasn't five days from 1976 until he came down with his disease that he was straight."[63] When Cash married Carter in 1968, she chose largely to sacrifice her own career to support his (she would later express some ambivalence about her choice in the song, "I Used to Be Somebody" on the album *Press On* [2003], where she recalled training at the Actor's Studio in New York with James Dean and a career not pursued).[64] They had a son together, John Carter Cash, who went on to produce and play on many of Cash's late albums. Cash presided over a large blended family that included their son, his daughters, and June's two daughters from her two previous marriages (including Carlene Carter, who also enjoyed fame as a country artist) as well as a string of sons-in-law (including the musicians Rodney Crowell and Marty Stuart, who remained connected to the family even after divorces). Members of Cash's family would perform in his road show, the Johnny Cash Show, over the years. Cash achieved international icon status with his network television show, but by the end of the 1970s his career was in decline, and, with the exception of "One Piece at a Time" (1976), he was scarcely producing any hits. After his long career at Columbia began cooling in the mid-seventies and floundered in the eighties, Rick Rubin of the American Recordings label afforded him renewed relevance in the 1990s, and in his final years he was showered with awards and attention.

A recurring theme in Cash's life narratives is his stoic response to health troubles and his will to overcome them, especially later in life, in order to remain a vital artist. In 1997 it was the onset of neurological problems eventually diagnosed as autonomic neuropathy that forced him to discontinue touring and turn his attention to recording; the disease contributed to his frail health after that point. During the last fifteen years of his life Cash was beset with numerous illnesses and constant pain. One particularly nagging condition, a jaw injury, affected his singing, making his pronunciation murkier and sometimes slurred. A botched treatment after a failed dental procedure in 1990 left Cash with a broken jaw; unsuccessful surgeries then resulted in nerve damage. He did not want to undergo further surgeries to try to repair his jaw, because he feared it might rob him of his ability to sing or send him into painkiller addiction; he also insisted publicly that the pain was only assuaged when he sang and enjoyed the adrenaline rush of the stage, but privately he said performing caused him immense pain, making him feel like his jaw was "on fire."[65] Weakened by years of drug abuse, Cash had open-heart surgery and a near-death experience in 1988, and he also suffered from asthma, diabetes, glaucoma that robbed him of much of his eyesight in later years, a bizarre tangle with an ostrich on his farm in 1983 that left him gutted and that could easily have killed him, and recurring bouts of pneumonia that prompted him to spend more time at his vacation home in Jamaica to avoid cold weather. He died of respiratory failure as a result of diabetes on 12 September 2003, several months after June Carter died of complications from heart valve surgery.

In terms of Cash's ongoing cultural legacy, to elaborate on the artistic and market contexts for Cash's work it is helpful to note how the form and content of his oeuvre imagine him as a border crosser, a category-breaker who merges musical styles, political stances, and social identities. His musical styles include gospel, folk, rockabilly, rock, blues, bluegrass, and country. His mix of cultural forms includes popular music, oral narrative, popular literary genres (autobiographies and historical novels), Appalachian and other folk cultures, film, documentary, and music videos. Again, Cash constantly bucked efforts to categorize him politically, and his stances varied from social protester and "outsider" populist critic of institutions such as prisons to a supporter of U.S. nationalism. In his work, Cash also positions himself as an iconoclast who upsets identity categories, from the progressive advocate of American Indian land rights and war protesters to the conservative patriot. In "Folsom Prison Blues" (1955), he famously sang "I shot a man in Reno, just to watch him die," and, less famously, wrote a novel about St. Paul and religious faith titled *Man in White* (1986).

Cash's vacillations, like his constant mixing of musical styles, kept people guessing about who the "true" Cash was. As Anthony DeCurtis remarks, Cash was both "Saturday night and Sunday morning," a dynamic that contributed to his worldwide success as well as to country music's fluctuating rejection and embrace of him.[66] He had to keep admitting that he never did hard time, because his songs and image made people think that he had. His jail time consisted of a total of seven overnight stays between the late 1950s and late 1960s for drug busts or drunk and disorderly conduct. False rumors abounded that a scar on his face was the result of a prison fight. Wildly disparate groups tried to claim him as their own, from fans of traditional country to indie rockers. In one notable example, MTV reports of his death genuflected to him as "the first punk" because of his projected attitude, citing his notorious amphetamine addiction in the 1950s and 1960s and his pioneering work in the area of rock stars trashing hotel rooms. As his wife June Carter Cash said: "He's always been a sneerer."[67]

Insofar as the market is a measure of popularity, Cash has proven a highly successful commodity; his widespread circulation, both domestic and international, has cast him as a worldwide ambassador for country music and one of the most recognizable stars of the genre. Cash's marketability intertwines with both his iconoclasm and this sense of him as a piece of Americana.

Cash first gained widespread fame alongside Elvis and the other members of the so-called Million Dollar Quartet of Sun rockabilly stars, Carl Perkins and Jerry Lee Lewis.[68] But his celebrity and notoriety burned brightest during his Columbia years. His high point was 1969, when his live prison albums made him the best-selling artist internationally that year, eclipsing the Beatles with 6.5 million albums sold. These two career-defining albums, *Johnny Cash at Folsom Prison* (1968) and *Johnny Cash at San Quentin* (1969), cemented his renown and his outsider, rough-hewn persona; both reached number 1 on the country charts, and the second climbed to number 1 on the pop charts as well. He had several notable crossover hits, such as "A Boy Named Sue" (1969). In his almost fifty-year career, he sold more than fifty million albums, recorded more than fifteen hundred songs, had fourteen number-1 country hits, won numerous awards, including more than a dozen Grammys, and was inducted into both the Rock 'n' Roll and the Country Music Hall of Fame as well as the Songwriters Hall of Fame (a distinction he shares only with Hank Williams and Jimmie Rodgers). Country Music Television designated him the top male country artist of all time, Rolling Stone labeled him the Thirty-first Greatest Rock 'n' Roll Artist of all time, and *The Guardian* named *Hurt* the greatest video ever made.

Cash's career successes include his popular network television primetime variety show, *The Johnny Cash Show* (fifty-six episodes on ABC from 1969 to 1971), which offers a telling example of his promotion of a contradictory persona, full of contending forces. There, he bucked conventions by featuring artists from diverse genres, embracing country, left-wing folk musicians and rock artists, gospel, soul, and rhythm and blues performers, with guests including Bob Dylan, Neil Young, Joni Mitchell, Stevie Wonder, Ray Charles, Linda Ronstadt, Neil Diamond, Derek and the Dominoes, and James Taylor alongside country regulars such as the Carter Family, Waylon Jennings, and Glen Campbell. He joined this unexpected cosmopolitanism with the seeming opposition of an equally unexpected on-air profession of his fundamentalist Christianity. To the chagrin of network executives, Cash introduced the hymn "I Saw a Man" at the end of one episode by saying, "I am a Christian" and citing his struggle between God and the devil, in typical Southern Baptist terms: "The number one power in this world is God. The number two power is Satan, and though he manages to fight for second in my life, I want to dedicate this song to the proposition that God is the victor in my life." Cash believed that this profession of his faith was unpopular enough to cost him revenues and to contribute to dampening his career in the 1970s.[69]

A range of other TV and film credits showcase his eclecticism as well as his predilection for embodying American archetypes. He was a violent bank robber and murderer in his first Hollywood movie role in the shlocky cult film *Five Minutes to Live* (1960), and firebrand abolitionist John Brown in the Civil War miniseries *North and South* (1985). He played cowboys in countless celluloid adventures, most notably opposite Kirk Douglas in the Western *A Gunfight* (1971), in a television movie remake of *Stagecoach* (1986) with Willie Nelson and Kris Kristofferson, and as Frank James in *The Last Days of Frank and Jesse James* (1986), with Kristofferson as Jesse. Linking to the Ur-movie cowboy icon, Cash did the theme song for the John Wayne Western, *The Sons of Katie Elder*. But Cash also played

American Indians, notably, the Cherokee chief John Ross in the TV movie about the Cherokee removal of 1838, *Trail of Tears* (1970).

His work with Rubin endeared him to a new generation of fans raised on alternative rock and rap, and Rubin encapsulated Cash's appeal to them as follows: "He makes outsiders feel like they're not alone."[70] A founder of Def Jam records, Rubin has been the producer of the rap acts Run DMC, Public Enemy, the Beastie Boys, and LL Cool J; the metal act Slayer; and alt-rockers the Red Hot Chili Peppers. Rubin quickly remade Cash again into a hipster taste marker, a symbol of cultural capital and distinction (and perhaps part of Cash's success with Rubin can be attributed to changes in music marketing and taste categories, which during this period included consumers eschewing older genre categories). Compilations of hits and his prison concert albums remain his most popular in terms of sales figures, but his output since the 1990s renewed his career through releases including four albums and two posthumous offerings: the box set *Unearthed* (2003) and the album *American V: A Hundred Highways* (2006). His first Rubin album, *American Recordings*, won the 1994 Grammy for Folk Album of the Year, and his second, *Unchained*, a classic, rollicking country album on which he is backed by Tom Petty and the Heartbreakers, won the 1997 Grammy for Country Album of the Year. *American III* (2000) won the 2000 Best Male Country Vocal Performance Grammy for Tom Petty's "Solitary Man." The fourth of the American Recordings albums (the last released while Cash was still alive), *American IV: The Man Comes Around* (2002), featuring "Hurt," has become his best-selling studio album with more than 1.4 million copies sold.[71] After American released it on 4 July 2006—a release date that can only serve to emphasize Cash's patriot-critic persona—*American V: A Hundred Highways* quickly reached the status of best-seller. It achieved the number-1 spot on both The Billboard 200 and the Top Country Albums charts in the first week of its release, making it Cash's first number-1 album following *Johnny Cash at San Quentin* in 1969. The album only sold 88,000 copies in its first week, making it the fewest-selling number-1 album since Nielsen SoundScan began tracking the sales of individual units in 1991, perhaps speaking to the 5-percent downturn in industry-wide CD sales between 2005 and 2006. Yet it has gone on to be certified Gold (500,000 units).[72]

Noting the unexpected interest MTV took in him, and the *Hurt* video in particular—which received extensive airplay and six MTV Video Music Award nominations in 2003, winning for Best Cinematography—some music journalists concluded, "Cash is cool again," and others argued that his cool is "timeless," thus registering the conviction that younger generations would discover him anew.

Even after *American V* (which includes his final composition, a train song titled "Like the 309"), Rubin still has enough recorded material for a planned sixth album.

Cash's albums surged in popularity just after his death; his sales doubled, and a number of biographies were published.[73] Record companies began launching career retrospective compilations several years before his death as his health worsened; Columbia reissued many of his classic albums as part of a "Johnny Cash 70th Birthday" marketing campaign. Since his death, reissues and compilations have flooded the market, including three particularly expansive compilations in 2005: Time Life's box set, *Johnny Cash: The Complete Sun Recordings, 1955–1958*; Sony Legacy's exhaustive *Cash: The Legend*, a career-spanning, multiple-CD box set that also comes in a special limited edition version with a lengthy coffee-table book and a commissioned lithograph of Cash; and Universal Music's *The Legend of Johnny Cash*, which reached the eleventh slot on Billboard's top music sales chart in its first week of release (and had a second, companion volume released in 2007). In 2004 his estate earned $7 million (*Forbes* magazine listed him as one of the highest-earning dead celebrities).[74] The Oscar Award–winning biopic *Walk the Line* (2005), which has earned more than $120 million at the box office to date, sparked yet another round of renewed interest in Cash, sending his second autobiography, *Cash: The Autobiography* (1997), to the best-seller list. The Man in Black has likewise sauntered onto Broadway. A jukebox musical in which a cast performs thirty-eight of his hit songs in vignettes, *Ring of Fire: The Johnny Cash Musical Show*, ran in 2006 on Broadway and continues to tour regionally. Another recent example of how the impulse to memorialize Cash (and a widespread emotional investment in this process) has continued is the response to the accidental incineration of his famous lake house outside Nashville. The home, which appeared in the *Walk the Line* film, featured a replica of the Lincoln bedroom and was the site of many of Cash's musical compositions and his frequent hosting of artists and even world leaders in salon-like gatherings. Barry Gibb (of the Bee Gees) purchased the house from Cash's estate in 2006 for more than two million dollars and was having it renovated when, in April 2007, it burned to the ground (in an unfortunate real-life disco inferno). In response to a renewed emotional outpouring from fans and musicians, Nashville journalists called for a memorial park on the site or even a name change for the Nashville airport to commemorate Cash's legacy.[75]

Although Cash will perhaps never become a marker of kitsch excess similar to Elvis, his booming merchandise sales illustrate his range of appeal, from faux black prison shirts marketed to indie rock fans at chain stores like Hot Topic, to T-shirts emphasizing his Christian and patriot image, picturing him staring at a cross or an American flag. Fittingly, there is even a Johnny Cash action figure, swathed in black, which strides both majestically and menacingly along a railroad track, guitar slung over his back, like a musical, train-hopping superhero. This plenitude of posthumous material may represent the most aggressive shaping of his image, because it makes assertions about the meaning of his work and legacy, claiming legendary status for him.

In the next chapter my reading of Cash's model of American ambivalence focuses on the issue of how Cash's image of authenticity is related to his projection of a contradictory persona. The book's subsequent five chapters trace the trope of contradiction through the major themes in his corpus, all of which involve polysemic constructions of identity in his fluctuating versions of Southern white working-class masculinity. Chapters 2 and 3 address gender in Cash's work and image, and chapter 4 centers on race and identity politics. Chapter 5 attends to class and Cash's "Outsider" social protests in relation to American patriotism, and compares, for example, the politics in his music to those of Merle Haggard, who has also been held up as an artist who plays to both the left and right wing, and to the far more explicitly left-wing politics of fellow Highwaymen Kris Kristofferson and Willie Nelson. Chapter 6 analyzes Cash's religious themes. The concluding chapter considers Cash's cultural legacies, with an analysis of the video for "God's Gonna Cut You Down," from *American V* (2006), as an example of how Cash's image in a wealth of posthumous material elucidates the continuing relevance of his oeuvre and iconography.

1

"WHAT IS TRUTH?"
Authenticity and Persona

I have been arguing that, in Cash, a large part of what counts as his projected "authenticity" is the image that he is a walking contradiction with respect to the different components of his performance. Precisely because his incongruities are what he and others portray as authentic in him, Cash is instructive in debates about the creation of authenticity in music and, consequently, in discussions of how country music formulates race, gender, and a Southern white working-class culture. In this chapter I question how Cash's oeuvre elucidates such debates, as I examine Cash's self-representation and others' accounts of him to determine how they establish that his contradictory persona is authentic. I detail how he stages his version of the market-versus-purity conflict and how his struggles over this tension speak to the political economy of the Nashville music industry. Concluding with an extended close reading of Cash's *Hurt* video (2002), I demonstrate how a nexus of authenticity issues becomes evident in his texts.

Cash's work is emblematic of the complexity in the country music genre that scholars must address. In calling for more attention to these complications, Barbara Ching has noted the problems with reifying country music's construction of simplicity, the dangers of trying to make the genre transparently stand for traditional virtues or a "simpler" life.[1] The complexity of Cash's work concerns, in particular, popular music's love affair with that hotly contested, endlessly debunked fantasy of what is authentic—meaning what is genuine. Theorists have long argued that authenticity is a construct of ideas and values reflecting specific socio-historical contexts of production and reception; thus audiences and record companies might deem artists or their music authentic because they seem to convey honesty, truth, and an organic relationship to their roots or fan base. Country music has been described as a genre of sincerity.[2] Yet one person's authentic favorite singer-songwriter is another person's manufactured country-pop star. The idea of authenticity involves various beliefs about taste, values, identity, and models of artistic creation. It is an arbitrary, constantly changing concept. By exploring what it means in specific instances, we can show what such ideas reflect about U.S. culture (as Richard Peterson has done for the institutional history of country music and as other scholars have done for specific country movements and stars).[3]

Cash's career illustrates what scholars have identified as the dialectical nature of authenticity narratives, because such narratives can frequently mean negotiating between seemingly opposed but actually interrelated ideas. As noted in the introduction, scholars in the field have detailed country music's familiar meta-narratives of a perceived opposition between market pressure and a nostalgic idea of purity, which may seem figured as the opposition between manufactured polish and hard-living roughness. In what Aaron Fox has called country's meta-narrative of "loss and desire," the genre stages the loss of a supposedly purer past, idealized as somehow counter to the market or commodity culture, bemoaning the falling away of traditional agrarian society in the face of urbanization and industrialization.[4] Yet country music articulates both parts of that dichotomy, the pull of the past and the longings of the market. In these paradigms we see a fluctuation between different imagined models of authenticity prevailing in various socio-historical contexts, as they coexist, compete, and evolve over time. Cash embodies both sides of cultural binaries. Thus, he can, for example, further illuminate the kinds of internal critiques of authenticity Ching has identified in country music.

Cash's variable image aptly addresses some of the dominant paradigms for authenticity in the genre, and he can add another difficult wrinkle to some of these tropes. Related to the market-purity dichotomy, for example, other key meta-narratives involve identifying a binary of stylistic differences that often take on gendered stereotypes. In Richard Peterson's "hard-core" versus "soft-shell" country dialectic, the "pure" roots of traditional country (Hank Williams) oppose the more "pop" or market-oriented form such as the Nashville Sound and its descendants (Jim Reeves).[5] Historians have noted how the "founding moment" of commercial country music, the 1927 Bristol sessions, generated two different paradigms of "authenticity": the Carter Family's home, family, and domesticity-focused traditional music (which they advertised as "morally good") versus Jimmie Rodgers's rambler, genre-crossing music.[6]

In this example, the careful fashioning of authenticity is readily evident. The Carter Family's "home" narrative is particularly striking for its extensive fabrication. The original trio (A.P. [Alvin Pleasant], his wife Sara, and his sister-in-law Maybelle) skillfully marketed an image of familial bliss, using their life stories as part of their public personae to become a symbol of the American family and domesticity. They were even scheduled to appear as such on the cover of *Life* magazine in 1941, although the onset of war changed editorial plans and the story never appeared. Yet the appearance of domestic tranquility was far from the reality. Beneath the semblance of family-values music we find something far more typical—blended, broken, dysfunctional, and nontraditional family arrangements. The married couple at the center of the act was estranged for much of their career. Sara actually left A.P. and their children in 1933 and went to live with her family. Her children describe her as a forward-thinking proto-feminist known to break gender taboos of the time by wearing pants and smoking. Granddaughter Rita says: "my grandmother was probably liberated before people knew the term, certainly for women in this area."[7] Sara and A.P. divorced in 1936 but continued to record and perform together, maintaining a carefully managed public image until 1943. In spite of A.P.'s efforts to reunite with her, Sara instead began an affair with A.P.'s cousin, Coy Bays. Although their families kept them apart and exiled Bays to California, she ultimately reunited with him through a Carter Family performance, throwing the artificiality of the act's familial image into stark relief. In 1938 the group was in Texas to perform on powerful border radio station XERA, earning them vast exposure. When introducing their song "I'm Thinking Tonight of My Blue Eyes," Sara dedicated it to Bays. He heard her on the radio, drove all night from California to Texas to reach her, and they were married three weeks later. In biographical narratives of the convoluted family ties, many accounts focus on the continued estrangement of A.P. and Sara and his bitterness at their divorce. Even given the strains beneath their public image of domestic harmony, the Carter Family managed to pitch an image of home-centered bliss and lend it staying power, achieving a definitive influence on country music notions of purity.

Cash illuminates the shaping of such domestic tropes in country music, and he more fully embodies the interplay of stylistic dialectics. He is knotty in some of these narratives. Cash actively helped to keep the music of both the Carter Family and Jimmie Rodgers alive, laying claim to competing authenticities at times, the family patriarch as well as the rambler. Cash's road shows featured, in equal parts, home-themed music backed by the angelic oohs and aahs of the Carter Family, and genre-bending rambler and railroad songs in the style of Rodgers. After the original Carter Family disbanded in 1943, later versions comprised of different group members and their children continued to play. Mother Maybelle toured with her version of the Carter Family (Mother Maybelle and the Carter Sisters, consisting of her and her daughters Helen, Anita, and June) with Cash into the 1960s, and Carter family members, in addition to his wife June Carter, continued to sing with him after that time. Cash also frequently performed Jimmie Rodgers songs and was often compared to him. Cash went so far as to attempt a Rodgers tribute at his 1962 Carnegie Hall concert. He emerged for one segment dressed in railroad gear as Rodgers the Singing Brakeman to perform Rodgers songs, but his New York audience for the most part did not recognize nor understand his reference (and the hoarse, drug-addled, incoherent performance he gave that night did not help his efforts).[8] Not only did he embrace both the Carter Family and Rodgers performance modes, but Cash also merged the family patriarch and the rambler in his projected image. While he and June Carter became like the second generation of the First Family of Country Music, he also maintained his outlaw persona, not least because they infamously became involved while both were married to other people and suffered public disapproval because of it.

Cash similarly illuminates the dialectical movement of other authenticity paradigms. For Ching, what she identifies as the subgenre of "hard country" critiques a projected authenticity in the sense that it responds to how a tourist's gaze might patronizingly frame a kind of abject "redneck" country image as "authentic." It expresses white working-class masculine frustration at disempowerment and claims an abject position in relation to the dominant, mainstream, middle-class bourgeois culture that ridicules it. Yet hard country also rejects this elitist putdown. Cash's performance both fits with and departs from this rubric. Ching, in arguing for a difference between mainstream, pop-oriented country and "hard country," notes Cash in passing as a hard country star in that his Man in Black persona "evokes bad boys and mourners." At the same time she observes that his "Man in Black" song confuses that picture, because Cash "righteously claims that his outfit signifies his mourning for the world's downtrodden."[9] Cash often voices working-class frustration in songs like "Country Trash," where he sings: "But we'll all be equal when we're under the grass / And God's got a heaven for country trash."[10] Yet his Man in Black persona clearly attempts to move beyond a restrictive version of white working-class masculinity (or associated stereotypes of sexism, racism, and violence) to engage in cross-racial class bonding as well as to express solidarity for various social movements, including the Civil Rights movement and antiwar protests.

The question of market versus purity in Cash is likewise exacting. He explicitly advocated certain anti-market constructions of authenticity. In one instance, he made it clear that he subscribed to some version of authenticity because when he felt threatened by market pressures at Columbia, he satirized his own image. In the mid-1980s, when he thought Columbia was trying to abandon him or get him to "sell out" and overproduce or water down his sound, he turned to burlesque. He recorded "Chicken in Black" (1984), a song parodying his image, in which the lyrics have his brain being transplanted to a chicken; Cash made a video for it featuring him dressed in a mock superhero costume, and the song actually became a modest hit, perhaps reflecting his audience's receptivity to his self-parody.

At the same time, however, Cash resisted efforts to script him into certain versions of authenticity. In one song, "I'll Say It's True" (1979), he satirizes press efforts to pin him down as well as all the false mythologies that circulate about him. In his lyrics, Cash dispels myths by singing "I've never been in prison," denying much knowledge about trains, noting that his Indian heritage claims came from "years ago," implying that he no longer makes those claims, and then establishing paradoxes for himself, noting that he loves New York City as well as the country, palatial homes as well as modest shacks; he says he will "let them old tales all stay twisted" but he will "set 'em straight" about his love for "his woman."[11] Cash the speaker expresses his weariness at all the same old questions, all the efforts to insist on certain versions of genuineness or to defrock his inability to live up to them, the criticisms of his mixture of wealth and folksiness, or his own identity formulations. As the press circulates endless stories about him, generating warped mythologies, he will only go on the record about his affection for "his woman."

Elsewhere, Cash explicitly pondered the question of authenticity in country music in a way that underlines the inevitable dialectic between the market and ideas of purity. In his second autobiography, when decrying how the country music establishment sometimes ostracized or abandoned him, dubbing him "not country," Cash slams commercialized, prepackaged "hat acts" that use props and turn the agrarian lifestyle that "country" music originally referenced into an empty fashion style. But as he engages in nostalgia for the agricultural roots of the music, he also wonders if market forces can produce the same feeling, and he leaves the question as an open one. Critiquing the country industry's production and marketing practices, Cash writes that "huge swatches of the blues and country music do after all come from the cotton fields in a very real way" and wonders if a sense of the country life has been abandoned for symbolic commodities:

> Country life as I knew it might really be a thing of the past and when music people today, performers and fans alike, talk about being "country," they don't mean they know or even care about the land and the life it sustains and regulates. They're talking more about choices—a way to look, a group to belong to, a kind of music to call their own. Which begs a question: Is there anything behind the symbols of modern "country," or are the symbols themselves the whole story? Are the hats, the boots, the pickup trucks, and the honky-tonking poses all that's left of a disintegrating culture? Back in Arkansas, a way of life produced a certain kind of music. Does a certain kind of music now produce a way of life? Maybe that's okay. I don't know.[12]

Here Cash contemplates whether the materiality of rural experiences that produced a collective sense of cultural expression will lose something in the translation into a commodified style and musical taste, yet he notes that this process is inevitable with historical change.

Cash's own music and its industrial context and reception here become a way to ponder that very process of social change—they become part of a historical discourse, particularly for audiences that might use his mass-marketed music to create their own sense of self-expression or identity. Obviously, while Cash's music and image are different from "hat acts," they are also mass-marketed and carefully constructed. Barry Shank notes that the market and authenticity have always functioned together in twentieth-century popular music, just as listeners re-create their own sense of self from the products of the culture industry.[13]

Cash's meditation on the sense of losing the past is essential to this dynamic. He sings nostalgically about rural life in songs like "Country Boy" (1957): "You gotta cut the weeds, you got to plant the seeds / . . . / But when it's quittin' time and your work is through / There's a lotta life in you." He concludes to the country boy, perhaps his earlier self, that "I wish I was you and you was me."[14] But the way of life he is nostalgic for can no longer exist precisely because of the economic conditions that make his mass-marketed song possible. Analyzing how popular culture responds to the ruptures of modernity, George Lipsitz has argued that historical discourse emerges as a way to provide a sense of continuity and memory in the face of modernity's break with the past, just as postwar mass culture fixates on the very loss it accelerates. As a hopeful Lipsitz argues, while mass media turns art into a commodity, which distorts and obscures artistic messages and contexts, it nevertheless can also indirectly provide meaningful connections to the past.

For him, some audiences "ingeniously enter those discourses to which they have access," and can make commercialized leisure into history (which he defines as "a repository of collective memory that places immediate experience in the context of change over time"). Thus popular music can profoundly expose "the tension between music as a commodity and music as an expression of lived experience."[15] As Brackett helpfully argues of the country genre, following in Hank Williams's mold: "The self-reflexive lyrics of much post-Williams country music comment explicitly on the inextricable links between country music and capitalism, thereby undercutting both the notion that music transcends its status as a commodity and the notion that it is wholly determined by it."[16]

Cash and some of his audiences could at times be seen to be engaging in this kind of process—again, using mass media forms to contemplate the loss that commodity culture is furthering (in this case, the loss of an agrarian past and way of life), yet also generating complex collective expression and re-created senses of identity from the mass music making and listening. Indeed, Cash's "walking contradiction" image itself often functions as a way to express the market-versus-purity tension, to hold both sides of the polarity together. Some of his American Recordings marketing, for example, projects his saint-sinner duality in terms of stripped-down, direct sincerity and purity, consciously making him a consumable icon, a hot, stylish commodity to purchase in order to express one's hipster taste. The picture of Cash as a category breaker has been one of the most successful marketing tools that producer Rick Rubin and the American Recordings label have used for Cash, both before and after his death. This vision of Cash as an artist able to combine distinct cultural traditions into new forms has contributed to his cultural impact and longevity. Claiming him as a murder-ballad forefather of the rap artists on his label, Rubin explicitly resurrected the old rebellious Cash from the dusty respectability of his 1980s aura, merging the drug-addicted wild man and the respectable father of country music into one paradoxical, Southern Gothic persona. The *Unearthed* box set, for example, includes an album of gospel songs alongside his covers of rock bands like Nine Inch Nails and U2.

The marketing for that box set, in particular, illustrates how Cash becomes a collectible taste marker and commodity. In the expansive, more-than-one-hundred-page booklet accompanying the set, the music journalist Sylvie Simmons provides sleeve notes for one disc, titled *Volume Four: My Mother's Hymn Book*. Cash anoints it his favorite album, his renditions of country gospel and church songs from his mother's old hymnbook, *Heavenly Highway Hymns*. Simmons discusses how Cash can sing both gospel and industrial rock on the same set of discs. She returns to a familiar selling point:

Cash's remarkable career has been full of these paradoxes and contradictions—
the country icon who rediscovered the soul of his music through working with
a heavy metal and rap producer; the symbol of stoicism who spent periods of his
life helplessly dependent on drugs; a man who'll sing a profound spiritual and
follow it with a piece of cowpony; the outspoken supporter of the downtrodden
and dispossessed who has a framed, signed photograph of Ronald Reagan on the
wall, etc., etc., etc. Johnny could tell you a whole lot more himself if he had the
mind to. He's always had a far better perspective on what he's done, and more
importantly, who he is, than anybody else.[17]

Simmons resolves this narrative of inconsistencies by coming back to Cash's own
insistence on self-definition. His icon status and personal mythology have turned
the contradictions into symbols of Cash's identity—the personal mythology necessarily leaves the incongruities unresolved because they are the substance of the
Cash symbolism. And it is through familiarity with that symbolism that audiences
can express their expert fandom (by buying this box set and others like it).

Epitomizing such marketing, the stark cover image for the first of the American albums, *American Recordings* (1994), pictures Cash in a black longcoat,
flanked by a pair of ominous dogs as he glares darkly. His hands grip the top of a
black guitar case balanced upright on the ground in front of him. He is backed
by an overgrown field and outlined against a lonesome sky, all in black and white
tones. He stands like a windswept outlaw holy man come for a musical reckon-
ing. Rubin admits to being attracted to Cash as much for his "timeless cool" and
outlaw incarnation as for his music, and the producer masterfully marketed that
persona in a way that fit Cash's mythology.[18] Digging into his rich treasure trove
of archetypes, Cash himself described this cover as an apt visual summation of the
album's themes as well as of his life narratives as a whole. Speaking to a *Rolling
Stone* interviewer, Cash said:

> You know my album cover with the two dogs on it? I've given them names. Their
> names are Sin and Redemption. Sin is the black one with the white stripe; Re-
> demption is the white one with the black stripe. That's kind of the theme of that
> album, and I think it says it for me, too. When I was really bad, I was not all that
> bad. When I was really trying to be good, I could never be all that good. There
> would be that black streak going through.[19]

In Cash's visualization, the sin and the redemption must always contain a part
of each other, both within himself and in his music. The cover representation
and his comments mark his symbolism of dark and light, badness and goodness,
and the idea that he inhabits both categories—and this semblance of him is also

melded with iconic celebrity and marketing imperatives. Columbia likewise released prison albums that played up the misleading idea that Cash had been a prisoner himself, yet they also peddled Cash as a religious patriot on his patriotic and gospel albums.

Insider/Outsider

I have been arguing that Cash stages the market-versus-purity dialectic as part of his projections of authenticity. His record labels often also emphasize this dynamic in his marketing. Providing fuller historical context, I will detail this dual image against the backdrop of Cash's fraught relationship with the Nashville music establishment over the years of his career, as it sheds light on the political economy of that industry. The discussion helps put Cash's negotiation of his insider-outsider status in a broader context, where Cash's efforts to gain autonomy or buck conventions resulted in serious conflicts that only emphasized his outlaw image. Some aspects of his career, in fact, reflect industry efforts to control his marketing image. Ultimately, of course, the multiple significations that "Johnny Cash" has as a media image, and the multiple meanings found in his work, are beyond any authorial or industrial control.

As a rockabilly singer, Cash began as an outsider, part of a musical movement that was highly threatening to the country music industry. Rockabilly threatened the industry because it challenged traditional social mores, but, more important, it threatened profits.[20] Cash was seen as more country than Elvis, and thus potentially less threatening, but he was still a longhair rockabilly singer from Memphis, and thus a disruptive force. Yet his sound made him distinct from his peers at Sun Records. Compared to them, Cash was never the balladeer that Elvis could be or that Roy Orbison epitomized, and he was never a singer who equally featured his instrumental talents, as Jerry Lee Lewis did with the piano or Carl Perkins with the electric guitar. His instrumentation was much simpler, his sound stripped bare, with his bass-baritone voice as the focal point, staying in a limited range, with straightforward singing and little vibrato or adornment, backed by the boom-chicka-boom of the simple guitar and rhythm section mimicking a train. The focus was always on his power as an empathetic storyteller. His signature songs also fit much more firmly in a country genre, while Orbison gravitated to pop music ballads and Lewis and Perkins had more driving rockabilly beats than Cash did. Although all these men began with Phillips's formula of having white singers popularize "black" rhythm and blues music, it was Elvis, unlike Cash, who went on to be dubbed the "King" of rock 'n' roll and to become a lightning rod for the continuing debates about racial and cultural appropriation (with critics arguing about whether Elvis was profiting from the music of black artists based on unequal power relationships, or if he was a charismatic musician who made his own new synthesis of gospel, rhythm and blues, and country). Fabian Holt notes that Elvis was the first to challenging the already permeable boundaries of the country genre, before moving quickly to pop markets, as he was never squarely a country act. Cash did not describe himself as country, but nevertheless his music was interpreted much more consistently in that category compared to his rockabilly brethren. As Holt observes, "few rockabillies committed themselves exclusively to country music," and no one calls Elvis "the king of country music."[21] In fact, it is a testament to the complexity of Cash's career that some have given him that moniker instead.

Cash did face resistance to the Phillips formula, however. As Streissguth recounts of Cash's first trip to the Grand Ole Opry in 1956, Cash made some initial efforts to gain acceptance in the country music establishment in Nashville but he quickly bridled under their attempts to make him conform to "purity" conventions. In attempts to appease alarmed industry insiders, Cash told reporters in Nashville that, even though his songs had "definite rhythm beat," that did not make them "rock and roll songs," and that even though he did a parody of Elvis as part of his own stage show, he was not doing an Elvis-style show.[22] But he felt their intense disapproval and quickly grew disenchanted; though Cash returned to play at the Opry several times through the late 1950s, he kept some distance from such establishment institutions (and, in the case of the Opry, was later banished for a time for his infamous stage light-stomping incident).

Precisely because of the market forces the rockabillies unleashed, the Nashville establishment changed what qualified as so-called authentic country music. As listeners deserted honky-tonk music for Elvis in the mid-1950s, and rockabilly and early rock 'n' roll developed, country music scrambled to provide a financially viable alternative that would succeed on radio. The Nashville Sound (Peterson's "soft" country) was designed to be a country-pop format friendly to radio; it strove for a smoother sound, eliminating the twang in singing styles, and trading the fiddle for a string section and vocal chorus. Developed and overseen by powerful producers such as Chet Atkins at RCA and Owen Bradley at Decca, the "countrypolitan" sound in general was highly produced, polished, and formulaic. It employed a stable of studio musicians, gave the artist very little freedom, and held sway in Nashville for twenty years. Singers like Eddy Arnold and Jim Reeves had mainstream success with this formula.

While Cash was eschewing this kind of "manufactured" sound, his engagement with the 1960s urban folk revival provides another cogent example of market-versus-purity tensions. As has been well documented, the folk revival grew out of a disillusionment with Cold War consensus culture and drew on the same energies of social protest and political criticism shaping the Civil Rights movement and the women's movement.[23] During the early stirrings of the 1960s counterculture revolution, the folk revivals of the late 1950s and early 1960s gave way to rock festivals such as Woodstock. By the latter part of the decade West Coast rock was protesting Vietnam, and the British invasion of the Beatles and the Rolling Stones was bringing blues-based rock back to the U.S. from its grand tour abroad. On the folk circuit from Greenwich Village to California, rafts of performers were thumping out folk songs in the earnest belief that folk culture was the country's cultural lifeblood and that, by turning to that wellspring passionately, they could achieve their own sense of truth and authenticity and embrace the popular in a way that the authoritarianism of Cold War culture could not. This idealistic search for purity in the face of the market is, as scholars have detailed extensively, an excellent example of the fantasy construction of authenticity, a nostalgic search for roots that were never actually pure in this way.[24] In the revival's search for authenticity, it is not surprising that it turned to the rich mix of Southern rural folk cultures, breathing new life into the careers of traditional country artists like Sara and Maybelle Carter and blues pioneers such as Son House (Robert Johnson's mentor), Howlin' Wolf, and Mississippi John Hurt. Major folk revival acts like Joan Baez, Bob Dylan, Pete Seeger, and Peter, Paul, and Mary shared stages with country fiddlers, mountain cloggers, gospel singers, shape-note choirs, and blues performers.

Cash gained attention from the folk movement and the counterculture, especially in his proletarian concept albums from the period and in his collaborations with Dylan, including Dylan's recording of the *Nashville Skyline* album (1969) in consultation with Cash (and featuring Cash's Grammy-winning liner notes for it). Dylan, seemingly trying to sound like Cash on this album, lionized Cash as a hero for folk music, just as Cash had earlier defended Dylan for his musical experimentation in going electric and embracing blues-based rock at the 1965 Newport Folk Festival. In response to outraged fans who believed that Dylan, by abandoning acoustic instrumentation and folk modes of address, had betrayed the folk revival and his status as the "voice of his generation," Cash was quoted in *Broadside* magazine as saying: "Shut up and let him sing!"[25] In his Rolling Stone article from 1968, Jan Wenner argued that Cash was Dylan's model.[26]

Critics have noted the Dylan-Cash musical exchanges as formative in the de-velopment of country rock.[27] Columbia, the record label for both men, quickly moved to capitalize on this connection in their marketing. For example, one ad for Cash's version of Dylan's song "It Ain't Me Babe" (1964), a full-page image in Billboard, pictures Dylan's face on one side of the page and Cash's face on the other, with the copy: "a new song from Bob Dylan on a new single sung by Johnny Cash."[28]

While Cash's engagement with the folk movement during this period high-lighted his folk roots, his dedication to participating in the long-standing folk mu-sic tradition of revising traditional American folk songs and performing new varia-tions on them or developing new songs in that vein was evident, as Don Cusic has noted, from the start of Cash's career.[29] The ongoing, evolving, participatory nature of folk music requires that singers bring new variations or improvisations to add to the stream of ideas, making their own innovations with well-known songs. During the 1920s, when country music was becoming commercialized, many singers would record their own version of a folk song classic and put their name on it. As Malone has noted, questions of authorship and intellectual property were not as important as folk traditions that prompted artists like A. P. Carter to treat the traditional songs he collected and arranged as public domain.[30]

In writing new lyrics to old folk melodies or elaborating on the basic contours of standard ballads, Cash was participating in and preserving working-class folk traditions. He thought of himself as a song collector in much the same way Carter was. His song "Going to Memphis" reflects this kind of composition history and speaks to the importance of folk music contexts for his career in the 1960s as well as in the 1990s. He first released the song on his *Ride This Train* concept album (1960) and rereleased it on his American Recordings box set, *Unearthed* (2003). Describing how he developed his version of this old folk song about a man escap-ing from prison, Cash said in the liner notes for *Unearthed*:

> This is a song that I wrote that got inspiration from Alan Lomax, who did a field recording back in the '40s. "Going To Memphis" was a partly finished song that was not really much of a song—just some talking about going to Memphis—and I took their words and made some lyrics out of it and added some music. That song became one of my best-sellers in the '60s. Alan Lomax was a song collector, so was A.P. Carter. I've gone through periods in my career when I've collected all kinds of old American songs—cowboy songs, blues, gospel. Collecting these various songs of various ilks, I find they all have a common thread. That there's love, there's hate, there's death, there's a lot of things in common in all of them. Sometimes you have to look for it, but it's there.

Here Cash emphasizes the thematic commonalities in the folk tradition and displays his investment in (and contribution to) its endurance.

Cash also made high-profile appearances on the folk circuit in the 1960s. Captured in footage included in Murray Lerner's documentary *Festival!* (covering 1963–65 at the Newport Folk Festival), a gaunt Cash performed "I Walk the Line" on solo acoustic guitar in singer-songwriter style at the 1964 Newport Folk Festival (where Cash gave Dylan one of his guitars in the traditional country star sign of respect). Cash also appeared on the *Hootenanny*, the weekly folk music concert television series featuring acts ranging from Judy Collins to the New Christy Minstrels.[31] In footage from a show broadcast from the University of Florida in April 1963, Cash, coughing, hoarse, and nervous from drugs, delivers a disheveled version of "Busted" by Harlan Howard (the songwriter who famously described country music as "three chords and the truth"). Cash also delivers a heartfelt rendition of "Five Feet High and Rising," his song about the flood that threatened his childhood home in Arkansas. As the microphone jumps during his first number, Cash jokingly growls "excuse me, mic, I'm busted." He sings with authority about the trials and tribulations facing the rural poor. The roughness of his delivery is followed by two smooth, melodic folk numbers delivered by Leon Bibb, a black folk singer Cash introduces by saying he saw Bibb in Greenwich Village. As Cash tells the white Southern college students in the audience about Bibb, calling him "one of our top favorites for about five years" and "one of the finest, most versatile entertainers," one gets a sense of the producers' determination to have these concerts cross 1960s racial barriers—and of the necessity of Cash making that case. Bibb sings "Adieu Madras" and "Little Boxes," the latter delivering a scathing critique of bad housing for the poor and conformity for the rich. Later in that show, Josh White Jr., a second-generation black folk singer, delivers a very smooth version of the traditional murder ballad, "Delia's Gone." As the audience sings along with folk contentedness, joining in their knowledge of a musical fable, one cannot help but think of Cash's 1990s version of the same song that takes this kind of folk tradition and roughens it up, making the song a bitter, jangling, Southern Gothic lament rather than a rousing folk sing-along.

Cash's engagement with the folk movement is itself evidence of his typical complications. Critics have noted how many counterculture enthusiasts (or even country music fans looking for a working class hero) hoped Cash could be a Woody Guthrie–style organic intellectual, particularly with the critical acclaim his prison albums enjoyed and because Cash vocally advocated prison reform.[32] But Cash's equally vocal support for Nixon (as I discuss more fully later in this chapter) and his ties to big business (as when he did commercials for American Oil Company) alienated many folk fans. Some were disconcerted over his conflicting investments, but Cash always insisted on his right to hold his paradoxical political positions. As Streissguth details in his extensive history of Cash's Folsom Prison album (1968), Columbia first promoted that album in the underground media and in alternative periodicals with an antiestablishment agenda, and they played up Cash's fantasy prison image and amplified the prison vibe of the record itself (dubbing in cheering prisoners in places). Although Columbia soon backed off its emphasis on the violence in songs like "Folsom Prison Blues" in marketing (and even censored the "shot a man in Reno" line in some copies of the single for fear of gun violence after the assassinations of Robert F. Kennedy and Martin Luther King Jr.), the company worked hard to reach a counterculture folk and rock audience. The alternative press initially saw Cash as a social protest spokesperson, but many writers were disappointed by his conservative comments, such as his statement at a 1969 New York concert that he was a "dove with claws," which was widely interpreted as his support for Nixon's Vietnam policies.[33]

In the context of the Nashville music industry, Cash both furthered and benefited from some market practices—yet he simultaneously criticized others and fought for the purity of more artistic freedom. In his crossover success in the late 1960s, Cash would contribute to the broadening of country music, which shifted sales practices and increased financial expectations. Cash would later suffer because of these very dynamics. In the 1960s Cash was an outsider to the Nashville establishment in that he identified with the urban folk music revival rather than with mainstream country music. Although he had a lucrative contract with Columbia and, especially with his prison albums, brought massive revenues to the company, he was still trying to define his own music without fitting any genre formulas. He had well-documented struggles with his record label over everything from his commercially risky concept albums to his desire to record live prison albums. Streissguth notes that it was only with Cash's network TV show in 1969 that he suddenly became "the ambassador of country music."[34] Cash's successes in the late 1960s and early 1970s, especially in 1969 when he was the best-selling act in the world, did much to help bring country music to a broader audience. Though Cash was not specifically part of the Outlaw Country movement of the 1970s, he was certainly sympathetic to founding figures Waylon Jennings (Cash's roommate for a time in Nashville) and Willie Nelson, and he became directly associated with them professionally in the 1980s with the Highwaymen supergroup. The Outlaw movement involved artists struggling against Nashville industry customs for creative control. Nelson and others wanted to produce their own records, use their own touring bands rather than studio musicians, and stray from the Nashville formula. The trend gained media attention with the 1976 release of the album *Wanted: The Outlaws*, with recordings by Nelson, Jennings, Jennings's wife Jessi Colter, and Tompall Glaser, which achieved sustained success on both country and pop charts; it featured edgy lyrics, a more driving rock-style beat on many songs, and an unbridled sensibility. The commercial success of such albums raised the financial expectations for country music and also marked greater nationalization of the market. James C. Cobb cites this period of expansion in country music as an example of what historians have called the "Southernization of America," as previously denigrated Southern culture gained increased respectability and relevance nationally during this time.[35]

Yet by the 1980s, in an industry increasingly focused on younger artists and commercial formulas, Cash was not receiving country radio airplay and was not selling solo albums, which led to Columbia abandoning him in 1986. During the 1980s the urban cowboy craze, sparked by the 1980 release of the John Travolta film, unleashed new industry practices and expectations, prompting the major record companies to begin targeting a specific demographic (twenty-five- to fifty-four-year-olds). In the mid-eighties Cash was averaging sales of only fifty thousand a year while the industry was looking for acts who could sell in the millions (such as Alabama, which was selling more than two million records a year then).[36] As Rick Blackburn, former CEO of CBS Records Nashville and Atlantic Records Nashville, says of the industry formula at the time, "it was just new faces, who's new," and Cash did not fit their model.[37] By the late 1980s a new generation of young artists who would sell more units emerged, most notably Garth Brooks, but also Clint Black, Travis Tritt, and Alan Jackson. Cash's success with the Highwaymen supergroup did not help his solo career. While band mates Waylon Jennings and Willie Nelson were strongly associated with the genre-pushing, forward-pushing, edgy Outlaw Country movement, and Kris Kristofferson came out of an evolving Lefty folk singer-songwriter tradition, Cash as a musician in the 1980s had begun to seem more like a singer simply recycling his early rockabilly classics.

Feeling disrespected by an industry he helped build, Cash signed with Rubin on the American Recordings label in 1993 and began recording with him in California. In a National Public Radio interview from 2002, he heatedly remarked of that time: "Yeah, I heard demographics, demographics, demographics, until I got sick of hearing demographics. Then I went to California and decided they could kiss my demographics."[38] Rubin gave him the creative freedom and inspiration to record any songs he wanted to do, and he marketed Cash to a younger audience and sent him out playing his spare, haunting songs on solo acoustic guitar at trendy clubs like L.A.'s Viper Room. Even as he was releasing these albums, they did not get airplay on country radio, and his first three, as noted above, won Grammy Awards (from the wider music community) but not awards from Nashville (Academy of Country Music or Country Music Association awards). Similarly, his controversial video from the first album, his version of "Delia's Gone" (1994), which portrays it as a grim Southern Gothic tale recounting the male character (played by Cash) killing and burying his girlfriend (played by Kate Moss), was played on MTV but censored by CMT (Country Music Television). The journalist Chet Flippo comments that the country music industry refused to acknowledge Cash's new work in this period, because many still resented Cash for his disdain for the Opry or old-fashioned conventions.[39] Cash ran into further problems with the industry as a result of changes in its political economy after the 1996 Telecommunications Act, which allowed corporations to own up to eight radio stations in any one market and resulted in the severe narrowing of playlists. In the country genre, it also resulted in an effort to target a new niche demographic: female audiences specifically. As the country music radio industry began focusing on niche markets, it followed a pattern common in the mass media after this federal regulation change, resulting in the conditions we see today, which is the dominance of huge companies such as Clear Channel and the practice of narrowcasting.

Cash's most notable act of symbolic resistance to the industry came in 1998, when American Recordings took out a full-page ad in music industry magazines. The ad pictured Cash's famous snarling image from his San Quentin live prison concert, when he flipped off the cameras, angry that documentary cameras were getting between him and his audience. The ad read: "American Recordings and Johnny Cash would like to acknowledge the Nashville music establishment and country radio for your support." This ad became a banner for many other artists frustrated with industry practices. Cash might have simply moved from one major record company to another (notably, Rubin now heads Columbia, alongside Steve Barnett, and, again, Columbia's parent company, Sony BMG, now controls a quarter of the album market share).[40] On another level, he did move to embrace an outsider approach in that his producer encouraged Cash's wide-ranging genre hopping, rejected the imperative to sell a large number of albums, and encouraged Cash to do material that other companies might have seen as unmarketable. Cash's rise with American Recordings coincided with the 1990s alternative country movement of acts that mixed country and punk sensibilities and influences to update the genre—acts that included Wilco, Ryan Adams, and Hank Williams III. It also happened during the revival of the Americana roots music, and many of these artists shared similar frustrations with the country music industry just as their fans sought a fresh revival of critical-minded, folk-based music (in some ways similar to the 1960s folk revival). In an act of genre busting that found sympathetic audiences, Americana musicians eschewed pop, rejected restrictive genre categories, and, rather than speaking directly to country music, used more general notions of the rural.[41] Cash's ad angered industry executives. The degree to which some of them refused to accept his criticism is evident in the comments of Ed Salamon, the executive director of Country Radio Broadcasters, Inc.: "People like to infer that that picture had something to do with Johnny's feelings towards radio or country radio in particular. Well it absolutely does not." Salamon instead asserts that Rubin was simply trying to create controversy in order to sell records.[42] Cash, meanwhile, in a later interview, insisted on his commitment to criticizing the industry: "I don't regret that I did it, I don't regret it at all. Because . . . it says a lot of things that other people wanted to say."[43] Indeed, the ethnomusicologist Aaron Fox has demonstrated that some working-class communities see Cash as a symbol of resistance to the corporate control of country music. Fox surveyed local bar owners in Texas, who were incensed that they were threatened with lawsuits because they did not pay licensing fees to ASCAP and BMI (for music played in their bars), and many summarized their feelings in sentiments such as "Johnny Cash wouldn't stand for this."[44]

It was only with the crossover success of *American IV* that the country music industry and country radio attended to Cash again. Rubin argues that the renewed interest was spurred by the album's economic gains (it was Cash's first Gold Record in thirty years, excluding his greatest hits albums).[45] The album won three CMA awards in 2003, Cash's first in thirty years. Country Music Television (CMT, a sister company of MTV, both owned by Viacom) created a Video Visionary Award for him at their 2003 Video Music Awards and thereafter named it in his honor (Cash's musical compatriot Kris Kristofferson was the recipient in 2006). Cash's checkered history with the Nashville music industry reflects the stresses of economic imperatives combined with creative expression and his labyrinthine negotiation of his insider-outsider status.

Voice and Sincerity

Cash's musical and performance elements contribute centrally to his authenticity effect, and it is important to note how they also involve a contradiction. Although

Cash had a comparatively limited vocal range and sometimes failed to hit or maintain the right pitch, he nevertheless mastered the art of conveying sincerity and suffering through singing in his distinctive bass-baritone voice. As William Echard has argued, the more idiosyncratic the voice, the greater the listeners' identification with the singer's persona (a multi-layered construction).[46] Fox, in his study of country music fans in working-class Texas communities, argues that Cash's voice signifies a working-class "structure of feeling" (pace Raymond Williams), that stands for "brooding darkness and historical marginality in every sung phoneme" and expresses solidarity with the world's poor and oppressed, the "sonic equivalent" of his black clothes.[47] Fox describes Cash's voice: "Low and gravelly and accented and weary and dour, Johnny Cash's voice will always signify pain and entrapment and struggle, the sonic equivalent of the black garments he always wore in solidarity with the poor and the oppressed of the world." Fox goes on to catalogue its musical elements: "its drawled, broad Ozark vowels, its hollow depth, its pungent back-of-the-throat midrange and gravelly texture, its complete lack of ornament or vibrato, and its deep, almost impossibly resonant low register, is so completely unique and identifiable and 'extra-ordinary' that it surely qualifies as one of the most inherently compelling voices in the history of recorded American song."[48] Fox argues that musical imitations of Cash are an integral part of working-class performance. In his study of the "poetics of direct mimetic quotation," he found that Cash's performance is only convincing to such audiences if the singer has a "biographically embodied voice" marking their own working-class experiences: "Knowing all the words did not mean knowing a song. The right words had to be saturated with the sweat and specificity of a particular body, a particular life, and a particular voice."[49]

A full musicological analysis of Cash's voice, including a spectral analysis, would be a productive undertaking. I do not have the expertise to engage in that project myself, but to point toward possible musicological research questions beyond the scope of this study I cite here the suggestions of the musicologist Denise Von Glahn, who comments on potential areas of interest regarding Cash's voice and sound. Her observations are meant to be suggestive, not exhaustive. She observes that Cash's sound is unique partly because the depth of his voice leaves more room for overtones. When other sounds are layered on top of it, the result is a singular, fuller, richer sound that ultimately signifies power. At the same time his voice has a flattened, direct, folk-like character, and possesses little of the vibrato that is generally associated with vocal training and is synonymous with the high arts. His voice is raw and grainy. She notes that Cash's unpolished sound, coupled with a defiant insistence on being heard, fits nicely with his image of speaking for the disenfranchised or the "common man."[50]

Cash's voice cuts through other sounds but also blends in with accompanying instruments on his recordings and performances. His longtime producer, Jack Clement, dubbed him "Captain Decibel," because his voice picked up remarkably well on sound recording equipment because his "apparent level" (versus actual level) records so well. Clement notes: "He's got the most amazing recording voice that I know of, in terms of getting on the tape." He adds: "It's a commodity. You just can't hardly cover it up. It's almost impossible to drown him out. You can put in lots of drums, horns, a roomful of guitars and everything else—he still cuts through. It's powerful. There's few voices I've ever heard like that."[51] Von Glahn points out that this effect is related to the fundamental low pitch of his voice and the play of upper partials. Yet at the same time, elaborating on how Cash turned his imperfect voice into a highly effective emotive vehicle, Clement notes how Cash blended in with the instruments of the band: "I wouldn't call him a great musician. I'd call him a great musical entity. He was a musical force and a great singer. People believed what he was saying. Most people don't understand that the voice is like an instrument and has to blend in with the other instruments. Somehow Cash understood that. Mostly because he didn't care. He would just sing. Somehow it worked."[52] Clement's comments underplay the extent to which Cash's sound is carefully fashioned, but they do point to Cash's singing as natural and effortless, which here functions as part of his authenticity effect. Clement's remarks also underscore how, as Albin Zak has detailed, popular music recordings function as artistic artifacts involving the collaboration of songwriters, musicians, engineers, and producers.[53]

The simplicity of Cash's music also contributes to a sense of sincerity, his ability to deliver emotional rawness and "truth." When a young Cash first arrived in Memphis in 1954 to try to break into music and got a hearing with Phillips, he apologized profusely for not having a "professional" band but just bringing in friends who played music with him. Luther Perkins (on electric guitar) and Marshall Grant (on standing bass) at times had trouble playing their instruments. Infamously Cash's signature "boom-chicka-boom" sound, mimicking the sound of a train (as many musical elements in traditional country music do), stemmed in part from their inexperience. Perkins was sometimes reduced to keeping time on the bass strings of his electric guitar. Cash put a dollar bill in his acoustic rhythm guitar strings to give it a percussive sound. The sparse backing rhythms highlighted Cash's deep, powerful, ominous voice, and Phillips dubbed Cash's ensemble Johnny Cash and the Tennessee Two ("Johnny" for the marquee appeal, as opposed to the name "J.R." from Cash's childhood, or "John R." as he was known during his Air Force stint). When they later added W. S. Holland on drums, the band became The Tennessee Three. Phillips marketed their unusual, plaintive sound—what the biographical movie *Walk the Line* has Reese Witherspoon, playing June Carter to Joaquin Phoenix's Cash, describe as "sharp like a razor, steady like a train."[54] Cash later explained how Perkins's curious sound came about: "Luther took the metal plate off the Fender guitar and muted the strings because he said he played it so ragged he was ashamed of it and he was trying to cover up the sound."[55] Grant noted: "We didn't work at that sound. It was all we could play."[56] This sound is evident from their first single in 1955, "Hey Porter" with B-side hit "Cry, Cry, Cry," to other hits including "Folsom Prison Blues" (1955), "I Walk the Line" (1956), and "Home of the Blues" (1957), from the first of his Sun albums, *Hot and Blue Guitar* (1957), and on through his other six at Sun. It remained Cash's touchstone throughout his career.

The idea of musical simplicity in Cash is also misleading, because his rudimentary sound is distinctive. Simple technique does not mean it is generic or always easily replicated. Colin Escott notes that Cash's sound was original but not as unique as Cash claimed; earlier artists, including Hank Williams, also featured electric guitarists keeping a ticktock beat on their bass strings, and singers such as Ernest Tubb and Jimmie Skinner both sang slowly in deep voices with little accompaniment.[57] Likewise, some scholars point to the influence of Maybelle Carter, who famously revolutionized country music by popularizing a guitar style called "The Carter Scratch." Speaking to the way country music has come to idolize her style, one recent documentary on the Carter Family memorializes footage of her guitar being placed in the Country Music Hall of fame, as the musicians Vince Gill, Gillian Welch, and others lovingly fetishize the instrument Carter played for fifty years. The musician Mike Seeger explains that Carter adapted a "banjo feeling" to the guitar. The guitar was only just beginning to become popular when she started playing it. Her innovation was to combine rhythm and melody in her playing, what Seeger describes as "thumb bass with rhythm lick in the treble." Carter developed this style because she needed to be able to accompany herself, playing both the lead and the rhythm line. She played melody notes on the bass strings and rhythmic fills on the treble strings, such as partial chords and runs (all designed to keep the rhythm line moving forward even while she attended to the melody). Carter had learned to play a banjo-picking style from her mother before she began playing the guitar, and when she moved to guitar, she adapted banjo techniques because she used a thumb pick for the bass note and her index finger for her strums and fills (sometimes a combination of strums and notes, or eighth-note strums; Carter also employed methods for making the notes resonate, like slides, hammer-ons, and pull-offs). Bluegrass players today who invoke the "Carter Scratch" usually do so using a flatpicking style, holding the pick between their thumb and fingers and rapidly executing downstrokes and upstrokes. Carter was the first recording artist to popularize her style, although others had been using similar styles. She put her own signature on it, giving it what Welch describes as a special, driving "bounce" that makes even dark, tragic lyrics less disturbing because the guitar is always moving forward energetically.[58]

Cash played rhythm guitar, and he mostly used standard, simple techniques. He most often used the I–IV–V patterns of chord progressions standard to blues and country songs and played alternating bass lines (in which the player plays the note that forms the root of the chord, then strums several designated strings in the chord, then hits another note in the chord, then strums again). He sometimes used walking bass lines (picking out notes between chords as the player moves from strumming chord to chord on the bass strings). But the influence of Carter's innovation is evident in Cash's propulsive sound and, perhaps, for example, using his thumb to strum his bass note.

In some of his songs Cash was also more complex. The notion of Cash's musical simplicity is deceptive. Consider, for example, the song "I Walk the Line." As the musician Guy Clark points out: "'I Walk the Line,' it just sounds like the simplest thing in the world, but it's really not. It's really a fairly difficult song to play and sing at the same time. To actually play it on a guitar and sing it is kind of like patting your head and rubbing your stomach."[59] This difficulty is partly because that song has a peculiar composition history. Cash got the odd chord progression during his Air Force stint. He was playing music with his cobbled-together guitar and string band, The Landsberg Barbarians, comprised of buddies in his barracks. A friend had used Cash's tape recorder to record himself playing guitar but put the tape in incorrectly, so when Cash played the tape, it played backward, sounding "otherworldly" to Cash. As Cash describes the sound: "All he was doing was strumming the chords on the guitar . . . and anyway at the end of the chords, he said 'Turn it off.' And as it happened, turn it off sounded like 'Father' played backwards. And it sounded like a religious ceremony or something. And it never got out of my mind and I never got that chord progression out of my mind—from E to A to D to A to E to B7th back to E."[60] Cash said his long humming between verses in the song resulted from his need to sound out the pitch of his next note in order to hit it correctly. While this song is one of his most elaborate ones, the key point here is that Cash's sound in his oeuvre is deceptive in its simplicity (it is both rudimentary and sophisticated), and the combination of components is unique.

Projections of Identity

The element of paradox in Cash's persona can be further explored by assessing how Cash is framed in autobiographies, biographies, media accounts, and marketing materials. Examining how the trope of contradiction appears in Cash's own self-presentation reveals key recurring themes, including, as mentioned above, his busting of musical genre categories, the tensions involving the commercialization of country music and the commodification of celebrity, country music's well-documented anti-modern criticisms and nostalgia for an agrarian past, and Cash's negotiation of identity politics (race, gender, and competing definitions of American patriotism).

In his own self-presentation, Cash insists on irreducible complexity. He goes so far as to create a model of multiple identities.[61] Perhaps most famous is his creation of "The Man in Black" narrative persona in his 1971 song as a conscious construction to speak for the impoverished and the disenfranchised: "But just so we're reminded of the ones who are held back, / Up front there oughta be a Man in Black."[62] He also imagines numerous selves in his two autobiographies. The first, *Man in Black* (1975), covers his childhood through 1975, and *Cash: The Autobiography* (1997) provides an overview of those years and then follows him through 1997 and the onset of the severe health problems that thereafter prevented him from touring.

In *Cash*, he explicitly addresses how he represents his identity differently in different contexts, noting how he uses different names for the different "Cashes" he played in different social settings, stating that he "operate[s] at various levels." He stages a struggle between "Johnny Cash" the hell-raiser, hotel-trashing, pill-popping worldwide star and "John R. Cash," a more subdued, adult persona. He also describes the names he uses as signifying his social role and relationships in assorted contexts. He writes: "I go by various names. I'm Johnny Cash in public and on record sleeves, CD labels, and billboards. I'm Johnny to many people in the business. . . . To June, I'm John, and that's my name among my intimates. . . . Finally, I'm J.R., my name from childhood. My brothers and sisters and other relatives still call me that." Not only does he distinguish between the public and private persona, but he also has what he calls "levels of intimacy" within his personal sphere. Noting that his family is aware of his different named personas and what they symbolize, Cash elaborates on how his wife calls him different names depending on his behavior: "Cash is her name for the star, the egomaniac. Johnny is her name for her playmate." In an interview with her father, Tara Cash once asked him, "Did you ever have an imaginary friend?" and he replied, "Yes. Sometimes I am two people. Johnny is the nice one. Cash causes all the trouble. They fight."[63]

Cash talks of moving in and out of character, whether in public or private dimensions of performance. He describes himself as "complicated," and endorses Kristofferson's walking-contradiction line, as well as daughter Rosanne Cash's depiction: "He believes what he says, but that don't make him a saint." Cash elaborates: "I do believe what I say. There are levels of honesty, though."[64] He delineates how he navigates his performance of identity: "I prefer to meet people before my shows, not after. When I walk off that stage I'm no longer the character I was in the songs I sang—the stories have been told, their messages imparted—but often it's a while before I'm J.R. again. When I meet people, it's important for both of us that I'm J.R."[65] His comments register how authenticity is always a constructed idea, rather than a naturalized one, that depends on the context, since both he and his audience need to be aware of his narrative persona, "Johnny Cash," as a character he slips on and then gradually sheds.

In the way that both autobiographies and biographies recount his familiar life narrative and rise to fame, they emphasize his vacillations and speak to the convolution of his image formulation. Cash frames his life story in terms of an ongoing spiritual struggle with his own inner demons: his drug addiction versus his Christianity, his sometimes depressive and destructive behavior against the angels of his better nature. In an authorized biography published after Cash's death, Steve Turner explains Cash's life as one "clouded by pain" (a high degree of physical suffering, such as the unmendable broken jaw he had to sing through for many of his final years, plus guilt over his brother Jack's tragic death as a teen, his alcoholic father's mistreatment, his infidelities and drug abuse) and "colored by grace" (Cash interpreted all his trials and tribulations along the lines of Job).[66]

In first wife Vivian Cash's posthumously published memoir, where she focuses on how Cash's drug abuse destroyed their marriage even though she never stopped loving him, she publishes Cash's voluminous letters to her from Germany. The letters capture the military man as a tentative, unsure youth eager to marry her; they show him getting to know Vivian through a culture of epistles, writing himself into being, trying on versions of selfhood, as he barely knew her before leaving for Germany. His volume of letters to her is striking (and is typical of him, as he wrote numerous letters to friends and associates—and even to himself—all his life). His letters focus on explaining and understanding his feelings, beliefs, motivations, and experiences through these written narratives to others, and they bespeak a writerly sensibility evident in the song lyrics, autobiographies, and his novel about St. Paul.

Locating his appeal in "his vast love and his vast acceptance of paradox," Rosanne Cash argues: "His heart was so expansive and his mind so finely tuned that he could contain both darkness and light, love and trouble, fear and faith, wholeness and shatteredness, old-school and postmodern, and sacred and the silly, God and the Void."[67] On the topic of juggling his private and public lives, the deep context for his identity construction, she suggests that Cash was only comfortable when he could keep his competing impulses in productive tension:

> It's weird. He's so comfortable living this public life for forty years that it's part of his private life. Real life tends to be disappointing for him a lot. I see him trying to get away from it. His impulses for healing and spirituality are constantly being pulled on by his impulses of self-destruction. They're the same thing. One is a warped attempt to do the other. The constant travel, the spiritual seeking, the drugs. It's too much to sit still and be on this planet.[68]

Her formulation is striking for how she sees Cash's opposing poles as versions of the same in his identity formation, the sacred and the profane as mirror images of each other. Implicitly, in her telling, as in many others, this tortured overlapping of healing and self-destruction, grace and pain—and the restless, seeking energy it generates—defines Cash.

Providing further examples of his ambiguous nature, Cash has often been marketed in terms of a trio of his favorite themes, famously encapsulated on his three-disc boxed set, *Love, God, Murder* (Sony, 2000; later joined by the posthumously released disc *Life*). We find contortions of the three subjects as we move back and forth across his lyrics, thematic content, autobiographical and biographical narratives, marketing, and public persona. Again, Cash sang "I Walk the Line" (1956) about marital fidelity (to his first wife), but his most enduring love story stems precisely from infidelity (the *Walk the Line* biographical movie turns on this issue, making epic drama from the Cash-Carter story line). As Merle Haggard said, the song was "kind of ludicrous for him to sing," because Cash "never walked any line."[69] Cash's anthem for fidelity is thus paired with infidelity, because of the open secret in his projected public image. This public image is a comment on the construction of gender and sexuality in country music, not to mention stereotypes of gendered behavior by star musicians on tour.

Cash's religious convolutions are also particularly powerful. As discussed further in chapter 5, Cash was a devout Christian (raised as a Southern Baptist) who took Bible classes, made a film about Christ called *The Gospel Road* (1973), and evangelized on the Billy Graham crusades. Yet he often avoided church and organized religion himself, excoriated religious hypocrisy, and encouraged his children to follow their own beliefs. The liner notes to his *God* disc market his religious thorniness. Cash writes: "At times, I'm a voice crying in the wilderness, but at times I'm right on the money and I know what I'm singing about." In liner notes for the same disc, Bono of U2, who recorded with Cash, writes: "Johnny Cash is a righteous dude . . . but it's the 'outlaw' in him we love."

Cash's outlaw image is entwined tightly to his murder ballads. Famous for singing about killing and violence, he never did hard time himself. His autobiographical narratives tie his concern with prisoners to redemption—theirs and his. He felt a kinship with them owing partly to what he termed his own religious fight between dark and light within himself, which some journalists attributed to the legacy of his father's alcoholism (though Cash himself downplayed its impact on him).[70]

His narratives of identity present his drug abuse as a key issue in his ability to identify with prisoners, and with human frailty and suffering more generally. He offers his first autobiography as a "spiritual odyssey," in which he argues that drugs and fame drove him from his Christian faith and upbringing, but once he returned to his religious beliefs, he was able to correct his path. Writing in the spiritual autobiography mode, Cash offers his conversion narrative as an example for readers. In a prefatory personal note that works to establish sympathy with the reader, Cash dedicates his book to his fans, to religious seekers, and to failed Christians like him, declaiming that "if only one person can be saved from the death of drugs, if only one person turns to God through the story which I tell, it will all have been worthwhile."[71] While his message is triumphal, he still emphasizes the constant struggle he faces with his drug addiction and inner demons, and his second autobiography underlines his unceasing battles with his own polarities.

His account in his first autobiography frequently pairs the issues of addiction with religion as a dichotomous internal struggle. He summarizes how his battle with drugs was serious and lifelong, beginning with the amphetamine addiction, which began in 1957 when he started taking pills to help him stay awake on the road during grueling tour travel. Cash writes that the drugs "turned me on like electricity flowing into a lightbulb."[72] He recounts how his years of drug and alcohol abuse, marked by drug busts (like his 1965 arrest for smuggling amphetamines across the border from Mexico), left him emaciated, barely able to perform, and suicidal. He wrecked cars and hotel rooms, set things on fire (including, accidentally, a national forest), played with guns (one quick draw with Sammy Davis Jr. got him ousted from a hotel), and even hauled around cannons and loaded guns. The incident he famously cites as his turning point occurred in 1967, when he attempted to kill himself by crawling into Nickajack Cave on the Tennessee River. Ultimately he crawled out of the cave because he felt that God wanted him to live. June Carter and his mother were there as he emerged from the cave, saying that he would quit drugs and commit himself to God because God had saved him.[73] Cash recounts how he went "cold turkey," suffering through withdrawal with the support of June Carter and her family. He claims he was able to eschew drugs for a period of time, but he had relapses throughout his life, necessitating interventions, including a trip to the Betty Ford Clinic. As we have seen, however, his biographer Michael Streissguth and band mate Marshall Grant claim that Cash was only drug-free for a six-year period and abused drugs heavily the rest of his adult life.[74]

Just as he frames his engagement with prison issues as part of his dark-light, addiction-religion polarities, Cash keeps ambiguity at play in his interactions with reporters on this topic. In interviews as well as in his autobiographical writings, he extensively contemplated his prisoner image alongside the reception of his Man in Black persona. The degree to which his symbolism weighs as heavily as his music in the public mind is evident in the three questions that, he says in his second autobiography, reporters always asked him throughout his career: Why was he in prison, how does he write songs, and why does he always wear black?[75] Dispensing with the song composition question easily by saying his practices vary, he addresses the sinuousness of his image in his replies to the other two queries.

The way that Cash answers these questions in his life narrative debunks myths but also perpetuates the idea of his own incongruities. Noting that people think he served time because of the prominence of "Folsom Prison Blues" (1955) and his Folsom Prison concert album, Cash observes that "there are those who just don't want to accept the nonfelonious version of me, and on occasion I've had to argue with people firmly convinced that whatever I might say, I once lived a life of violent crime." He points out that his most famous line, "I shot a man in Reno just to watch him die," is "the one that still gets the biggest rise out of my audiences, especially the alternative crowds," but that the line is obviously "imaginative, not autobiographical." Cash—perhaps thinking he was following the folk ballad tradition of synthesis—lifted many of the lyrics from an earlier song, Gordon Jenkins's "Crescent City Blues," and he later settled a lawsuit with Jenkins over it, paying out almost a hundred thousand dollars. Streissguth notes that Cash later told Marty Stuart that he had developed his own signature line by revising two lines from Jimmie Rodgers's famous "Blue Yodel #1 (T for Texas)": "I'm gonna shoot poor Thelma / Just to see her jump and fall."[76] Cash gained inspiration for the song upon seeing the Hollywood film *Inside the Walls of Folsom Prison* while in Germany and reacting with sympathy to the drama about corrupt prison conditions. Despite the well-documented media sources for his song, Cash, in recounting how he got into the mind-set to compose the song, wants to maintain the emotionally resonant idea that he identifies with prisoners and killers: "I sat with my pen in my hand, trying to think up the worst reason a person could have for killing another person, and that's what came to mind. It did come to mind quite easily, though."[77]

Cash characterizes his most enduring symbol, his signature black garb, as one that involves an oppositional struggle over meaning. He emphasizes that, although it eventually came to signify his Man in Black persona, he first started wearing black out of necessity: he and his band wore black at their first public performance because they were the only matching clothes they had for their "band outfit." His comments implicitly establish his working-class status (they could not afford to buy other outfits) and his struggle to replicate the performance codes required to break into the hierarchical recording industry (one with manifold approaches to class and authenticity, as discussed earlier). Cash writes that he maintained the black except for a brief early period when he wore "flashy outfits" that his mother made for him (like a white rockabilly suit). In his first autobiography, Cash also explains his vestments in terms of somber religiosity. He notes that his initial performance in black was in a church, and that he would sometimes reply to the black-clothes question simply by telling reporters: "Black is better for church."[78] Elaborating in his second autobiography, he says he also, however, wanted to turn the black clothes into a message, given the consistent queries from reporters, especially during the time he had his network television show on ABC, and he did so with his Man in Black persona. Framing the persona as an oppositional symbol for contesting official discourse, he insists that wearing black is "still my symbol of rebellion—against a stagnant status quo, against our hypocritical houses of God, against people whose minds are closed to others' ideas."[79] Thus, in different narratives circulated by Cash, the costume has multiple significations, from ideological protest to support for religious observances to straightforward pragmatism linked to class status.

The context for his initial performance of "Man in Black" and the lyrics themselves emphasize the persona as one that attempts to script audience responses to it. Cash wrote the song for a special episode of his television show filmed at Vanderbilt University in Nashville and in explicit support of the right of students to protest and question their government. The subsequent album release, *Man in Black* (1971), also included a song about a trip Cash took to visit the troops in Vietnam in 1970 (during which he suffered a drug relapse), and his urgent cry for the war to end, "Singin' in Vietnam Talkin' Blues." Cash frames the "Man in Black" song lyrics as a response to the endless questions about his garb, opening with the sentiment: "Well, you wonder why I always dress in black," and going on to explain, "Ah, I wear the black for the poor and the beaten down." His song references a variety of social ills (poverty, Vietnam, prisoners, the sick and elderly), calls for social change, and insists on his own performative response to these problems: the song's narrative speaker promises to maintain a black stage costume that signifies resistance to oppression, the song itself incites listeners to advocate for social change, and the singer incorporates this protest stance as part of his representational strategy. Singing that "I'll try to carry off a little darkness on my back," Cash merges autobiography, narrative persona, social message, and political critique into a pedagogical message about how listeners should inter- pret his black clothes. Similar lines in his final two stanzas suggest the speaker's hopeful yet pragmatic call for social change, and his insistence on his stage per- sona, enacted in the song, as a symbol for that need for change, describing how he will not wear a white suit until things are changed and made "right." As he turns himself into a walking symbol in this song, Cash develops his iconography further, in imagery journalists continued to elaborate. Even given his multiple explanations for his stage clothes, the symbol is never static but is, instead, layered and multivalent.

Depictions of Contradiction

In others' depictions of Cash, the sheer wealth of references to his contradictory nature is staggering, but so, too, is the sense that Cash is someone to fight over and defend. Equally noteworthy is how often accounts make him a metonym for America. In Steve Turner's biography, Kris Kristofferson's foreword enshrines Cash as "a true American hero, who rose from a beginning as humble as Abraham Lincoln's to become a friend and an inspiration to prisoners and presidents."[80] Kristofferson maintained that Cash's "face ought to be up on Mount Rushmore," a line journalists and biographers like to repeat (and one that echoes, perhaps, a Highwaymen video in which Cash, Kristofferson, Nelson, and Jennings are depicted as the faces of Mount Rushmore).[81]

The music journalist Brian Mansfield, in his compilation of quotations about Cash, discusses Cash's mythology in ways that are typical of other journalists' accounts in that he posits the essence of Cash's social presence as an icon representing America's irresolvable discrepancies. Mansfield writes: "perhaps no other singer in American popular music has crossed as many boundaries as Johnny Cash." He goes on to locate the source of the singer's appeal: "Cash was seen as a poet, patriot, preacher, and protestor. He absorbed the images the way black absorbs light. He was all those things—and, by being the sum of them, he became something entirely different. Cash, with his overpowering presence, was large enough to encompass such paradoxes. . . . Did he contradict himself? Very well then, as Walt Whitman might have said of him, he contradicted himself. He was large. He contained multitudes. He was, after all, Johnny Cash."[82] The comparison to Whitman is apparently an easy shorthand for referencing a writer who himself included multiple vernacular voices and not, of course, an in-depth correlation between the two men.

In another variation on this theme, Mansfield's November 2005 *USA Today* cover story about Cash, prompted by the *Walk the Line* movie release, imagines Cash as both rebel and guru with a pedagogical message to be gleaned from his inner turmoil: "Both icon and iconoclast, Johnny Cash began his career as a tormented superstar possessed of a black-clad, James Dean cool. He ended it as a soft-spoken sage who showed future generations of musicians how to stare down age and death with dignity." Mansfield goes on to strike the Whitman multitude chord again when he argues: "Cash tapped into so many streams of the American myth—self-made man, gold-hearted rebel, champion of the underdog—that he became Everyman, not because he was like just any man, but because he was like all of them."[83] Such massive claims for Cash's ability to embody all elements of a cavalcade of American mythic types might seem untenable, yet they recur so frequently in music journalism about him that this idea of Cash encompassing and transmitting the lifeblood of American character and folk culture is a truism in his iconography, almost a cliché.

Similarly, the writer Nicholas Dawidoff, in his 1997 book on country music, frames Cash in terms of warring personality traits that mirror America.[84] Dawidoff argues that Cash is as much a "piece of Americana" as the objects Cash collected, like "John Wayne's pistol, Frederick Remington's cowboy sculptures, Buddy Holly's motorcycle, and Al Capone's chair."[85] Cash as American folk hero becomes a national collectible. The link critics make between Cash and his country is both thematic and musical. Dawidoff argues that Cash's voice is a metonymy for a certain version of the South: "Lodged somewhere between talk and music, his singing is flat and artless and grim, the way the white poverty-stricken South was flat, artless, and grim."[86]

In yet another posthumous tribute that interprets Cash through the cultural vocabulary of contradiction, the *Rolling Stone* book *Cash* collects music journalism from that magazine spanning much of the man's career as well as posthumous remembrances. The editor Jason Fine lauds the singer for "the darkness he struggled with, the America he believed in and the peace he wished for all of us," and DeCurtis delights in his "glorious mess of contradictions," and the pull of both violence and religion in Cash's "divided soul."[87] In his biographical overview, Mikal Gilmore underscores key moments in Cash's personal and artistic history that embody polar opposites.[88] Gilmore cites Cash's 1969 session and collaboration with Bob Dylan on "Girl from the North Country" for Dylan's *Nashville Skyline* album. This musical meeting of the minds yoked together icons of country and rock, melding the supposedly conservative, nostalgic values of the country genre with rock's revolutionary, avant-garde critiques in a collaboration that was somewhat shocking to some audiences at the time. Yet, as we have seen, Cash's longer connections to the folk revival movement, and his dedication to preserving the folk culture of early country music, are solid grounds for that collaboration. More important, from the viewpoint of American controversies, Gilmore notes Cash's stance on Vietnam and his 1970 invitational performance at Nixon's White House as examples of his ambiguity.[89]

Indeed, if we look at Cash's oeuvre as a whole, the Vietnam/Nixon issue is a particularly good example of how Cash troubles categories with his multiple significations. Cash's stance eventually alienated him from the Lefty urban folk revival, as these revivalists were looking for an organic intellectual and were disappointed in him. Cash supported the office of the president and the troops, but he also sanctioned the right of students to protest the Vietnam War, especially as so many of them faced being drafted and killed. He famously sang, in "What Is Truth?" (1970) (one of the songs included at the Nixon performance), that one cannot blame young men of draft age for questioning the truth of what they are being told, since they may have to "lay down" their lives for it.[90] His "Man in Black" lyrics similarly decry the pileup of scores of dead soldiers each week. For the Nixon performance, Cash declined to play Nixon's requests: Merle Haggard's "Okie from Muskogee" and Guy Drake's "Welfare Cadillac." Haggard's complex populist song was commonly interpreted at the time as an anti-hippie, pro-war song, and Drake's was seen as a racist anti-welfare song that satirized supposed welfare abuses. Cash reportedly refused the Drake song because he thought it was racist, and headlines gleefully decreed that Cash had snubbed Nixon.

Yet, in later lyrics and comments, Cash playfully avoids resolving the tension between his patriotism and his social protests. He ridicules efforts to spot his discrepancies, ducks any attempt to script him into consistent political positions, and insists on his ability to fashion his own variable stances. An early draft of the song "I'll Say It's True" refers to the Nixon White House incident and resists the narrative that his refusal to play the requested songs was intended as a direct criticism of Nixon; one stanza includes the lines "I like Okie from Muskogee" and "I like Welfare Cadillac."[91] Although the published version of the song omits these lyrics, the original lines seem incongruous, contrary to his other public stances on the issue of social protest, counter to his Man in Black outsider persona. In what seems like an apolitical retreat that deflects any truth claims about him, Cash's draft lyrics use the White House event as an occasion to criticize the effort to turn him into an icon. More than that, however, the lyrics reject efforts to hold Cash to a resolved, coherent narrative about his life experiences, his musical tastes, or his political beliefs.

When addressing the Nixon incident in his second autobiography, Cash similarly performs a double move—he both articulates his politics and insists that no one else can inscribe those politics for him: "The issue wasn't the songs' messages, which at the time were lightning rods for antihippie and antiblack sentiment, but the fact that I didn't know them and couldn't learn them or rehearse them with the band before we had to leave for Washington. The request had come in too late. If it hadn't, then the issue might have *become* the messages, but fortunately I didn't have to deal with that."[92] Cash explains his views, but then again he does not; he resists reporters' accounts but leaves his own version ambivalent precisely on the issue of how others will frame his actions and beliefs—he claims he did not have to go "on record" with his politics at the White House, but he leaves open the possibility that he might have.

In my reading of Cash here, I again depart from Malone, who argues that Cash resolved the tension between his support for student protesters during the Vietnam War and his patriotic support of Nixon by allowing the patriotism to win out. For Malone, Cash's real emphasis was always on the dominance of his patriotism, not on a call for social justice. This argument fits well with another paradox that Lewis sees in country music: the unquestioning acceptance of authority and state in the political realm as patriotic, and the idea that this capitulation to power actually supports individual freedom.[93] Indeed, when Cash did things like perform for Nixon's White House or support the office of the president or participate in commercials for Standard Oil, he disappointed counterculture supporters in the 1960s who, again, saw him as potentially the next Woody Guthrie, a proletarian popular hero, or what Gramsci would term an "organic intellectual," or a leader organizing his class.[94] On the one hand, Cash did make comments that were interpreted as hostile to the cause of the labor movement, for example: "If you're not going to support the president, get out of my way so I can stand behind him."[95] Yet his commitment to the folk movement and to counterculture causes and social justice can be seen throughout his long career. The newsletters and publications of his fan club, archived at the Country Music Foundation, emphasize Cash's ongoing efforts on behalf of the "underdog." Fans routinely sent in newspaper clippings, reprinted in the newsletter, of Cash singing for local chapters of labor unions and raising money for anti-hunger and anti-poverty campaigns as well as American Indian advocacy efforts.

Malone insists that when Cash was asked to play Nixon's White House and refused to perform the two songs cited above, the liberal media mistakenly trumpeted that act as a rejection of Nixon. Malone contends that Cash refused to perform the songs simply because he didn't know them.[96] Malone's assertion is not the whole story, however, since Cash makes it clear that he wished to dodge being categorized but that, if forced to do so, he may well have taken a political stand. The markers of the narrative are Cash's insistence on retaining his own political affiliations, sympathizing with both left- and right-wing causes, and refusing to be placed in any one political category. Cash refuses to resolve the tension between social protester and government supporter, and in order to deal adequately with Cash's complexity, we must resist the temptation to force him into an easy resolution.

Many reporters have unsuccessfully tried to fashion a clean story for Cash, the one dramatized in the film *Walk the Line*—a story of redemption in which Cash moves from rebel youth druggie to dramatic recovery through the help of God and June Carter. Although Cash approved the film's script and sometimes supported the narrative, at other times he did not. Noting how Cash delighted in thwarting reporters, an early biographer, Christopher S. Wren, notes that Cash "has never been able to explain himself," and the star's deflection of easy answers or story arcs "usually sends reporters frustrated to their typewriters."[97] More often Cash kept his own vacillations active.

Some journalists actually go so far as to label inauthentic any portrait of Cash that is not about contradiction. In a *New York Times* editorial criticizing the film *Walk the Line* for downplaying Cash's religious faith, Robert Levine notes that the Broadway show *Ring of Fire* (2006) itself downplays Cash's bad behavior. Sounding the common note about Cash as paradox, Levine says that perhaps "Cash's life is simply too big for one movie" and "different fans could remember him in different ways." He goes on to argue: "But he was far too complex a figure to be claimed by either side in the culture wars. Although he was guided by faith, he never cared much for organized religion; he had a sense of himself as deeply flawed, but not beyond hope of redemption. Those contradictions, as much as the compelling story of *Walk the Line,* are what make him fascinating."[98] His comment registers the complex, subjective, contextual nature of any act of interpretation. But *Walk the Line* and similar biographical narratives do not so much ignore Cash's contradictions as they try to find explanations for them that are ultimately unsatisfying because his ambiguities foil closure.

Hurt Video and Projections of Identity

Concluding this chapter with an emblematic reading of Cash's *Hurt* video, the text is analyzed for how it perhaps best synthesizes many of these biographical and autobiographical narratives. Directed by filmmaker Mark Romanek, the award-winning video for "Hurt" (2002), Cash's cover of the Nine Inch Nails song by Trent Reznor, summarizes Cash's life and career in a striking visual montage. It entangles layers of fact and fiction, and renders Cash's constructions of identity and authenticity as a theme embodying American contradictions. The elderly, frail star sings in his wobbling baritone Reznor's lyrics about a regretful junkie: "What have I become / My sweetest friend / Everyone I know goes away in the end," and his pitch wavers over "What have I become."[99] As the song's persona, Cash sings of his own mortality and regrets in life, offering listeners his riches as an "empire of dirt" and focusing instead on a wish to do things over. The song itself emphasizes Cash's singular authenticity by emphasizing his lone guitar playing (using finger-style picking) at the beginning, then adding his voice, and then overlaying piano in rising crescendos, which give the song a sense of hopefulness even in the face of the despair communicated by the lyrics. The song also opens with three minor chords, but then shifts to major chords for the chorus, underscoring a sense of movement and hope. It concludes by subtracting all elements other than the man and his guitar, and then finally only his voice. The vocal timbre of Cash, singing here as an old man, sounds rougher than his voice does in earlier recordings.

The video illuminates how commercial representations of Cash present him as a border-crossing icon. The text won awards (including the Grammy and Country Music Association Award for best video and an MTV Video Music Award for Best Cinematography) as well as emotionally charged responses from viewers and critics. Many applauded its treatment of mortality and death in Cash's self-referencing rendition of Reznor's industrial rock drug song—serious points not usually seen on MTV.[100] It would be wrong, however, to read this video as simply a romanticizing project. More important is how the text tries to make sense of Cash through his own mixture of forms and paradoxical themes. Indeed, the video critically explores the process of turning an artist like Cash into an icon, part of what Sut Jhally terms the commodity-image system.[101]

In its form and content *Hurt* imagines Cash, who crosses both musical and political categories, as multifarious. Romanek's use of montage conveys this sense of fragmentation and multiplicity through scenes of Cash performing as the song's narrative persona intercut with Cash's own home movies, concert footage, and previous film and television appearances. Like Cash's multiple selves in his autobiography, the video builds on themes of the "real" Cash blurring into the "fictional" one, as his movie characters become a version of him, or his home movies become part of his fictional icon persona. A fictional video that uses documentary forms, *Hurt* is what the media studies critic John Caldwell would term a "docu-real" text.[102] The energetic footage of Cash from his much younger days contrasts sharply with scenes of him acting as the song's ailing persona.

The video depends on the juxtaposition of themes, anchored by images of Cash in black clutching his guitar or playing the piano, his hands trembling when not playing music. It features an extended visual metaphor of material wealth and stardom as a decaying, lonely, opulent feast, where he pours out the wine on the banquet table. In contrast, we see uplifting pastoral images of religious hope and rebirth, for example, a dove flying over a river. The video intercuts footage of the suffering Jesus on the cross from Cash's film *The Gospel Road* with prison footage of Cash playing San Quentin and from the video for "Folsom Prison Blues." *Hurt* references Cash's struggles with his own personal demons, often through his familiar cultural vocabulary of religion versus drugs. Cash increases the religious imagery. In the song's third stanza, for instance, Reznor's original lines discuss a "crown of shit" the speaker wears, while Cash changes the crown to one of "thorns" (just as Cash likewise eschews the discord Reznor used in the original, instead eventually focusing on hopeful major chords). Shots of the statesman are intercut with shots of the wild man. The elderly Cash with June Carter Cash and their awards, the fleeting acclaim of the culture industry, appear beside performance footage from his amphetamine years, a young, haggard Cash projecting intensity and violence. We see an image of the American flag, but it appears next to a disintegrating House of Cash museum (once home to his offices and recording studios), a building meant to stand as a monument to his legacy but instead closed down because of flood damage. The subversive, reversed, upside-down American flag logo of American Recordings itself implicitly flies over all the proceedings.

The video captures significant recurring themes in Cash's oeuvre, given its attempt to summarize his entire career. The frail present-day Cash juxtaposed with the virile young star jumping trains, for example, speaks to his charged construction of a Southern white working-class masculinity as it appears in country music, which, again, is in tension in his corpus with a postmodern questioning of identity categories.

Pastoral nostalgia is another key trope in the video, fitting in nicely with how country music idealizes the pastoral to bemoan industrialization's destruction of tradition. The video, mining this vein, features images of a forlorn, young Cash visiting his childhood home in Dyess, Arkansas, and the fields where his family worked as sharecropper cotton farmers. On one level, this footage is a nostalgic return to his youth, but it also marks how country music articulates the nostalgia that many Americans have for the rural, agrarian past. These shots capture the U.S. movement from a rural agrarian to an urban industrial and post-industrial society, and the cultural expression that this shift engenders. The video here borrows from Robert Elfstrom's 1969 direct cinema documentary of Cash, *The Man, His World, and His Music,* which trails Cash making a trip to the abandoned farmhouse of his childhood while on tour.[103]

As we have seen, Cash himself tried to preserve older proto-country music forms, such as nineteenth-century ballads and the early-twentieth-century Carter Family standards. Yet he also embraced a modernist, avant-garde mixture of forms and an urban cosmopolitanism, and his collation reflects national tensions around emergent and residual ways of life and cultural forms. The video references the materiality of rural life with the documentary images of his old home and cotton fields, as well as footage of floods like the one that threatened his childhood home when the Mississippi River flooded in 1937, immortalized by his song "Five Feet High and Rising" (1959). Thus Cash typically confronts this theme with a combination of nostalgia, ambivalence, and regret, and his stance hails his interpretive community.

If, as I have been arguing, Cash embodies a model of placing competing American ideas in a productive tension, *Hurt* demonstrates how contradiction is evident in both the form and content of Cash's music. Regarding musical form, as discussed above, we find productive tension here in how Cash combines musical styles. The video depicts Cash's cultural syncretism of genres not only because it positions him as the Man in Black, wearing a black, fringed Nudie-style suit (named for the tailor who designed the signature opulent, rhinestone-covered

suits of country music) in a country star mode of address, covering Reznor's industrial rock song about drugs, but also because the interspersed historical performance footage refers to his career-long mix of styles.

Scholars have long shown how American popular music is deeply mixed—and
how that cultural mixing of European and African forms both inscribes American
history and often replicates problematic race relations, such as whites appropriat-
ing black music for profit.[104] Since mixture permeates American popular music,
Cash is not unique in his own boundary crossings. I believe, however, that Cash
is an important model of cultural mixing and ambivalence because he stages the
pleasure that audiences take in both transgressing and reasserting categories like
musical genres, styles, and traditions. As he violates category boundaries—like
country and rock music or progressive and conservative politics—he also calls
the original categories into being. He himself rejected music genre boundaries,
famously bringing folk, rock, country, gospel, R&B, and soul artists onto his television show and, at various points of his career, collaborating with musicians as
diverse as Dylan or Rubin's stable of artists like The Red Hot Chili Peppers. Yet
even as Rubin marketed their American Recordings albums as crossover roots
music, journalists were still asking Cash to address the category issue. When
MTV's Kurt Loder, in Cash's final interview, asked him how he classifies himself, Cash said, "You got to call me like you see me." Loder was rejecting strict
genre boundaries, yet he nevertheless asked the same question journalists had
been asking Cash for fifty years.[105] Though Cash often found the country label
too limiting for his music, he still wanted recognition from the country music
establishment that had largely ignored him as a solo artist during the 1980s and
1990s. His Grammy success with his American Recordings albums (specifically
his 1998 Grammy for Best Country Album for *Unchained*) prompted the famous
1998 advertisement that Rubin ran in *Billboard* of Cash flipping off the camera
from his San Quentin concert as they changed the purpose of the famous image
to chastise the country radio and music industry for its provincialism—and as its
anti-music industry message has inspired legions of musicians to post the ad on
their tour buses since then.

We know that musical genres serve as organizing principles—they hail audience segments, imagined communities, subcultural affiliations, marketing categories, radio play, industry labels and awards—and they also signify musical
and lyrical forms that artists choose to respond to in some way, even if their
response is to reject the conventions. Genres are fluid, changing, and indeter-
minate, based on the socio-historical contexts of production and reception and
the uses to which they are put (much like the concept of authenticity itself). The

scholar Simon Frith notes that through "genre rules," genres "bring together the aesthetic and the ethical" and convey "ideological and social discourses" about value and meaning and who has the power to judge.[106] Cash's work and image stage an intricate double movement, a pleasure in transgressing but also identifying with these genre categories and genre rules.

These formal issues are, of course, linked to content. As we know, the very idea of mixing musical styles raises larger ideological issues about cultural mixture. Here again, Cash exposes false oppositions and binary thinking in favor of ambiguity. Most important in this regard, Cash's long-running engagement with American Indian–white race relations illuminates how his incongruities are a crucial component of his ability to scrutinize the sociopolitical tensions that popular music both shapes and reflects. Turning to a consideration of race and gender in Cash's oeuvre, the next two chapters examine his formulation of Southern, white, working-class masculinity and then discuss his depictions of American Indians.

2

"A BOY NAMED SUE"
American Manhood

Nothing is as macho as Johnny Cash's voice.

—**Bono, U2**

He was one of the originals. He was one of the first guys
to embody that "Don't mess with me" image.

—**Kirk Hammett, Metallica**

He's such a man to look up to, just for a male to look up to a man, you know,
you can't think of anyone more inspiring than that. People should get down
on their knees in front of him for what he's done and the songs he's written.

—**Jack White, The White Stripes**[1]

Johnny Cash is an icon of Southern white working-class masculinity. The embodiment and performance of that masculinity—in his persona, lyrics, and biographical and autobiographical self-presentation across the second half of the
twentieth century—are multilayered and raise key issues for the study of masculinity in U.S. popular culture generally. Cash performs a version of heroic
masculinity, and the popular connotation of his media image is the idea that

he is a "man's man," that is, a virile masculine role model. The components of that version of Cash include his outlaw status; his Man in Black persona as an anti-authoritarian voice for the poor, the prisoners, and the disenfranchised; and an exemplary speaker for the "common man." As indicated by the epigraphs to this chapter, expressing the sentiments of Cash's fellow musicians in the wake of his death, the macho image stems from aspects of his musical performance, especially his signature deep voice, as well as from his rebellious attitude and the kind of proletarian advocacy he infused in his songs. Thus he can be seen as a forefather for musicians ranging from Irish protest rockers to heavy metal "axemen" (in that highly male-centric genre) to indie rockers. At the same time, however, Cash also questions this construction of masculinity and also gender codes more generally. In some of his lyrics and performances, Cash conveys an uncertainty about gender norms, questions what constitutes manhood, and portrays a suffering and fraught masculinity. These thematic contradictions speak to the social construction of masculinity in popular music, specifically in country music, as well as to the changing formulations of Southern white working-class masculinity during Cash's more-than-fifty-year career.

In keeping with the focus on complexity and conceptual flexibility in his oeuvre, Cash is a key case study because his work simultaneously stages and questions this iconic masculinity and presents an ambivalent version of Southern white working-class masculinity. Barbara Ching has argued convincingly that "hard country" artists respond to outsider attempts to frame Southern white working-class masculinity as abject by incorporating a critique of outsiders in their defiant articulation of this masculinity, and, as noted earlier, Cash could be included in this model.[2] In Cash's versions of masculinity, however, the critique involves more than that dynamic. His texts question gender binaries to some degree or, at the very least, suggest that gender roles are arbitrary social categories. As Sheila Whiteley has observed, traditional gender codes in country music are so rigidly patriarchal, presenting the active male and passive female as the norm, that drawing attention to uncertainties in those codes denaturalizes them.[3]

Cash's engagement with substantive issues of masculinity is an essential element of his paradigm of contradiction. Like the other key themes that he explores through this vernacular, Cash's representations of gender offer opposing forces and competing tendencies that are not easily resolved. Instead, his texts examine some of the difficult tensions that inhere in the performance of gender in different socio-historical contexts, treating the paradoxes and oppositions with respect, exploring them in all their polyvalence. In so doing, his work speaks cogently to the quandaries of Southern white working-class life in the twentieth century.

The masculinity he performs is, of course, tied to the masculinity he assigns to the characters he writes and sings about, characters with which he encourages his audiences to empathize and identify. He sings of common men who are often heroically masculine. Some of his lyrics, implicitly or explicitly, are about his own life, invading the speaker in his song with his own persona. This kind of identification between speaker and subject is common in country music and contributes to the genre's projections of truthfulness and sincerity.[4] Cash's commentary on his male characters may not always display approval of their actions, but, ultimately, it is deeply sympathetic to them; thus his portrayals of these men model and validate certain versions of gender role performance.

The version of Southern white working-class masculinity in Cash's lyrics portrays hard-working, hard-bodied men struggling to provide for their families, even if that means breaking the law, men who suffer and are prone to violence but are always admirable in their travails. They are conflicted about the migration from the rural farm to the bustling city, from tradition to modernity, and their focus is always on physical labor rather than movement into the Information Age. Declaring their loyalty to mother and wife, and often seeing women as ministering, domestic angels, they also sometimes see women as a source of problems, as a possession liable to stray, and as a target for their violence.

But even when Cash's signature songs stage this version of masculinity, often they also question it and emphasize its uncertainty. Cash's men alternately boast and worry about manhood. Some of his characters try to be godly men or follow what they see as a Christian model of manhood, but they also express perplexity about their faith or how well they are embodying Christian ideals, instead suffering in their negotiation of faith and manhood. Some express both the desire for marital fidelity and the impossibility of living up to that ideal. Many dwell on the inevitability of roaming, the lure of the rambling life that undermines a normed model of masculinity based on the domestic family unit, such as the modern nuclear family that achieved center stage in the postwar 1950s, as Cash was launching his career. From sharecroppers to train jumpers to working hobos to hardened criminals, Cash's men negotiate their own version of identity that is in dialogue with dominant cultural norms but frequently departs from or is marginal to them.

Theories of Gender and Popular Culture

Why does this examination of Cash matter to the larger analysis of gender and popular culture? I join several other scholars who have looked at key male figures in country music and shown how their expressions of masculinity are more complex than one might think, and how these figures shed light on the gender constructions of this popular music genre. [5] Given the genre's wide circulation in popular culture, such case studies also illuminate the popular formulations of masculinity in key socio-historical contexts. Given the long-running stereotypes about country music as a male-dominated field that pushes conservative, patri- archal values, the genre is clearly an important one for understanding changes that have occurred in constructions of manhood across the twentieth century, beginning with the early stages of country music's commercialization in the 1920s. This inquiry can tell us how popular forms impact specific versions of masculinity in American cultural and social history. Broadly speaking, the study of gender and popular culture can tell us how texts enter into a circuit of mean- ing-making in which gender is one of the key cultural ideas being shaped and reflected through the various stages of production and consumption, as these texts circulate through industries and audiences. Scholars of this subject in vari- ous fields have noted that popular culture is a key space where gender ideology is formed and expressed, and where the varied negotiations of masculinity— through vernacular, folk, popular, and mass media culture—constitute a con- voluted history.[6]

My study joins an emerging body of scholarship on gender and country mu- sic. Charles Wolfe has observed that scholarship on country music has only developed since the late 1960s (with Bill C. Malone's *Country Music U.S.A.*, in 1968), and that some of the first generation of historical scholarship perhaps inadvertently reinforced popular ideas of gender stereotypes and the emphasis on country music as a male-dominated field. Newer scholarship emerging from me- dia studies and feminist studies, particularly since the 1990s, has been addressing gender more critically. It has revealed women's contributions, recovering their ef- forts to succeed as country musicians despite the well-known industrial practices barring them (such as limits historically on the number of "girl singers" played on country radio). This work builds on Mary A. Bufwack and Robert K. Oer- mann's important history of women in country music.[7] Kristine M. McCusker and Diane Pecknold's vibrant collection, *A Boy Named Sue* (taking its title from Cash's song), questions the industry's stereotypes and how some scholarship has reinforced these rubrics.[8] In other key examples, Joli Jensen has examined the negotiations of gender imagery by female stars such as Patsy Cline, and Pamela Fox has explored gender-coded notions of authenticity in the autobiographies of Dolly Parton, Loretta Lynn, and Reba McEntire, while David Sanjek has demonstrated the contributions of women in honky-tonk and rockabilly.[9] The call for more scholarship on gender that examines nuanced imaginings of both femininity and masculinity echoes larger discussions in popular music studies. These trends include recent efforts to decenter "rockism" paradigms (defined as a focus on rock as a masculinist musical and scholarly formation) as well as crucial studies of gender in popular music.[10] Important investigations of masculinity in popular music include genre studies such as Rob Walser's research on masculinity in heavy metal, and investigations of key artists such as Whiteley's assessment of Mick Jagger's shifting performance of masculinity in rock and Gareth Palmer's discussion of working-class masculinity in Bruce Springsteen.[11]

These efforts in gender studies have broader applicability. For example, George Lipsitz and others have criticized Richard Peterson's influential account of authenticity in commercial country music on the grounds that his paradigm of "hard country" authenticity versus "soft" country-pop sounds (like the Nashville Sound) makes unexamined gender assumptions, with the "pure" masculine-associated styles enjoying greater credibility and the feminized styles being seen as "sell-outs."[12] This discussion recalls Andreas Huyssen's examinations of a masculinized, modernist celebration of a "pure" or "high" art in danger of being diminished by a feminized mass culture.[13] Those larger cultural issues would have had currency in the 1950s, when Cash was breaking into the popular music industry. Of course, country music is a particularly interesting case here, as the masculinized pure art would be the residual, supposedly pre-modern folk culture sounds such as the "high lonesome" pitch and "twang" in the voice that can also be stereotyped as feminine. Indeed, because the intricate staging of authenticity in country music has been a topic of much critical debate, gender becomes an important site for this discussion, as gender paradigms are strongly linked to authenticity issues.

In what follows, Cash's gender themes are analyzed by placing his texts in key socio-historical and cultural contexts. Cash's work is framed in terms of the American ideals of manhood, which is the broadest relevant rubric. A discussion of scholarly accounts of American manhood will reveal that Cash's working-class masculinity is both marginal, and resistant, to middle-class ideals, especially as it is presented in his train songs.

Marginalized Masculinities

Cash's work implicitly considers what constitutes manhood and questions what critics would term "hegemonic masculinity," defined as the construction of masculinity that is privileged in a particular historical and power context, up-

holding instead "marginalized masculinities." Specifically his texts establish a
marginalized, working-class masculinity as defiant and critical of middle-class
norms, while also considering the uncertainties of that working-class manhood.
R. W. Connell and Michael Kimmel have demonstrated the need to account for
multiple masculinities and how masculinity is always defined in opposition to
a feminine "Other." Erving Goffman satirically describes this hegemonic male
in a twentieth-century American context as "a young, married, white, urban,
northern, heterosexual, Protestant, father, of college education, fully employed,
of good complexion, weight, and height, and a recent record in sports."[14] This
model is defined to contrast with "emphasized femininity," an ideal where women
comply with male desires, emphasize social over technical skills, accept gender inequality, and comply with the hegemony of a patriarchal social and labor
organization.[15]

Connell has detailed how the idea of hegemonic masculinity draws on Antonio Gramsci's Marxist concept of hegemony in class relations, where a dominant
group establishes social leadership and secures the cooperation of subordinate
classes.[16] Marginalized masculinities, in Connell's paradigm, include manhood
as "Othered" by class or race; for example, black masculinity defined in opposition to white masculinity, or working-class manhood in opposition to the middle
class. Connell notes that working-class masculinities (of the kind relevant to
Cash's oeuvre) are often subordinated to middle-class bourgeois ideals, and thus
some working-class celebrations of manliness and self-respect, beginning in the
nineteenth century, grew out of a resistance to middle-class management.[17]

In U.S. history hegemonic masculinity, since the nineteenth century, has
meant a middle-class ideal of the self-made man, the white bourgeois breadwinner who embraces individualism and competition and who benefits from a race
and gender hierarchy. Cash's sharecroppers, prisoners, and impoverished rural
Southern men certainly do not embody this type of masculinity. As a writer,
Cash emphasizes the common man's valor as the bedrock of America. His songs
are infused with a working man's ethos and frustrations, and they often express
resistance to middle-class ideals. But when Cash himself embodies a masculinist
performance persona, he does not embody hegemonic masculinity. Instead, he
emphasizes his relationship to a Southern white working class, not only in his
themes but also in performance elements such as Southern pronunciations (dropping "g's" at the end of -ing words or singing words like "horse" as "hoss," as in
his cover version of Jimmy Driftwood's song "Tennessee Stud") or his boisterous
"suey" pig-calling yell that punctuates many of his songs in performance. Cash's
Southern accent is one significant quality of his vocal timbre.

In order to contextualize how Cash's working-class heroes negotiate American models of masculinity, and use strategies of accommodation or resistance, it is necessary to outline key issues in masculinity studies and some general narratives of how manhood ideals evolved in America. Cash's men are laborers, railroad men, farmers, and truckers—hard-working men who enact a version of masculine pride. His insistence on the dignity of these men and his celebration of them speak to multiple models of masculinity in America's cultural history. The men use their hands and bodies, again focusing on manual labor rather than techno- logical "skilled" labor of the Information Age that has become one of the defining models for middle-class manhood in the late twentieth century. Meanwhile, the distinction between different kinds of labor and salaries marks an increasing gap between the classes. However, Cash's songs include a number of different mascu- linities, which are contextualized below, for example, a working-class manhood of pride, hard work, and functioning as the male head of the household supported by the "love of a good woman"; a residual artisan manhood; manhood defined through war and soldiering; heroic frontier masculinity; and a working-class mas- culinity that celebrates women as laborers alongside men (as in Depression-era families or in the newer postmodern family patterns of working-class men strug- gling to survive in a globalized market economy).[18]

Michael Kimmel, Anthony Rotundo, David Leverenz, and Dana Nelson have shown that the history of manhood in American society centrally involves the emergence of the middle-class "self-made man" ideal from the early Republic to the present. Although that bourgeois ideal has taken on different dynamics over time, it has become firmly connected to state power and the development of market capitalism, resulting in what has variously been described as an entrepre- neurial manhood, or the rationalized manhood of the professional managerial class. This paradigm of manhood emphasizes individualism and competition, an effort to define one's manhood against other men, a patriarchal hierarchy, a racial hierarchy (where white men dominate men of other races), a vision of the man as the breadwinner, and an investment in the legitimization and cultural validation of the structural conditions of patriarchy (male-dominated institutions, homosocial institutions, etc.). This middle-class masculinity has direct links to national ideologies. For example, Nelson traces the emergence of what she terms "national manhood" from the 1780s to the 1850s as an ideology linking white manhood as a fraternity to civic identity and forming the root of later middle-class professionalization.[19]

In the nineteenth century the emergent bourgeois masculinity competed with other forms of masculinity. Many of the different models for thinking about this competition and evolution suggest that the Industrial Revolution supported the rise of a northern middle-class manhood over earlier colonial models of, in effect, aristocratic manhood (landowners like George Washington), as well as an artisan manhood (self-sufficient workers such as shopkeepers or farmers, like Thomas Jefferson's yeoman farmers, who pride themselves on hard work and independence).[20]

These paradigms are relevant to Cash's oeuvre, particularly since he projects so many of the men in his songs into the past. The working hobos from the Depression era in many of Cash's songs have lost their farms or their claim to some kind of residual artisan culture of manhood (in "When Papa Played the Dobro," such a man turns to the folk traditions of music as a comfort, even when he is unable to play skillfully). Joining the working hobos are men forced to work as sharecroppers, robbed of their independence, the working poor whose labor is exploited by the "self-made men" ("Come Ride This Train," "Face of Despair"). Sometimes these men have traded the ideal of independence on the farm for urban life, but, in a dynamic common to country music, they regret their move to the dehumanizing, alienating city and want to return home again ("The Ballad of Barbara," Cash's version of the "Barbara Allen" ballad). Most of Cash's male heroes are the working-class "Others" against which the hegemonic middle-class male would define himself. Many of them express their frustration at the disempowering class relations and masculine competition they experience, and they often criticize hegemonic masculinity and emphasize the internal discrepancies of that model.

The frustrations that Cash's working-class heroes face under urbanization and increasing industrialization are also relevant to the evolution of the bourgeois, self-made man. These forces impacted middle-class manhood at the turn of the twentieth century and grew more intense as they combined with internal pressures—freedom versus competition, the emphasis on individualism versus the connection of manhood to the state—and pressures from "Others" such as women agitating for more rights.[21] Connell asserts that as hegemonic masculinity became more rationalized, masculine violence was pushed symbolically to the frontier (enabled by the historical imbalance in the numbers of men versus women on the frontier), resulting in the shaping of frontier masculinity in, for example, James Fenimore Cooper's novels, Buffalo Bill Cody's Wild West shows, and Hollywood Westerns. This ideology of manhood, embodied by figures from Theodore Roosevelt to John Wayne, constituted what Connell calls a "self-conscious cult of inarticulate masculine heroism."[22] Cash's sustained exploration of frontier masculinity follows in this pattern, most notably in his concept album, *Ballads of the True West*, which embraces cowboy mythology.

By the postwar 1950s middle-class manhood, as mentioned earlier, is connected to the modern nuclear family ideal and the kind of suburban domesticity that Cash and his rockabilly brethren threatened. But the 1970s and 1980s witnessed the start of what scholars term a "crisis in masculinity," which created links between the middle class and an aspiring working class that are particularly relevant to developments in country music. Challenges to patriarchy, such as the women's and gay and lesbian movements, prompted various responses such as the men's liberation movement of the 1970s, the Robert Bly mythopoetic men's movement of the 1990s, and the "metrosexual" image of the 1990s and 2000s. Meanwhile, the economic stresses of deindustrialization and globalization have also caused marked downward mobility in the lower middle classes.[23] These gender developments are also affected by a shift in demographics and cultural norms from what sociologists term the "modern family," an older nuclear model emerging from industrialization that became a culturally idealized form in the Victorian period and peaked in the 1950s. A diversity of "postmodern family" forms emerged in the second half of the twentieth century. Social historians define the modern family as a nuclear unit with a male breadwinner, female homemaker, and dependent children; its gendered division of labor was largely only an option historically for the white middle class where the male head of the household had access to the "family wage."[24] Although this pattern was upheld as a dominant cultural ideal, it never represented a majority of people.[25] The 1960s and 1970s saw the emergence of diverse family arrangements, comprising what the historian Edward Shorter termed "the postmodern family."[26] Families labeled blended, single-mother, post-divorce, and gay and lesbian have materialized, spurred by increases in divorce rates, single-parent households, women's entry into the labor force in large numbers after 1960, the decline of the "family wage," and the pressures on labor caused by post-industrialism and globalization.[27] Such demographic changes sparked a political backlash beginning in the 1970s, notably in the form of the "family-values" media debates that have intensified since the 1990s.

These combined challenges have resulted in white male anger in the 1990s, especially in the middle class (office workers, salesmen) and the lower middle class (small farmers, shopkeepers), who feel that the structures of patriarchy or their sense of social identity are threatened. Kimmel describes these angry groups as "the 'Pa' in the Ma and Pa store, Richard Nixon's 'silent majority,' and Reagan

Democrats."[28] In response to the trend of downward mobility, the self-made man is in crisis; as the journalist Susan Faludi argues in *Stiffed* (1999), these men are experiencing a sense that they are losing "a useful role in public life, a way of earning a decent and reliable living, appreciation in the home, respectful treatment in the culture."[29] This masculine frustration impacts middle-class men, most acutely the lower middle class, but also has implications for white working-class men with mobility aspirations, too.

We can see the traces of the "national manhood" that Nelson identified in various political appeals to cross-class gender bonding, especially Ronald Reagan's 1980s appeals to white working-class men to support his Republican agenda on the basis of shared patriarchal "moral values," even though his economic policies were severely detrimental to that group. Jefferson Cowie and Lauren Boehm have studied Reagan's efforts to co-opt Bruce Springsteen's music in the 1980s, even though some of Springsteen's working-class aesthetic would seem counter to the Reagan agenda.[30] Linking this paradigm to Cash, I argue that Republican National Party efforts to uphold Cash as a symbol of patriotism and solidarity at the convention in 2004, despite left-wing efforts to claim Cash as a proletarian advocate, constitute an example similar to that of Bruce Springsteen. Such efforts to co-opt Cash perhaps work on the same logic: an appeal to patriarchal patriotism that tries to co-opt the white male working class.

In developments particularly since the 1980s, country music has become a repository for perceived conservative, patriarchal values and the feeling among some white men that they have been disenfranchised. Some scholars see this trend as a betrayal of country music's earlier potentially progressive working-class roots. For example, along with the hypermasculinity he sees staged in heavy metal and hip-hop, Kimmel identifies the surging popularity of what he calls "rockified country and western" music as a symptom of the rage of "NASCAR dads" who are turning to nostalgic songs that offer both fantasy resolutions to their identity crises and an aggressive rock attitude (songs about lost love, about turning to simpler pleasures like cars and beer to cope with economic troubles).[31] Kimmel distinguishes this new trend from traditional country music, which, as the "music of America's rural working class," can explore the realities of working-class life and gender, including trepidations about the challenges involved. He argues that, unlike a slightly earlier superstar like Garth Brooks in the 1990s who combined bravado with compassion as a "sensitive S.O.B.," a new generation of stars in the 1990s and 2000s such as Toby Keith focus on white lower-middle-class resentments with unbridled masculine aggression, glorifying the Everyman father, husband, and soldier who does not get the respect he deserves and threatens male violence in response (witness any of Keith's post-9/11 anthems to the "American way" of macho violent retaliation).[32]

Cash occupies a unique place in this welter of masculine ideals. Although I would not place him in the Keith category of reactionary response to displacement, there are songs where Cash voices some version of white male working-class aggression. He has become a common symbol in some recent country songs— those with a strong rock flavor of the kind Kimmel isolates—that stop short of Keith's specific political aggressions and instead invoke Cash as an icon of masculine rebellion. Jason Aldean's song "Johnny Cash" (2006) fails to address Cash with much specificity, instead repetitively invoking him in very general terms for his outlaw "badass" cachet. The lyrics tell of a male protagonist who quits his job, grabs "his woman," jumps in his car, and hits the open road, fleeing to Las Vegas to escape his troubles, cranking up Cash on his radio to signify his masculine anger and disaffection. Similarly, Montgomery Gentry's "Hell Yeah" is emblematic of a number of bar party songs that offer a "shout out" to Cash as a symbol of a rebellious, hard-living man.

"Locomotive Man"

Although these invocations of Cash are largely escapist in their resolution of the tensions in working-class or lower-middle-class masculinity, Cash himself is more wide-ranging, substantive, and investigative in his own treatment of these themes. Some of his songs actually examine the historical evolution of working-class labor, capturing the sweep of some of the narratives cited above. Many voice the marginalized masculinity of working-class pride in one's labor, or a valuation of residual artisan values, and even a sense of how working-class gender roles sometimes differ from dominant middle-class roles in needing women to labor alongside men. Two of the best examples are his version of the most popular American ballad, "John Henry" (about the famous train worker and "steel-drivin' man"), and one of his train songs, a medley titled "Come and Ride This Train." Cash recorded both songs in the 1960s, his period of association with the urban folk revival movement.

His deep fascination with trains and railroad culture as symbols for American working-class ideals is evident in his dedication to this topic throughout his composing career, from his first released single ("Hey Porter" in 1955) to his final composition ("Like the 309" in 2003), with many rambling men ("Locomotive Man") and working hobos ("Ridin' on the Cotton Belt") in between. His television show included a segment called "Ride This Train," for which the song

"Come Along and Ride This Train" (1969) was written. The segment, which Cash had to fight his network to keep on the show, featured historical material about trains and documentary footage. It follows on his earlier album by that name, *Ride This Train* (1960), which includes songs about escaped prisoners ("Going to Memphis") and working hobos trying to support families ("Papa Played the Dobro"). Cash also starred in a 1974 documentary, *Ridin' the Rails: The Great American Train Story*, which used Cash's patented formula of presenting historical material "in story and in song." He narrates and sings while the documentary intercuts historical reenactments set to Cash's songs. Written and produced by Nicholas Webster and Dyann Rivkin, and directed by Webster, the documentary argues for the importance of trains in building modern America. Emphasizing the idea that trains represented opportunity for poor Southerners, Cash begins his narration, walking down a train track and saying: "There's nothing that stirs my imagination like the sound of a steam locomotive—that lonesome whistle cutting through the night and that column of black smoke and steam throwing shadows across the land. When I was a boy the trains ran by my house and they carried with them a promise that somewhere down the track anything would be possible."[33] Covering the late-eighteenth-century invention of steam engines and railroad history highlights such as Lincoln's Railroad Act (1862) and the meeting of East and West in the transcontinental railway (1869), the documentary includes reenactments of major events (including a segment featuring a crew of African American "gandy dancers" laying track by hand, with a caller singing songs to provide rhythm to work by). All are accompanied by Cash's renditions of railroad songs. It also includes reenactments of Cash's version of folk ballads such as "John Henry," "Casey Jones," and "Wreck of the Old '97," all lauding heroic feats of train workers who died in their work.

In "Come and Ride This Train," Cash's driving boom-chicka-boom sound mimics trains. Thematically, he uses a train as a unifying, omniscient perspective from which to view America's growth and the evolution of its labor practices. He calls listeners to journey, figuratively, on the train with him to witness how it links all parts of the nation, including American Indian reservations and sharecroppers toiling in the cotton fields of the Mississippi Delta. He describes how "life is pretty hard" for such denizens. Cash urges his audience to see how the interstate highways now provide the road over the same ground where "the lonely pony express rider carried the mail." He then describes westward expansionism and settlement, and concludes by praising the truck driver who carries on the tradition as the "modern mover of America." These lyrics suggest that America's growth, as indicated by developments in transportation, is linked to the tradition of the working-class man making the system function.

In Cash's oeuvre as a whole, trains are multilayered symbols. They can signify national unity, a desire for mobility, and a barrier to mobility for poor men who cannot afford a ticket. His hobos jump trains to look for work and ramblers board them to flee stable family units. Perhaps most important, however, trains crystallize a key contradiction in working-class life. Train workers are celebrated as symbols of authentic working-class labor and part of an anti-modern critique. Trains brought new job opportunities to the working poor, but trains are also part of the mechanization process; they also displace human labor and bring more poverty. In the working-class tradition of "Ride This Train," transportation is the labor of working-class men. The men who make the system function are paid low wages and are often replaced when labor processes become mechanized.

Aaron Fox argues that, musically, "Folsom Prison Blues" exemplifies working-class views of trains. For him, the song signifies the train of progress leaving the working class behind via Luther Perkins's electric guitar riff and the common country "train" beat of the song ("slightly uneven sixteenth notes accented on the second and fourth beats of the bar"). Fox insists that Perkins's riff is one of the genre's most "symbolic musical figures," because it stands for a "whole rural, working-class structure of feeling." Fox describes it musically, with Perkins

> repeating the low B like a machine gun, pouncing upward onto the D-sharp which always seemed dissonant because it didn't resolve immediately to the E above it, instead slinking back down through the low B to a slurred, bent blue-note G moving almost to a G-sharp, marking the ambiguous tonality of the song, halfway between E major and E minor, symbolizing the "blues" of the title and of the song's narrator, then winding down through a bent F-sharp moving almost to the G, and finally sliding off that bend into a sharply attacked open-string tonic low E on the downbeat.[34]

On that final downbeat, the band comes in with the train beat. For Fox, Perkins's insistent, off-kilter bluesy riff, the full band sounds that mimic a train, and the lyrics all signify the tortured working-class sense that mobility and progress are happening just beyond their reach. It is also notable that the live recording of Folsom from the prison concert has a faster tempo than the studio version, and the percussive speed emphasizes the train feeling as well as the sense of a faster tempo and the focus on Cash's voice as the elements that will most appeal to that live audience.

As Malone notes, jobs on the railroad represented an important alternative to farm work and even through the early twentieth century these jobs were the apex of respectable wage labor for both black and white male laborers.[35] Malone argues that folk and country music tend to celebrate the railways more than criticize the abuses of the railroads (some of which sparked dissent such as Populism), instead seeing trains as a symbol of the Industrial Revolution and the access of the Southern poor to those changing conditions. Malone sees such ballads as "John Henry" as celebrations of individualism and manhood, as Henry will die to protect his manhood.[36] Again, although Malone sees Cash's working-class songs as escapist in this vein, I disagree and argue instead that Cash does make structural criticisms here.

In the case of "John Henry," Cash's elaborate version of the traditional ballad comments on working-class history, the evolution of labor and technology, and marginalized masculinities. The folk ballad (drawing on early Anglo-American ballads) eulogizes John Henry, a black man famous for his strength who toiled as a railroad worker in West Virginia in the 1870s on the Big Bend tunnel.[37] Cash's version, "The Legend of John Henry's Hammer," is a lengthy eight-minute song in which the tempo speeds and slows with the action described. It incorporates Cash's oral storytelling recitations, dialogue, and sound effects (such as hammers hitting steel, train whistles, and steam) to approximate the action taking place. It appeared on Cash's labor concept album, *Blood, Sweat, and Tears* (1962), which includes his cover of Jimmie Rodgers's "Waiting for a Train" and his version of the "Casey Jones" ballad that recounts how the famous engineer was willing to die at the controls of his engine. Cash's version of "The Wreck of the Old '97" similarly emphasizes the idea that the engineer dies on the train because he is pushing it so hard to stay on time.

On one level, "John Henry" tells the story of a man's individualistic triumph through masculine competition. As Henry's boss challenges him to drive a superhuman amount of steel, Henry does so, and women come to admire his hard-bodied strength. The jealous boss, eager to demean Henry, has him compete against a machine, hoping to emasculate him. Engaging in mock masculine jests with the machine itself, Henry beats it but later dies from the exertion, and his admirers make him a folk hero, honoring his grave.

Cash, on the other hand, emphasizes a stringent class critique throughout. In criticizing a mechanization that invokes religion, Henry asks his boss if it is God's will for machines to replace working men with families to feed, wondering: "Do engines get rewarded for their steam?" Cash's song begins with sympathy for impoverished men struggling to support their families, and it continues the Southern working-class tradition of empathizing with such men when they break the law under these conditions. Henry's father is the one who gives him the hammer so he can work to help support his eleven siblings; the father has escaped from jail twelve times trying to provide food and medical care for his twelve children.

The song examines marginalized masculinity, here in a black working-class hero. Henry chooses his heroic death in defiance of his boss in order to make a symbolic point. He tells the man that even though he might die beating the machine, he will die laughing, with his "hammer in his hand," because while a man "ain't nothin' but a man," he will still triumph over a machine. Henry will show that a "steel-drivin' man" is not replaceable. Such a focus on the body in manual labor, which entails both the potential for heroic exploits as well as injury and death, reflects on the tenuousness of working-class masculinity associated with the male body.[38] Cash's lyrics speak to the fragility of hard-bodied masculinity in this context when he describes Henry's grave as the place where the legendary hero is lying, finally receiving respite for his injured back, and a place where trains slow and men remove their hats in deference when they pass by it.

The critique of machines and technology that Henry offers from the point of view of an authentic, hard-working man is ironic, because he is toiling to build the very railroads that will make him obsolete. The paradox of his anti-modern critique involves the more general core paradox we see in country music (premodern nostalgia articulated through the very forms of modernity that are erasing the premodern). Henry's victory is that he will live on as a folk hero, an alternative vision of heroic masculinity who dies resisting his subordination, who "talks back" to the professional managerial class of bourgeois men. Here, Henry also represents a marginal version of masculinity in his relationship with his female partner. Like the folk tradition of women seen in songs as labor partners (and carried on by singers like Hank Williams), Henry sends his woman to work in his place once he knows he is dying. Because she is John Henry's woman, Cash sings that she will be able to perform heroically and carry on his steel-driving tradition, which is better than any machine; when the other men see her swinging his hammer like Henry did, they will know that she is Henry's woman. Henry here imagines that he can bequeath his masculine prowess to his female partner and she can carry on the working-class protest for him. The ability to drive steel with heroic strength also appears as an almost artisanal, craft-like skill; the father passes the hammer and skill to his son, who teaches it to "his woman."

Here, if the railroad boss is implicitly trying to rise in the managerial ranks of the self-made man, he does so only by exploiting the labor of his workers, and his boasting will never triumph over working-class, hard-bodied manhood. The song's criticism of exploitative industrial bosses becomes even clearer in one verse in the song where Henry, before the contest, sleeps briefly in a coal mine for his supper (implying that he goes hungry). The mine boss wakes him up, yelling for him to start working to dig out enough coal with a pickax to approximate another "hell" for him with its burning fires. This description of the coal mine as a burning hell and the boss's aggressive attempts to exploit any nameless, faceless laboring man he can find (and from whom he will demand subservience) speaks to the exploitation of the more noble working-class men. As we will see, this trope permeates Cash's corpus and illuminates American ideals of manhood in different eras.

3

GENDER AND
"THE BEAST IN ME"
Ramblers and Rockabillies

As Cash develops his theme of manhood, reflecting the specific socio-historical contexts in which he is writing and performing, his representations also embrace the broader sweep of country music's treatment of the tensions in Southern working-class life. Each section of this chapter considers a key recurring gender theme in Cash's oeuvre and examines it both from the viewpoints of specific moments—paradigmatic examples of songs or albums in their immediate sociocultural contexts—and in the broader frame of Cash's lyrics in relation to country music's traditional depiction of rural Southern life. The first section analyzes Cash's rambling-versus-home theme in his earliest performances of this motif— his Sun singles and 1950s rockabilly—and its threat to postwar middle-class domesticity. The next section examines Cash's depictions of prisoners—a variation on the rambler—in the context of his 1960s prison albums and the folk revival. The last section assesses Cash's treatment of tension in love relationships—his version of the "battle of the sexes"—in *American Recordings* (1994), especially "Delia's Gone," in the context of the 1990s Americana roots movement.

Roaming versus Domesticity

Cash's combination of opposing forces and a concomitant questioning of gender performance and norms recurs in his corpus in particular contexts. The rambling-versus-home theme is evident in his earliest singles with Sun, and his output for Sun (1955–58) points up the conflicts in masculine roles. As discussed earlier, "I Walk the Line" pledges masculine fidelity while suggesting its impossibility. Other Cash-penned songs portray similar themes. "Come in, Stranger" captures the marital alienation caused by a musician's life on tour. Some songs crow about masculine prowess in love ("Straight A's in Love"), and others pledge devotion but note constant temptation ("You're the Nearest Thing to Heaven"). Many of these songs focus on ramblers, both men and women, who are torn between home and roaming, and reject domesticity or only fitfully embrace it. Some male protagonists roam yet feel pulled home ("Hey Porter"), and others are left to chase their roaming women or wait for them to return, all while feeling a sense of dislocation and identity trouble because of the woman's departure ("Big River," "Wide Open Road," "So Doggone Lonesome," "Port of Lonely Hearts," "Don't Make Me Go," "Next in Line," "There You Go," "Two-Timin' Woman").

These themes are amplified by rockabilly performers, as these perceived incendiary types were seen as threats to postwar suburban middle-class domesticity. As carefully marshaled by Sam Phillips, the rockabilly movement was youth-oriented and featured disruptive expressions of masculine sexual energy. This dynamic is epitomized by Elvis, whose gyrations infamously prompted moral panic about his exhibition of a teen idol male sexuality. Mary Bufwack and Robert Oermann, as noted earlier, assert that the rockabillies departed from gender norms in their performance tropes, from hip shaking to yelping.[1] Michael Bertrand has argued persuasively that their merger of "white" country and "black" rhythm and blues was in part an effort to take on some of the gestures of black urban masculinity as a way of coping with their postwar Southern white rural migration to cities. As Bertrand details, Elvis also represented a threat because of the way emerging rock 'n' roll audiences were crossing racial lines and younger generations began questioning the Southern racial etiquette of previous generations.[2] This antiauthoritarian, hedonistic movement was explosive. The rockabillies are described as "wild boys" who brought an arrogant swagger to the stage and prompted girls in the audience to scream.[3]

Although Cash always produced music more squarely in the country music vein as compared to Elvis and his other Sun label mates such as Jerry Lee Lewis, Carl Perkins, and Roy Orbison, he nevertheless projected the same rockabilly youthful "wild boy" aggression in his performances, and he embodied the rockabilly "look" with his pompadour, swagger, and energy. He and Elvis would compete with each other to see who could drive their audiences wilder, and his competition with Elvis extended to women. June Carter had earlier toured with

Elvis before she met Cash; Elvis wrote her love letters and pursued her, but Cash would later burn Elvis's letters to her. In her liner notes for Cash's *Love* compilation album (2000), June Carter Cash remarks that while she was on tour with Elvis, he tried to tune his guitar to sound like Cash and would mimic Cash's singing on "Cry, Cry, Cry" (the B side of Cash's first single), humming "Ah-ummm, Ah-ummm" like Cash did. When she asked what the humming was for and who Cash was, Elvis replied: "That's what drives the girls crazy. Cash don't have to move a muscle, he just sings and stands there. . . . The whole world will know Johnny Cash. He's a friend of mine." Cash's charismatic performances thus followed the rockabilly dynamics of disruptive sexual energy.

At the same time Cash's life narratives about this period—memorably circulated in the Cash-approved *Walk the Line* biopic but also catalogued in biographies like Michael Streissguth's—demonstrate his own attempts to negotiate tension between the rambling life of the road versus his first wife's attempts to model middle-class domesticity. As they began having children and moved from a Memphis apartment to what could be considered a suburb, Vivian Cash pursued the kind of middle-class aspirations and familial roles idealized by the postwar modern nuclear family unit of male breadwinner and dependent housewife and children. Streissguth quotes Marshall Grant who heard her say during this time: "He could retire and not ever had to be on the road again. We could live off of what he has already made."[4] The biopic argues that Vivian was happier when Cash was a salesman who could be at home more and that she resented the way his music career took him out on the road and away from their family; meanwhile, Cash's conflict over his competing roles of rambler versus domestic patriarch caused him great stress.

We find a reversal of these traditional gender roles in Cash's rockabilly songs about female ramblers. When the woman leaves, the male protagonist often responds with both masculine aggression and uncertainty. "Mean-Eyed Cat" (1955) epitomizes this dynamic. There, the woman defies the male speaker's control. Angered that she spent his grocery money on cat food for her pet (after he insisted she not do so), the male speaker gives her more money for a "one-way ticket." She leaves him with a "Dear John" letter and takes a train out of town, and he is left flustered at her departure: "I was scared as I could be." The lyrics emphasize his insecurity and fear as he spends his last dollar getting his own train ticket to retrieve her, even though he will need to buy another return ticket for her. The slightly humorous implication is that she has pledged her loyalty to the ornery cat over him. But the deeper implication is that his masculine gender role performance depends on her feminine performance and her acceptance of him. He expects to be the household provider while she manages the domestic sphere, and he is destabilized by her rejection of him and of those roles. A rockabilly song with a fast, driving rhythm and rollicking electric guitar, Cash sings with brio. Yet, thematically, the speaker's confidence in his role is as uncertain as his female partner's commitment to domesticity. As he aggressively chases her, trying to assert his masculine dominance, the song ends with doubt; the male speaker is penniless and unsure of where to find her. His boasts ring hollow.

Cash later added another verse to this song for its re-release on *Unchained* (1996), and the new conclusion emphasizes female authority. Finding out that "his woman" has fled to Arkansas, the speaker summons the courage to call his mother-in-law, who only agrees to reveal her daughter's whereabouts if he will agree to "act right." Thus he must capitulate to this female authority figure. The man learns "his woman" is working as a waitress at a truck stop, and when he arrives, she quickly comes with him, although she buys her own return ticket with her tip money. The song's happy ending only occurs with his compliance to her desires, because, although they return home to take up their cozy places on the sofa together, the two are joined by the ornery cat in their scene of domestic bliss. The happily ensconced cat emerges victorious. But the deeper point is that domesticity is either tenuous or produces uncertainty in gender role performances. Like many of Cash's other characters, this duo does not fit domestic ideals.

Richard Leppert and George Lipsitz have shown, relevant to my own discussion of Cash, how Hank Williams's music, which became popular in the early 1950s, bucked the dominant cultural narratives of gender at that time. As the postwar baby boom saw a promulgation of the modern nuclear family unit, this development signaled an uncomfortable return to patriarchy and the home, for during the war many women worked outside the home.[5] Williams articulated the frustration of the Southern poor and working class toward the middle-class norms of a nuclear family unit, consumerism, and the suburban expansion. He undermines an emergent masculinity of middle-class domesticity because he represented the troubled drifter (in his "Luke the Drifter" persona) who resisted the modern nuclear family. Leppert and Lipsitz argue convincingly that rather than embracing a return to patriarchy, Williams's themes featured an effort to get closer to women, not to dominate them, often as working-class partners (perhaps a residual reference to the Depression-era South where women frequently presided over extended families when the men had to roam looking for work). Williams's identification with a Southern white working class was expressed through musical elements that have been typed feminine (such as a high pitch)—here the "high lonesome" voice and the "twang" of the Southern white folk culture.[6] While Cash uses rockabilly rather than Williams's "high lonesome" mode of address here, he articulates similar themes that trouble the modern nuclear family, although his characters are more clearly torn between rambling and home.

In contrast, Diane Pecknold has analyzed how the Nashville Sound era, emerging in the late 1950s, navigated this Cold War, postwar emphasis on middle-class masculine domesticity by using gender imagery to further their product and develop their industry by getting country music on the radio (and casting industry professionals in these terms). Pecknold traces how the Nashville Sound tried to appeal to blue-collar audiences by imagining men as Western gentlemen and yet male breadwinners with a family, a housewife, and aspirations to enter the middle class. As Pecknold writes: "If honky-tonk had been the lament of men displaced by war and economic upheaval, and rockabilly the sexual braggadocio of their adolescent sons, then the Nashville Sound, with its angelic backing vocals and orchestral strings, was the soggy reverie of the postwar suburban wife."[7]

Cash the irreverent rockabilly depicts the rambler in his lyrical output across his career. Treating these songs like folk poetry, as Cecelia Tichi has done with country music more generally, allows us to analyze how these texts both shape and reflect popular ideas about Southern working-class manhood in the nineteenth and twentieth centuries, as well as American mythologies and ideals such as frontier mythology, national symbolism, and patriotism.[8] Cash's representations constitute a twist on long-running country music traditions of expressing Southern working-class tensions. Thus he suffuses the common trope of the rambler versus the family man throughout his lyrics and performing persona, even going so far as to record an album called *The Rambler* (1977), which followed the story of a roamer through songs such as "Hit the Road and Go," and eight interspersed dialogue tracks in the form of a radio play. Cash's oeuvre joins a long tradition in the genre but is also distinctive for the way it troubles gender. His songs do not resolve the opposition between rambler and home but, as they explore both sides, they leave the two poles in productive tension, sometimes using it as grounds for criticism of class hierarchies or social injustices. The songs often question gender role conventions and identity categories.

This common conflict between home and rambling that grips the author and journalist W. J. Cash's "man-at-the-center," battling between hedonism and piety, Saturday night and Sunday morning, is a symptom of the social history of Southern working-class masculinity.[9] Malone has demonstrated how ramblers could be vehicles for expressing, in popular culture, Southern working-class resentment and anger over class privilege, a set of trickster figures with whom audiences might vicariously identify as they defeat rich people through homespun ingenuity.[10] Southern literature is populated by a wellspring of these characters, such as Flannery O'Connor's conniving hucksters who turn stereotypes of the ignorant country rube to their advantage in, for example, "Good Country People," thus leveling a stinging criticism of class prejudice.

As Malone has illustrated, in country music the rambling man is often a vehicle for expressing nostalgia for some sense of lost working-class freedom and individualism. Taking the ideals of masculine dominance and patriarchal hegemony from the shaping influence of British folkways, rural Southern culture adapted codes such as patriarchal "honor" over the law in both upper- and lower-class contexts. For the lower class, however, the rambler or outsider motif, which would include the outlaw and sometimes even musicians, took on a special valence as a way to express class frustrations. Scholarship in Southern history has shown that white Southern working-class men historically enjoyed a wide degree of freedom, even given class hierarchies, given their access to a patriarchal order; they also engaged in masculine rivalry and physical competition outside women's domestic sphere.[11] Malone notes that the Southern working-class machismo was often diverted into popular culture, sports, music, religion, entertainment, boasting, and practical jokes. Along with his large body of songs that fretted about masculinity, Cash also perhaps speaks to this tradition in his many joke songs ("Flushed from the Bathroom of My Heart," "Dirty Old Egg-Suckin' Dog"). He also engaged in some legendary practical jokes—from setting chickens loose in hotels to throwing televisions out of windows—and aggressive pastimes such as firing Civil War–era cannons with his buddy Hank Williams Jr. Some of the pressures in Southern white working-class masculinity were amplified by the rapid social changes of the late nineteenth century: western migration, sharecropping and tenancy after the Civil War, and less freedom in work under a more constricted economy and labor market as an increasing number migrated to urban centers at the start of the twentieth century. Malone notes that these tensions also exploded into violence such as lynching and domestic abuse.[12]

Drawing on long-running tropes in Southern culture, Cash does more than examine both sides of the rambling-versus-family dichotomy. As noted in the introduction, Cash departs from typical genre conventions in songs that give women characters access to the rambling life in ways similar to male ramblers. In many of his songs, male speakers lose their woman because she is a rambler. It is much less common to see rambling as an option for women in country music lyrics. When this dynamic does appear, the woman is usually framed as a destructive force threatening the family. Lewis cites a few country music songs in the wake of the women's movement in the 1970s that featured women roamers, but the women are mostly castigated for threatening the domestic sphere or abandoning their family in their quest for freedom rather than being seen, like male ramblers, as symbols for the cultural tension between rambling and home.[13]

Both male and female ramblers populate Cash's songs in great numbers, and the lover who is rambling often breaks the heart of the one who is left behind. The rambling man is sometimes the macho, hard-bodied drifter who will never be pinned down by domesticity or family and instead demands freedom. Sometimes this man is aggressively hostile to the woman he is leaving and spews misogynistic complaints at her ("Understand Your Man," "I'm Leaving Now," "Too Little, Too Late," "Cry, Cry, Cry"). Yet, in other songs, the rambler is surprised by his own vulnerability; he leaves his woman with hubris but then is shocked when he feels emotional pain after his departure ("Hurt So Bad"). Cash explores the angst of working men who feel trapped by their existence, unable to break out of their poverty, and resentful of both the privileges of the rich and the deprived domestic life that binds them to their fate, which they wish they could leave. In "Hungry," the male figure is weary from "carryin' the same ole load" and yearns for "something [he] ain't got." Other Cash songs sympathize with the men who do uproot and leave but still experience anguish concerning the home-versus-freedom opposition ("This Town," "Hit the Road and Go").

The dynamic of vulnerability in male protagonists is not unique. It is evident in earlier genres, such as 1940s honky-tonk and in that era's Tin Pan Alley songs, as David Brackett has shown.[14] But Cash is more distinctive in how he treats his suffering men with a touch of existential alienation.

In several train songs typical of his themes, we are encouraged to sympathize with a male protagonist who is broken-hearted at being left by a woman rambler. In Cash's "Southwind," the male speaker is jilted when his woman takes the train from Jacksonville to Nashville, because she "always likes to go" and has the money for the ticket. He, meanwhile, does not have the money to go, but would follow her if he did; as it is, he is left waiting and watching to see if she returns. If he did have the money for a ticket, he would purchase "a smile to carry on," implying that he would be flush with masculine bravado with that train ticket, but he is barred from such freedom because of his working-class status. The man has become passive, awaiting the actions of the woman to exercise her free will.

Similarly, in "Train of Love," trains are symbols of mobility, freedom, and roaming, and the urge to roam is universal—it includes women. The song uses trains as a metaphor for love relationships, and when it argues that "everybody's baby" will sometimes have the "urge to roam," it refers to infidelity. The male speaker laments that other people's women come back home on this love train, but his has not, although he will wait for her forever. But the sexual metaphor is only plausible if one grants the comparison to actual rambling on trains (a life usually rife with licentiousness), which would also involve a universal urge to have all the opportunities the mobility of trains provides. Cash similarly portrays a woman as a rambler in "Daughter of a Railroad Man." Here, the woman bucks conventional gender roles and roams, having learned this lifestyle from her railroading father. The idea of a woman rambling by train is again turned into a sexual metaphor, because her roaming specifically involves her breaking hearts with one-night stands. Refusing to settle down with any one man, she's always "outward bound," never remaining in "any station," and is never lonely because she can always find another man "on down the line."

Many of Cash's songs about women ramblers emphasize the vulnerability and suffering of the jilted man. Sometimes a new love relationship is defined as a positive one in contrast with a man's previous experiences with a cheating woman. In "You're My Baby" (also known as "Little Wooly Booger"), the working-class man announces that he is poor but, unless he gets chased down to pay his bills, he will spend all his money on his beloved because she is far preferable to the previous woman who cheated on him. When a woman has mistreated him, Cash's male speaker feels a lingering pain and an agitated emotional state ("Cold Lonesome Morning," "It Comes and Goes"). Often the woman leaves and breaks the man's heart ("You Beat All I Ever Saw," "Lonesome to the Bone," "It's All Over") or the man dejectedly waits for her ("Port of Lonely Hearts," "Next in Line") and only rarely does she return ("Kentucky Straight"). Frequently Cash's male protagonist keeps taking his woman back even though she has cheated on him ("There You Go," "Time and Again," "After the Ball"). Sometimes the woman chooses some other pastime over the male protagonist. In "Rock 'n' Roll Ruby," the speaker's girlfriend loves to dance at a juke joint. Although at first the man enjoys her display (it "satisfies" his "soul"), he eventually suffers because she brushes him off, claiming her own freedom when he tries to make her leave. In a number of Cash's songs about rambling women, the man tries to bring the woman back ("A Certain Kind of Hurtin'" "The Wind Changes," "So Doggone Lonesome," "I Do Believe," "Mean-Eyed Cat"), hoping that she will remember their happy times together as he does, and relent.

Occasionally the male protagonist uses violence to try to force the woman to return. In "Two-Timin' Woman," Cash's male speaker sings about a woman who cheated on him because she is a rambler who "drifts around the country." He hopes she will drift back where he is, not so that they can have a happy reconciliation, but because if he finds her, he plans to "chain her to the floor" to tame her and "make [her] understand." As the man threatens violence toward the rambling woman, he implicitly enforces a double standard in which the male rambler is much more accepted and less troubling. In "How Did You Get Away from Me," a song Cash wrote with June Carter and Anita Carter, this kind of situation is played for humor. The song's male speaker describes all the outlandish ways he tried to keep his woman to stay (a moat, window bars, a "moss-covered monster," a rattlesnake pit, a sniper, a tiger in the car, dynamite, an electric fence, handcuffs, swarms of bees) and wonders how she managed to escape from him anyway. The woman jokingly "talks back," saying: "You said I'd die if I tried." The song reverses chivalric romantic imagery (castles and moats) and uses hyperbole to poke fun at the lengths to which the man will go to keep his woman versus her ability to defeat all his attempts if she is determined to leave. Yet, placed next to the far more Gothic "Two-Timin' Woman" or Cash's rendition of "Delia's Gone," this song, on one level, seems to turn real situations about domestic violence into an exaggerated novelty joke song in a way that is somewhat jarring. However, the parody in the song offers some commentary on gender codes, drawing attention to how they are constructed by its exaggeration of them.

Cash's rendition of "A Boy Named Sue" is another example of Cash's moments of parody where he mines humor from gender role stereotypes. Sheila Whiteley has noted that, given traditional patriarchal gender codes in the genre that are strict and naturalized, country stars typically perform heteronormative "family values" and invite identification with these codes from fans. Because these codes are so rigid, parodies of them can denaturalize them. Whiteley argues that k. d. lang's early performances parody these gender codes in precisely this way, because while lang adopted elements of excessive femininity (wearing cowgirl skirts and singing about love and longing), she also parodied them by incorporating a camp butch identity (excessive country-punk touches like torn stockings and sawn-off cowboy boots as well as a satirical singing style that combined jazz and country, what lang marketed as "torch and twang"). As Whiteley notes, Dolly Parton also flaunts excessive femininity, drawing attention to its artificiality (as in her famous tag line: "It costs a lot of money to look this cheap"), although Parton's parody is praised in the industry because it is not threatening to dominant gender codes in the way that lang's is. Cash's moments of parody also do not threaten dominant codes, but, at the very least, they show gender to be a constructed performance or a socialized behavior. In his 1973 appearance on *Hee Haw*, Cash offers up such a parody of his own macho persona. He jokes that his impressively macho image is exaggerated to the point of parody.

Like "Sue," Cash's parodic delivery of "My Old Faded Rose" jokes about gender role stereotypes in ways that draw attention to their constructedness. In his lyrics the male speaker has rejected his lover because she is growing older, and he offers increasingly ridiculous analogies of her to a rose with faded petals "hangin' down." When he notices that other men are chasing her, he returns to her, insisting that she should ignore him if he ever jokes that she needs "prunin'." The implication is that she is a prostitute, because the protagonist concludes by saying he "is back in line for one more time" with his "old faded rose." In his recording of the song, Cash sings while June Carter joins him on the chorus, and he plays it very broadly, like a parody. Over a bouncing drum beat, Cash exaggerates his delivery, lowering his voice to deliver deeper pitches while humorously singing "ah ummm, ah ummm" between verses, almost making fun of his own delivery. On one level, the song is a catalogue of male sexual privilege and objectification of women. But through exaggeration, Cash's song makes this account extreme and parodic in performance, playing these gender tropes for humor and yet effectively drawing attention to their status as stereotypes.

Prisons and Masculine Frustrations

In other themes that question gender, Cash's prison albums, seen in the context of the 1960s folk revival, highlight Cash's use of the saint-sinner binary and the outlaw as a variation on the rambling-home dichotomy. This example also stresses how Cash models a resistant working-class masculinity that eschews middle-class domesticity. The folk movement and the 1960s counterculture were both outsider movements not invested in upholding the modern nuclear family unit, although, as critics have shown, the counterculture movement was sexist whereas the folk movement allowed a few more opportunities for women.[15] Cash's live prison albums from Folsom and San Quentin made both these movements embrace him enthusiastically as a symbol of social protest. Both emphasize his hyper-masculine identification with a suffering working-class masculinity as embodied by the prisoners in his audience.

A particularly stunning example of this projection and identification is Merle Haggard's recollection of seeing Cash perform in San Quentin as the turning point in his own redemption and eventual move from a jail cell to country superstardom. Haggard, who saw Cash perform on New Year's Day in San Quentin in 1958 when Haggard was in jail for burglary (he was later pardoned by California governor Ronald Reagan), emphasizes Cash's macho arrogance in his performance and his ability to communicate his identification with the prisoners. Haggard once mused about Cash's performance: "He was chewing gum and he was the most arrogant son of a bitch I think I've ever seen on stage. But somehow he pulled it off."[16] Elsewhere elaborating on the vagaries of sympathy sparked by that performance, Haggard asserts:

> What stood out about Johnny Cash when I saw him at San Quentin, more even than his music, was his demeanor. He was a bit cocky and a bit arrogant—his voice was shot because he'd been up too long the night before. He was supposed to be there to sing songs, but it seemed like it didn't matter whether he was able to sing or not. He was just mesmerizing. There was just this excitement. It didn't even matter that *he* was free, because there was a connection there, an identification. This was somebody who was singing a song about your personal life. Even the people there who weren't fans of Johnny Cash—it was a mixture of people, all races—were by the end of that show.[17]

Crucial to Cash's identification with prisoners was his empathy with their masculinized frustration over a lack of mobility and freedom, a theme he expresses powerfully in his most famous prison songs ("Folsom Prison Blues," "San Quentin"). The image of Cash raising his middle finger at the camera at his 1969 San Quentin concert similarly symbolizes his devotion to his audience and their frustrations. Cash's insolent act was prompted by a camera man, filming for the BBC documentary, who was blocking Cash from his audience. The power dynamics in such settings are thorny. While, as Haggard says, Cash is free and has a charismatic hold over these men, they can also choose to riot. Cash later recalled being tempted to start a riot at the concert after his encore performance of "San Quentin" riled the prisoners and left them jumping on tables and yelling—and left the guards arming their guns; Columbia producer Bob Johnston, who was at the concert, would later excoriate Cash for being so drunk on power that he would even consider it: "All he had to do was say something. It would have been a huge riot, and Johnny and all his family would've been dead out there."[18]

June Carter Cash later described her fear that day when faced with the violence and intensity of the inmates, but she underscored her religious faith and her empathy with the prisoners as fellow sinners as well as her belief that Cash's performance allowed them to express their masculine frustrations. Describing the crowd's response as Cash "slung his guitar across his back, slithered like a snake onto that stage, and said, 'Hello, I'm Johnny Cash'," she writes: "Some kind of internal energy for those men, the prisoners, the guards, even the warden, gave way to anger, to love and to laughter. It all came together. A reaction like I'd never seen before. I was enraged inside, a feeling of fire, dangerously tense." She interprets

Cash's performance of "San Quentin" as the inmates' chance to assuage their hu-
miliation with some masculine acting out, and she again empathizes with them,
imagining herself in their place in their desire to perform a defiant masculinity:
"This sore made by chafing it in the most humiliating place, you add bitterness
and bile. You find yourself walking, trying to strut and swagger. But about all that
you can do is spread your legs and swagger."[19]

In the midst of his hyper-masculine displays (involving gender as performance),
Cash also wrote songs that decried the dehumanizing treatment of inmates and
emphasized their desire to be connected to family despite their status as prisoners.
In his live performance, he included gospel tunes that focused on the prisoner's
ability to be redeemed (the set list at San Quentin in 1969 included "[There'll Be]
Peace in the Valley," "He Turned the Water into Wine," and "The Old Account
Was Settled Long Ago"). His prison albums emphasize the saint-sinner dualism,
just as his reform advocacy moves beyond the mores of middle-class domesticity
by identifying with convicts.

In his lyrics as a whole, Cash often links sympathy with working-class men
to structural social critiques. In Cash's prison songs, he castigates members of
Congress who fail to comprehend that the prison system, as he maintains, dehu-
manizes prisoners rather than rehabilitating them. In "San Quentin," he sings,
"Mister Congressman, you can't understand," and he accuses politicians and
elected leaders of oversight in horrific prison conditions. He calls for listeners
to advocate on behalf of young men abused in prison. In "Jacob Green," a song
based on real-life events, a young man arrested for drug possession is awaiting trial
but hangs himself after his jailors humiliate him by taking his clothes and shaving
his head. Cash makes his appeal for prison reform advocacy through this personal
story, but he urges social justice action from his audience, arguing that "it could
be someone that you love" who suffers Green's fate and that "if you turn your
head away" this scene will continue to happen because it happens throughout
an abusive system. Cash sings that although Green's father sued and the sheriff
retired and two guards were fired, if you look inside jailhouses everywhere "you'll
find corruption never seen."

In an iteration of the rambling-home binary, many of Cash's songs establish
that prisoners have committed violent acts but also portray their love for their
families. These men represent both masculine aggression and a devotion to family, and Cash uses these opposing tendencies to argue for humane prison conditions and for some degree of sympathy for prisoners who have been arrested
because they are trying to provide for their families. He valorizes the lengths men
will go to succor their families. "Give My Love to Rose" (adapted from the folk

song "Give My Love to Nell") sympathizes with an ex-convict in California who has been trying to get home to Louisiana but is instead dying in the cold by the train tracks; he wants the speaker to send all his money to his family so they can continue on without him. At his most polemical, Cash criticizes the legal system and questions who is on the right side of the law when poverty forces men to break the law to provide food for their families ("This Side of the Law"). He understands when some men try to escape harsh chain gang conditions ("Tell Him I'm Gone"). He even appeals for sympathy for violent, forgotten men who will die in prison but who nevertheless miss families who have stopped communicating with them ("Dear Mrs.").

Cash's prisoners are the most extreme example of a saint-sinner tension, but his working men and ramblers exhibit similar conflict. His songs voice the masculine frustrations of men who cannot afford to buy the goods they labor to produce—and who sometimes steal those goods in protest. In Cash's famous rendition of "One Piece at a Time," an auto worker steals a car from the factory piece by piece over many years. In "Strawberry Cake," a former farm worker who has now migrated to the city steals cake from the decadent Plaza Hotel in New York City in frustration over his hunger and dislocation. Cash's lyrics describe the man's time as a strawberry picker in California as "hard work with no future" (just as Cash had worked briefly as a strawberry picker in Arkansas after graduating high school). The lyrics criticize the opulence of the hotel by juxtaposing it with the man's starvation, highlighted by the irony that the man cannot afford to buy the very food that he himself harvested.

Elsewhere Cash complains about unsafe working conditions while applauding the valor of laboring men who are merely trying to care for their families—and will go to extremes to do so. In "Call Daddy from the Mine," a man's daughter awakens and cries for him to leave the mine because she fears a collapse. Because he heard her crying for him, the man finds an air pocket and survives the mine disaster, crawling out from the rubble two weeks later, determined to return to his fatherly duties. The song implicitly decries unsafe working conditions. Likewise, in "The Timber Man," Cash emphasizes a man's masculine prowess and working-class pride in the face of labor exploitation. The timber cutter gives his boss "more than his hire," working so hard that the sweat from his brow "turns the ground to mud." But he takes pride in his work, because he can cut down any tree and people seek him out to ask him to teach them this skill.

Similarly, in "Cisco Clifton's Fillin' Station," a song inspired by a real gas station in Dyess, Arkansas, Cash sings about the nobility of a small gas station owner who never makes a profit but instead gives back to his community in the form of loans that will never be repaid and even through providing a space for people to gather and play checkers. When an interstate highway is built and "progress" displaces him, Cisco works odd jobs at night to keep his station open and be able to support his family. Cash frequently uses internal rhyme in his lyrics, and here he uses that poetic technique to highlight the frustrations of Cisco's situation: he takes on extra work "to keep his will and to pay his bills" and his livelihood is threatened because "the cars flew past on high test gas." Cash uses recitation in this song, as he does in many, which highlights the oral narrative and storytelling components. The album context for this song emphasizes men like Cisco as American heroes (the song appeared on Cash's concept album about American life, *From Sea to Shining Sea* [1967]).

Love, Murder, and Musical Roots

One of Cash's more controversial performances of a violent, outlaw masculinity is the song and video for the murder ballad "Delia's Gone," from *American Recordings* (1994). This song epitomizes the conflicts between Cash's symbolic themes of love and murder by exploring the linked desires for violence and marital union in his vengeful male protagonist. A folk ballad attributed to Karl Sibersdorf and Dick Toops, it was a popular song on the folk revival circuit in the 1960s. Cash had previously recorded a version of it in the 1960s, on his album *The Sound of Johnny Cash* (1962).

It is not surprising that Cash would record another version of it for his first album with Rick Rubin in the 1990s, particularly since this murder ballad invokes basic Cash touchstones, such as folk traditions of fallen, conflicted manhood as well as a dangerous, outlaw force. This song is representative of Cash's divided man in his output with American Recordings—his man torn between rambling and home, between being a saint and a sinner. Rubin returned to Cash's outlaw image to market it, calling him the "Godfather of Gangsta Rap," and linking him to the frustrations of the disenfranchised. But as Rubin himself observes in the *Unearthed* liner notes, Cash departs from gangsta rap in his focus on remorse and the hope for redemption. As discussed earlier, the pictorial cover for this first album crystallizes that marketing, with Cash portrayed as an outlaw in a black long coat flanked by two dogs (animals he later nicknamed "sin" and "redemption"). Again, like the 1960s folk revival, the Americana roots music movement in the 1990s was in search of a fantasy of folk purity in the face of trivialized commercial popular music. In this epoch, Cash rearticulated a frustrated working-class masculinity in a new musical context. Yet the vision in his songs is not that of the

"NASCAR dad" of the 1990s angry at his own downward mobility, a vision that Kimmel finds in mainstream country songs.[20] Cash is no Toby Keith. Instead, he invokes folk traditions to explore a Southern Gothic saint-sinner, examining an aspect of society in the trials and tribulations of a mythical common man. But, again, he does so in the context of remorse and an overwhelming desire for redemption, so that the violence of his male protagonists is depicted in the rubric of prohibition tales.

The song itself offers a disturbing story of a working-class man acting out his anger in misogyny and domestic abuse. The male protagonist recalls catching "his woman" cheating and killing her; but he recounts this story from the perspective of his own remorse, because she now haunts him as he sits in jail. Adding to the long tradition of love linked to domestic violence in murder ballads, Cash amplifies the violence and the Southern Gothic elements here. As noted earlier, his version includes lines describing Delia as the "kind of evil make me want to grab my submachine."

Cash's song depicts this extreme example of love-hate, violence-remorse, through the lens of gender relations. The song sets up these tensions carefully in its narrative and musical elements. It has six verses, each followed by the refrain, "Delia's gone, one more round, Delia's gone," which is repeated twice at the end of the song. It opens quietly, with soft dynamics, as Cash sings solo and accompanies himself with gentle strumming on acoustic guitar; the first line sets up an almost romanticized love song in a folk singer–songwriter tradition singing Delia's name. The next lines quickly juxtapose that devotion with aggression: "If I hadn't have shot poor Delia / I'd have had her for my wife," followed by the refrain. Cash underscores the theme of aggression in that second line by singing and playing more loudly, speeding up the tempo, and erupting into an alternating bass line whose emphatic rhythm drives the song forward. Throughout the rest of the song, he frequently includes eighth-note strums (playing down and up on the strum) for emphasis at the end of lines. The next three verses describe how the speaker travels to Memphis to find Delia, then ties her to a chair and gruesomely shoots her twice. His justification is that Delia was "low and trifling," "cold and mean," and that her evil prompted his violence (as in the "submachine" line quoted above).

In his phrasing in the fourth verse, Cash underscores the irony of the speaker's mingled love and hate. He sings: "First time I shot her, I shot her in the side / Hard to watch her suffer / But with the second shot she died." Cash draws out the word "hard" for emphasis, making it heavy with the irony that the speaker caused Delia's suffering—and that his response to recognizing her pain is to shoot her again. In the fifth verse, the speaker's attitude shifts to remorse, complaining to the jailor that he is sleepless because he hears her walking around him. Cash marks this emotional change by stretching out some of the words, lingering over his cry to the jailor to denote the speaker's suffering and second thoughts. The final verse ends with an admonition to other men, telling them that if their woman is straying, they can either let her stray or kill her as Delia was killed. Since the previous lines focus on his remorse, the song is ultimately a warning against the latter; the lyrics implicitly suggest that if other men murder their female lovers, they will suffer similar agony. Emphasizing an attitude of sorrow as Cash closes the song, he sings the refrain in decreasing volume, the second delivery much quieter than the rest of the song, as is his guitar accompaniment.

Cash's narrative techniques capture this mixture of ferocity and regret, particularly in his use of the Southern Gothic elements, including the horror of the speaker's excessive, bloody violence, the supernatural in Delia haunting him as a ghost, and the premise of a destructive, possessive love. Cash's lyrics set the song in the South with its references to Memphis. Similarly his performance emphasizes Southern pronunciations (dropping "ing" endings, pronouncing "submachine" as "submochine," singing "hadn't have shot" as "hadn't a-shot," and "I'd have had" as "I'da have"). The ballad's connections to long-running rural Southern folk traditions also place its integral Southern links in the category of regionalism rather than the mere window dressing of local color.

Although literary genres are notoriously permeable and arbitrarily defined, the Southern Gothic subgenre in literature and popular culture is generally seen as focused on elements of horror and the supernatural, often using them to question rationalism, emphasize the limits of human knowledge, express ambivalence about Southern history, or sometimes assail Southern cultural norms and inequities concerning, for example, race, gender, class, religion, and politics. Tennessee Williams famously described the Southern Gothic style as capturing "an intuition of an underlying dreadfulness in modern experience." In her study of the generic impurity and fluctuating conventions of the American Gothic, Teresa Goddu argues that the South, "identified with gothic doom and gloom, . . . serves as the nation's 'other,' becoming the repository for everything from which the nation wants to disassociate itself," such as irrational impulses that run counter to Enlightenment ideals.[21] She argues, for example, that the Gothic tales of Southern writers such as Edgar Allan Poe are shot through with ambivalence about ideals of white racial purity and are haunted by the ghosts of slavery.

Cash's song, functioning in this Southern Gothic subgenre, focuses on masculine amorous and murderous tendencies in a broader framework concerning Southern white working-class anxiety about changing male roles (as the result of the kinds of changes to labor and demographics that I have already detailed) and a tenuous social status. As this male fear is projected onto the woman, the song brings out the cultural contradictions of patriarchy—particularly through the male speaker's implicit insistence on white male privilege in the face of their abject class status, and in his acts of domestic violence combined with later regret and admonitions against it. The speaker enacts the structural violence of patriarchy. As Goddu argues of the Gothic genre more generally, "American gothic literature criticizes America's national myth of new-world innocence by voicing the cultural contradictions that undermine the nation's claim to purity and equality."[22] Arguably Cash's corpus of work can be seen to do the same in popular culture; he is not alone in doing so, but he is at least distinctive for his specific articulations. Cash also amplifies these effects in "Delia's Gone" by using the grotesque, which offers another aesthetic turn of the screw by combining unusual images or an excess parody of Gothic elements to evoke both fear and laughter. Cash's lyrics hint at the grotesque when the speaker incongruously imagines peppering Delia with a submachine gun (a literal overkill), or in the bloodily humorous lines where he finds it hard to watch her suffer and yet he shoots her again.

In keeping with Southern Gothic conventions, Cash's protagonist is an example of fallen humanity, a mixture of good and evil. Rather than judging the character's offenses, the song sees his struggle with his demons as a reflection of society's similar struggle. The director Anton Corbijn's video emphasizes these Gothic components, portraying the male speaker losing his sanity. Haunted by flashbacks of his violent act, he is disheveled and agitated, frequently putting his face in his hands as, implicitly, reason and rationality abandon him. Cash plays the male speaker who is pictured in a decaying graveyard where he buried Delia, played by supermodel Kate Moss. The video is in black and white but uses sepia colors in what seem like "flashback" sequences of the killing and burial, where Corbijn's images have the brownish tinge of old photographs. It becomes clear, however, that these are not actual flashbacks but mental reenactments of the murder in the speaker's mind, as he is old (the same age as the "present" tense scenes) and the woman remains young.

In a decidedly ominous, Gothic setting, Cash stands by a burly oak tree in the bleak cemetery, dressed all in black in his long coat being whipped by a fierce wind. He sings and plays his signature custom Martin black acoustic guitar in a graveyard full of leaning wooden crosses, choked by weeds, sticks, and underbrush. Cash stares menacingly at the camera in a series of shots that alternately have the viewer, more omnisciently, looking down on him (with a shot looking down from slightly above him) or that bring the viewer closer to his perspective,

in close-ups where he fills the frame. The intercut flashback/reenactment sequences include footage of him reenacting the murder; he is distraught and looking around wildly, and then, later, fearfully drives away toward the cemetery with
the body. As the video cuts back to the present of the graveyard, Cash is behind
bar gates that symbolize prison. In the flashback/reenactments of Cash burying
Moss, he puts her frail body in the grave and throws dirt on her. The video also
accentuates Delia as a haunting ghost, because it opens and closes with images
of her out of the grave, both in the brown film grain representing the speaker's
mental reenactments of the past. In the initial shot, she stares down at the camera.
In the final one, she is standing outside the grave kicking dirt down into it as the
camera looks up from the perspective of being inside the grave; she covers it with
the same dirt her killer used to bury her. In some sense, Delia gets the last word,
because she has figuratively escaped the grave as a haunting presence that buries
the speaker in an endless loop of images of the murder.

In the flashback/reenactment of the murder itself, Corbijn includes a striking
shot where the camera adopts her point of view; we see Cash filling the frame,
coming toward us with a rope that he puts around "our" neck as the rope moves
into and beyond the frame. As the viewer is placed in the uncomfortable position
of the female object here, the video encodes intricate dynamics involving gender
and visual culture. If, earlier, the video had followed the conventions of the male
gaze of the camera as it objectified Moss (and as her body becomes a literal object
that the man throws in a grave), shot from this vantage point it de-familiarizes
that male gaze. Momentarily unlinked from the camera's perspective, that gaze
is now trained violently on the viewer.

The reception of the song and video exposes the political economy of the
music industry in the 1990s. Country Music Television (CMT) banned the video
as offensive. More important, the video did not fit in with CMT's commercial
focus on country-pop at the time; country radio largely ignored the song for the
same reason. MTV (again, also owned by Viacom) aired the video and celebrated
its appeal to punk and indie rock fans intrigued by Americana roots music, thus
fitting MTV's different marketing imperatives.

In some ways CMT's censorship of the video involved taking Cash's lyrics
literally and rejecting any metaphorical complexity in them, which is precisely
the kind of simplification of country music that Barbara Ching argues against.
Although the video is disturbing, it is a Southern Gothic lament and prohibition
tale. CMT's censorship, in contrast, is a symptom of the channel's commercial
move away from a strong connection to country music's roots in folk culture.
Similarly the song was largely rejected at the time by a mainstream country audi-

ence that did not recognize the murder ballad tradition. Instead, the larger music community recognized the controversial album by awarding it the Grammy for Best Contemporary Folk Album, and *Rolling Stone* later ranked it on its list of the greatest albums of all time (364 out of 500).

CMT later memorialized its censorship of the video in a 2004 documentary, *Controversy: Johnny Cash vs. Music Row*, about the tempest surrounding the video as well as Cash's long-running conflicts with country music's industrial practices, including limited song rotations on consolidated radio stations, and record company conglomerates following a commercial formula that rejects risky musical innovations. Having by then cashed in on his renewed commercial and critical appeal, as they aired tributes to him after his death and enshrined him as their number one on their list of "40 Greatest Men in Country Music," CMT distances itself from its own past rejection of Cash and emphasizes its more recent wholesale embrace of the man. Although the documentary is critical of the earlier censorship, it fails, perhaps not surprisingly, to reflect upon CMT's later opportunistic hagiography of Cash. Still, the documentary incorporates comments from talking heads who note how the "Delia's Gone" video controversy signifies an ignorance of folk traditions among newer entertainment industry executives. Traci Todd, CMT Director of Program Planning, recounts how, at the program committee meeting where members review new videos to determine if they fit the channel's programming profile, she was surprised by responses to *Delia's Gone*: "The reaction in the room, it really caught me off guard. Because there were at least one or two people who were definitely offended. It became clear to me that not everyone working in country music television had the historical perspective of the heritage of the music and where it came from." Similarly Robert K. Oermann, noting the ignorance of folk traditions among a new crop of industry professionals focused on a certain commercial formula, asserts: "The people that refused to air *Delia's Gone* by Johnny Cash were of that new generation. It's a bad thing when an art form loses sight of its past."[23]

In the context of Cash's whole album, this song engages powerfully with such stubborn folk traditions. The song's pressure points involve competing impulses that are not settled into a convenient package; thus the incongruities that the text represents more forcefully address larger contradictions in American ideologies, precisely because the song refuses to paper over them.

The album's other tracks are also about conflicted souls who desire redemption but remain torn. Cash includes tunes addressing conflicted misogyny and an acting out of working-class male aggression ("Delia's Gone," "Let the Train Blow the Whistle"), but they are also framed more broadly by remorse. Several of his cover songs here (from alternative rock and heavy metal artists to contemporary folk singers) focus on the idea of a divided soul, a man who fears his own competing impulses, and the struggle between good and evil within himself (Nick Lowe's "The Beast in Me," Leonard Cohen's "Bird on a Wire," the heavy metal artist Glenn Danzig's "Thirteen," which he wrote for Cash). Cash's male protagonists look for redemption from wars, literal or metaphorical, through social understanding or the support of a woman. These include his suffering Vietnam veteran in "Drive On"; his man weary from the wars of daily life, such as drugs and rambling, who finds solace in "his woman" in "Like a Soldier"; and the murderous sinners throughout history looking for redemption in Tom Waits's "Down There by the Train." Cash joins his own song about religious salvation ("Redemption") with a cover of Kris Kristofferson's famous song about his religious conversion, "Why Me Lord?" in which the unworthy speaker is amazed by his own redemption. He also adds the "cowboy's prayer," "Oh, Bury Me Not," his version of a famous folk song collected by the Lomax brothers, which he originally recorded on his *Ballads of the True West* album (1965) with the input of Tex Ritter. Cash pairs the famous country standard, "Tennessee Stud" (by Jimmy Driftwood, a 1959 Eddy Arnold hit), where a virile man happily finds his female match, as do their horses, with Loudon Wainwright's "The Man Who Couldn't Cry," a joke song about masculine stereotypes. These two songs were both recorded live at the Viper Room, which at the time was a chic Sunset Strip club owned by Johnny Depp, and the happily roaring audience of young hipsters signifies their appreciation of both.

Expanding the discussion to Cash's lyrics in his corpus as a whole, even in songs that do not so explicitly address violence or relationships that end with such Gothic horror, many of his lyrics, arguably, express an existential sense that love always entails unsolvable contradictions between patriarchal structures and egalitarian ideals, freedom and roaming, and companionship and isolation. In terms of the gender role constructions in his songs, Cash frequently imagines gendered power struggles in love relationships. The core issue in many of his songs about love is that the romantic relationship is supposed to assuage loneliness and isolation, but that relationship is also always under threat, as the temptation of others never ends. The relationship is seen as potentially transient and, even more important, it does not always cure the man's existential sense of isolation. The dynamic between men and women is repeatedly depicted as a central factor defining their gender role performances and sense of identity. Thus his songs fit the cultural model described earlier, where masculinity is defined in relation to femininity, but the definitions are uneasy.

Some of Cash's most famous duets with June Carter Cash innocuously partake of a familiar country music tradition of "battle of the sexes" jousts, such as their signature, show-stopping rendition of "Jackson," as well as other covers like "Long-Legged Guitar Pickin' Man," and their duet of Bob Dylan's "It Ain't Me, Babe" (all featured on the album *Carryin' On with Johnny Cash and June Carter*, 1967). In another duet that Cash and Carter wrote together, "Oh What a Good Thing We Had," the male and female speakers trade verses cataloguing an ideal romantic relationship ("everything was milk and honey" and it made the "whole world jealous"), until the refrain, "Oh, what a good thing we had," includes the tag line sung in unison "gone bad," which jokingly reverses the initial romantic fantasies. In several songs, Cash claims to be explicitly autobiographical; he defines happiness as his love with June Carter ("Happiness is You"), argues that he was once a sinner saved by the love of a good woman ("I'm Alright Now"), and insists that he will ignore any unfounded press reports or mythologies about himself, but the one issue on which he will not suffer lies is the truth of his love for her ("I'll Say It's True"). In a more conflicted autobiographical song about their adulterous love affair, Cash's celebrated rendition of "Ring of Fire," written by June Carter and Merle Kilgore, the speaker suffers from a passionate burning love that overcomes him and he cannot escape, as he is suffused by this sublime mixture of love and pain. The song's instrumentation amplifies that feeling. In the studio recording, the Mexican brass Cash adds to the song, along with background vocals, makes for a bigger, more majestic sound, worthy of an epic topic, juxtaposed with his low, staccato lead vocals.

Considering the body of Cash compositions as a whole, however, neither the man nor the woman always gains the upper hand and the lyrics highlight ambivalent emotions—love and mistrust, braggadocio and vulnerability. "Don't Make Me Go" depicts a seesaw battle of the sexes, where the man begs his woman not to make him leave. Even though he can tell she would prefer to be with someone else or even alone rather than with him, he loves only her and dislikes "tradin' love for sympathy." In several rhymed couplets, Cash describes the woman's power over the male speaker, has the speaker apologize for taking her for granted and not knowing "the way to show love," and imagines an ideal love situation as a balance between the two partners: "Two hearts in love must give and take / When one heart fails the other breaks." It is the man's mistreatment that has alienated the woman, and he will reveal his vulnerability to her to beg her to let him stay.

Cash does include optimistic love songs. In some, it is their love for each other that defines a man and a woman in terms of their gender ("WOMAN"). Several songs emphasize the idea that a woman's dedicated love is worth more than riches, fame, or any earthly power ("I'd Rather Have You," "What Do I Care," "My Treasure"). This committed love is seen as something that can be renewed or reaffirmed ("All Over Again," "Cause I Love You"), or that enjoys a continually reignited passion ("You've Got a New Light Shining in Your Eyes," "Drink to Me").

But even in songs where Cash expresses a dedication to fidelity or a joy in his love relationships, he sometimes simultaneously explores intractable tensions. He lauds romantic love and deploys terms such as "true love" in some of his songs, yet he also explores in great detail the ambivalence of relationships or marriages and the existential alienation his characters sometimes feel in the context of those relationships. In "Flesh and Blood," the speaker talks about his struggle between the need to be alone, to enjoy his solitude, and his need to have another person. In the song's three verses, the speaker describes with nostalgia his time spent in pastoral, rural spaces. Near a mountain stream he carves a whistle and listens to a mockingbird, then reluctantly leaves when darkness falls. The chorus juxtaposes this masculine freedom in pastoral solitude with his desire for the comforts of "his woman" and human contact, because "flesh and blood needs flesh and blood" in spite of the solitary time spent in nature that feeds the "mind and spirit."

Similarly, even when the male speaker in Cash's songs pledges his love and finds sustenance in it, he nevertheless faces constant temptation that requires him to reaffirm his love, or he senses that the love he focuses on could be fleeting. The romantic love he celebrates does not prevent temptation from occurring, and it may not have the power to ward off the passage of time and human emotions (as in "I Walk the Line"). In several songs, the speaker declares that his romantic love brings him happiness, even if that happiness is for a short time or even if he is unable to keep this woman ("What Do I Care"). In "You're the Nearest Thing to Heaven," even while the speaker is exalting his romantic love in religious terms, he also notes that he's "been tempted"; though he evades the lures because he loves her, he lives in a state of temptation that will never be resolved. Even in songs where the speaker says he is willing to forsake earthly treasures, such as the song "My Treasure," where a woman's love is a treasure "from above," he eventually admits that he wants both worldly possessions, "like any man would," in addition to the love of his woman.

Elsewhere, Cash details the dysfunctionality of marriages or relationships. In some cases, the tension between rambling and home (or touring and home) contributes to a sense of alienation between husband and wife ("Come in, Stranger"). In others, it is the tedium of quotidian domestic life that leads to boredom and a sense of being trapped ("Hungry").

In songs about failed relationships, the male speaker often expresses a deep sense of vulnerability. The speaker focuses on his feelings of loneliness while missing a lost love ("I'll Remember You") or sometimes even apologizes for not treating the lost love as well as he should have when they were together ("You Remember Me"). "You Remember Me" critiques the insensitive man who takes the woman for granted while the woman is always left caring for the man's emotional needs. Another criticism of gendered double standards of moral judgments comes in "The Baby Is Mine," where the speaker claims his woman's child as his own; even though the child is not his, he insists that society not judge her harshly and grants her baby his patrimony. Highlighting an ideological contradiction, the song effectively criticizes the hypocrisy of gender roles even while affirming the man's power to legitimate the woman.

As Cash's oeuvre both stages and questions a Southern white working-class masculinity, it underscores the uncertainties and socio-historical pressures inherent in that identity construction. Similarly the category of "whiteness" in these texts is also placed under stress, most directly by Cash's intricate depictions of American Indian themes, as I examine more fully in the next chapter. As the American studies scholar Josh Kun observed in his discussion of the foundational ties between music and race, "there is no history of racial formation in the Americas that is not a history of popular music, and there is no history of inter-American popular music without a history of racial formations."[24]

4

RACE AND
IDENTITY POLITICS

Broadening the discussion, this chapter considers how Cash's work and career are a forceful comment on identity politics. I examine his complicated identification with American Indian cultures and his long-running engagement with America's frontier mythology, that deep national story still informing country and western music. Cash, in typical equivocating fashion, plays both cowboy and American Indian, a dynamic I investigate as a paradigm of how he stages American ambivalence. Notably, four of his concept albums from the 1960s created a cycle of American history linking proletarian and American Indian struggles while also celebrating the cowboy aesthetic. He explored train-fueled western expansion in *Ride This Train* (1960) and working-class folk songs in *Blood, Sweat, and Tears* (1963); he decried American Indian land and cultural dispossession in *Bitter Tears* (1964), and then celebrated the cowboy in *Johnny Cash Sings the Ballads of the True West* (1965). Cash's albums attempt to fashion a revisionist, multivocal narrative of American history, linking proletarian and racial struggles in both powerful and problematic ways. Cash exhibits aspects of a more positive cultural dynamic of collaboration, but at the same time he displays aspects of appropriation, replete with a power imbalance between himself and his American Indian collaborator (on *Bitter Tears*) and audiences.

On the one hand, Cash can be read as an example of romanticizing, white liberal guilt. He sometimes claimed Cherokee heritage and later admitted it wasn't true. He dressed like an American Indian for the *Bitter Tears* album cover and the album's liner notes insist that Cash is justified in singing about Indian-white relations from "the Indian's viewpoint," because he has "Cherokee blood." This false claim is part of what Vine Deloria Jr. calls the "Indian grandmother complex," where whites claim an Indian heritage that has more truth in fantasy than in fact.[1] Cash later professed merely to be toying with reporters ("That's something I used to say back when I was squirreling reporters").[2] He also said he "thought" he had "Indian blood" until he checked his family tree; he demurred that his drug abuse at the time added to his confusion: "when I was on the pills, the higher I was the more Indian I thought I was."[3] Nevertheless, his identity claim is a modern-day variant on white liberal guilt toward Indian dispossession and genocide. This kind of white guilt is problematic in the sense that it does not significantly alter dominant power relations and instead amounts to appropriation and paternalism. Claiming a false Indian heritage is a trope that hearkens back to that which Leslie Fiedler and others have pinpointed in nineteenth-century American literature— the "Cult of the Vanishing American." Here the white absorbs the Indian who is, naturally and ineluctably, destined to die as white civilization displaces him but preserves him as a noble savage who lives on in the whites.[4] Cash's false claim also references deeper American history, such as Frederick Jackson Turner's "frontier hypothesis" that the frontier and Manifest Destiny formed American exceptionalism.[5] Indeed, Cash was fascinated by James Fenimore Cooper's frontier novels and by pioneer folk ballads.

On the other hand, Cash makes his own combination of European and American Indian cultural forms and critiques. Collaborating on *Bitter Tears* with folksinger and songwriter Tewa Indian Pete LaFarge, Cash merged European ballad forms and American Indian oral storytelling to address American Indian themes in aggressive political critiques of Manifest Destiny and racial oppression. Perhaps the most famous song on the album, "The Ballad of Ira Hayes," asserts that the titular drunken Pima Indian World War II hero, who helped raise the flag at Iwo Jima but years later died drunk and forgotten, should not be erased from American history. Another of the album's tracks, "As Long as the Grass Shall Grow," castigates the hypocrisy of U.S. treaties that were supposed to hold indefinitely but were quickly broken, and the song became an anthem for some American Indian audiences.

To make sense of Cash's difficult model, I draw on the use, in American studies, of postcolonial theory, which views the U.S. as a special case: a former colony that became an imperial power and practices "internal colonization" in the form of American Indian reservations. I invoke Mary Louise Pratt's concepts of "con-

tact zones" between cultures and of "transculturation," where a subordinated culture appropriates a dominant power's culture and changes it, generating cultural
mixtures that include a political critique of the dominant or imperial power.[6] I
do not argue for Cash as an example of transculturation, as his collaborative work
on *Bitter Tears* does not achieve that level of cultural syncretism. However, the
paradigm is still a useful tool for assessment here because it illuminates both the
potentialities and restrictions of Cash's texts which do more than simply reinforce
American frontier mythology. Ultimately Cash examines the deeply ambivalent
histories of the tropes of the cowboy and the American Indian in U.S. folk culture. In so doing, he sheds light on the nation's ideological paradoxes, engaging
profoundly with them but not resolving them.

Critics have demonstrated an identification between Southern white working-
class communities and American Indian communities.[7] This sympathy is evident
in country music ballads that compare the two groups, although these songs often
feature problematic, highly romanticized depictions of American Indians.[8] The
ethnographer David W. Samuels has also found a significant interest in country
music among some American Indian populations.[9] In national narratives, American Indians join poor Southern whites as fellow marginalized or abject "Others"
who are sometimes used, paradoxically, to represent American distinctiveness
and exceptionalism.[10] Cash's texts celebrate both cowboy frontier mythology and
American Indian rights, but, again, his advocacy moves beyond simple romanticism. His two contrary impulses remain in difficult tension, counterbalancing
each other in ways that elucidate American incongruities such as "free" land
gained through violent dispossession. Cash's texts both support and contest founding national fictions. As a case study, he can speak to both the possibilities and
the limits of cross-racial class bonding through popular music.

Race in Cash

Although Cash's treatment of race focuses most strongly on relations between
whites and American Indians, an earlier context for race in his oeuvre involves the
theme of black-white relationships in his career and his engagement with ongoing
tropes in country music. Here Cash again equivocates. As he sings the words of a
"shoeshine boy" who works to the sound of blues rhythms in "Get Rhythm," he
reflects the legacy of blackface minstrelsy and its problematic politics in country
music, as noted earlier. Yet, he also spoke publicly against the Ku Klux Klan when
a white supremacist group targeted him because his first wife, Vivian Liberto,
appeared "dark-skinned" in newspaper photos. The rockabillies practiced the

love and theft of minstrelsy, but they also were the targets of racist slurs because their integration of white and black music symbolized social integration in the segregated 1950s.

Cash's identification with Jamaica is another case of competing politics. He wrote a song highly critical of bloodthirsty colonial slave owners ("The Ballad of Annie Palmer"). He famously covered one of Bob Marley's signature compositions, "Redemption Song," performing it as a 2003 duet with The Clash's Joe Strummer. George Lipsitz has shown how indigenous musicians in different countries have often turned to reggae and appropriated it strategically for political ends, identifying it as "black."[11] Addressing country music's circulation among indigenous populations, Aaron Fox maintains that country music has also become a globally popular genre among groups who are, like the Southern white working class, "victims of progress," including Native North and South Americans, Aboriginal Australians, and many black Africans.[12] Fox's comments speak to the hope for a cultural syncretism that might critique the center from the margin, as Mary Louise Pratt describes transculturation. Cash's duet seems to express an attempt at cross-racial class bonding. It appears to have had some success in securing that kind of response. The left-wing musician Tom Morello of Audioslave, commenting on the Cash cover of Marley, exclaimed: "There is something in the soul of the music of Johnny Cash that has something very much in common with Bob Marley and Joe Strummer. Though they are artists from different continents and completely different genres of music, there's an honesty and an integrity to the music that they make. I think that if Johnny Cash had been born in Jamaica, he could have been Bob Marley."[13]

By the same token, however, Cash is a tourist looking out from his vacation home, the rich owner of a "grand house," an eighteenth-century sugar plantation in Montego Bay named Cinnamon Hill (built in 1747, the original owners were the Barretts, the family of Elizabeth Barrett Browning). In his second autobiography Cash criticizes pampered tourists when he imagines that the plantation's former slaves haunt the home and the golf course that now covers the soil they toiled on. He writes: "I doubt that the vacationers playing those beautiful links have any idea, any concept, of the kind of life that once teemed where they walk—though perhaps some do, you never know."[14] Yet his comments fail to account fully for the dynamics of power, politics, and appropriation. As Cash writes in his autobiography, it is his vacation home in Jamaica and his romanticized gaze on the black agricultural workers there that make him feel some connection with the cotton fields he worked in as a poor white youth in Arkansas. He writes: "Jamaica has saved and renewed me more times than I can count," and that he loves

Jamaica for "deep reasons" such as "the lushness of the vegetation, the purity of the air, the rainwashed hills, the sparkling sky at night—these are pieces of my childhood in Arkansas."[15]

In the way that Cash addresses the legacy of colonialism in Jamaica, he enshrines a history that is more about his ability to be a philanthropic tourist, thus the historical nostalgia he is enshrining is a dubious nostalgia for colonial privilege. The ambivalence in his framing of Jamaica and his status there is found most vividly in his description, in his second autobiography, of a home invasion by robbers on Christmas Day in 1982. Several armed men invaded the home, held Cash and his family captive for four hours, demanding millions of dollars. As they threaten his wife and child, Cash explicitly feels his white masculinity threatened and violated. They men took what they could, locked Cash and crew in the basement, and left them some turkey to eat. During the robbery, Cash notices their probable drug addiction and feels an affinity with them, just as one gunman chats with Cash's son, who was eleven at the time, asking him: "What do you do down here? What do you like to do in Jamaica? Do you snorkel?" and the boy exchanges pleasantries with him about tourism and guns, prompting the man to exclaim: "Hey, I like you, man!"[16]

After the young men leave, the Jamaican police quickly catch them. Cash is told that all "died resisting arrest," and he recalls that the police told him, when they first went after the robbers, that "these people will never trouble you or your family again." He writes: "Looking back, I realize he was saying more than I understood him to mean at the time. Or perhaps I understood him just fine, but preferred to imagine otherwise."[17] Cash guiltily notes his complicity with "unofficially sanctioned summary justice in the Third World," asking himself what his stance on it is and what his reader's is:

> What's my emotional response to the fact (or at least the distinct possibility) that the desperate junkie boys who threatened and traumatized my family and might easily have killed us all (perhaps never intending any such thing) were executed for their act—or murdered, or shot down like dogs, have it how you will?
>
> I'm out of answers. My only certainties are that I grieve for desperate young men and the societies that produce and suffer so many of them, and I felt that I knew those boys. We had a kinship, they and I: I knew how they thought, I knew how they needed. They were like me.[18]

Cash, after empathizing and identifying with the murdered robbers, tries to note the ways in which he fits into the local Jamaican culture and how he could have seen those boys growing up, how he feels like "family" with the people rang-

ing from "the police and the Rasta men and all the other factions in Jamaica's
political struggles and ganja wars," whose representatives came and went every
day near his home. Cash feels "victimized *and* guilty" after the robbery.[19] Deciding not to leave Jamaica, Cash finds "some good" from it all: local people
offer "gratitude for my decision to stay in Jamaica" and he has been spurred to
be "more involved in Jamaican life" such as in charity work. He writes in 1997:
"Today I feel truly at home in this beautiful country, and I love and admire its
proud and kindly people."[20] For all his efforts to empathize with the desperation
spurred by poverty and imperial exploitation, Cash does not leave the comfort
of his paternalism. When he compares Jamaican life to Arkansas cotton fields,
he elides his own power position. Indeed, after Cash's house was robbed, the
state intervened to save its tourism. Cash writes: "The prime minister was very
upset—and of course concerned that we might flee Jamaica for good, and create
tourist-discouraging publicity—so he ordered fully armed units of the Jamaican
Defense Force into the woods around our house until it was time for us to go back
to the United States."[21] Cash here is the beneficiary of Western hegemony and a
witness to its abuses.

This case of an intersection of reggae and country, Jamaica and Arkansas,
Marley and Cash, does not evince a coherent critique of racism, imperialism,
and global capitalism. But the episode does illustrate how the possibilities for a
cross-cultural, cross-racial class critique are, in the case of Cash's appropriation
of Jamaica, fatally limited because of the legacy of colonial discourse and the
continued exploitation of the West Indies by the West. It illustrates the limits of
attempts at transculturation or cultural syncretism that fail to confront structural
racism and the legacy of colonialism but instead reinforce Western hegemony,
just as Timothy Brennan has long warned of the dangers of fetishizing hybridity
that unproblematically reproduces imperial and colonial power relations.[22]

The Wild West

Compared to the Jamaica example, Cash's American Indian album and songs
make a somewhat more effective critique of hegemony, but the pairing of his
cowboy and American Indian albums together offers a paradigmatic sense of his
treatment of racial themes in the United States. It is noteworthy that Cash's four
1960s concept albums attempt to establish a bond between American Indians, the
working class, and prisoners (Cash addressed prison farm labor on *Blood, Sweat,
and Tears*). The albums were received as part of the 1960s folk revival movement, and Cash sometimes insisted that *Bitter Tears* and *Ride This Train* were the

height of his artistic achievement.[23] Regarding these albums, Cash argues: "They brought out voices that weren't commonly heard at the time—voices that were ignored or even suppressed in the entertainment media, not to mention the political and educational establishments—and they addressed subjects I really cared about. I was trying to get at the reality behind some of our country's history."[24]

The American Indian album, *Bitter Tears*, and the cowboy double album, *Johnny Cash Sings the Ballads of the True West*, released in consecutive years, offer competing visions. Although his criticism of U.S. government policies—especially the continuing string of broken treaties with American Indian tribes—is sweeping and insistent, the following album consecrates the ways of the cowboy (which implicitly depend on those very same policies).

Biographical and music-journalist accounts of his work on these two albums emphasize his own struggles with the idea of "pure" authenticity versus the market. Perhaps partly because of Cash's own claims to authenticity with both, the albums had a surprising degree of commercial success (in keeping with the industry's desire to market authenticity), especially given country radio's resistance to the albums. The music journalist Phil Sutcliffe argues that these concept albums stemmed partly from his guilt over career success with his Columbia records and his struggles to reconcile fame and fortune with his roots in poverty, not to mention the torment over his forbidden love for June Carter. The guitarist Norman Blake, who often played with Cash, worked on many of these concept albums and offers his psychological evaluation: "I suspect he found it hard to accept the fame and fortune he was handed and it was when things got too nice he made these albums, half-expecting them to fail commercially."[25] This notion of a conflict between the market and some kind of traditional American folk culture is, of course, fabricated. As Bill C. Malone has detailed, even in early American folk culture, the popular was always mixed with the folk; there was no noncommercial "purity" or split with the market, since early folk music was always simultaneously folk and popular, just as there was never any racial or cultural "purity" in folk practice (as Southern folk music is comprised of a syncretism of Old and New World, African- and European-derived influences). Malone argues that the purity-versus-market conflict shows up only in the early bias of academics and song collectors (as in the interest in folk music at the turn of the twentieth century), not in folk practice itself.[26]

On *Ballads of the True West*, Cash makes aggressive claims for authenticity. The album grapples with the Old West in terms of emotional realism, reflecting on a certain "structure of feeling," meaning the shared felt experience of living in the late-nineteenth-century Old West. Cash explicitly sets out to access the feeling of living in the West as a cowboy or pioneer through the songs, narratives, and folklore of that era. As his album offers a version of that experience, it expresses a doubled structure of feeling—it is a fictional text, its own piece of what Williams would term "documentary culture," that implicitly works through the historical contradictions of both the earlier era and the 1960s America.[27]

In the track "Reflections," Cash delivers a spoken-word meditation, backed minimally by harmonica and five-string banjo (the sounds of the open range), that considers how one accesses the past from the vantage point of a century later. The track argues that lived history can best be discerned through popular culture, as in ballads and storytelling. Although legends are only one way of locating the past, Cash argues that they yield greater truths. As he discusses what is unique about the pioneer and the cowboy, groups the world did not know before and will not know again, he points to his clothing and daring as well as his "unique brand of lingo," but, above all, the "six-gun dangling" for quick access. Cash tries to pinpoint this material culture by reenacting it himself—playing "dress up" by wearing cowboy props—and he argues that, by retracing the steps of this earlier group of people and listening to the legends, listeners can draw their own conclusions about the true West. He encourages listeners to do so, to disprove the facts or legends, but only after they have walked over these trails in moccasins and listened intently, "Really listened to the west wind / And to everything it whispers."

On the one hand, Cash urges an almost Emersonian self-reliance, in which listeners should not allow experts or history to tell them what the West was about, but they should develop their own perspectives by engaging with documentary culture. He writes that such legends are only one version of a particular moment in history. On the other hand, although he suggests that his listeners do not have to agree with his presentation of the West, still he implies that his view has higher claims to authenticity. He claims that by listening to what he has to say, his audience will be able to see the West as it really was—although he does not insist they agree with him but only that they use what he says to help them look into the past. He presents his true West almost as a product of nature, telling us that we will hear the legends through "the wind that breathed these tales."[28] Cash's track here becomes a historical discourse offering an explanation for the culture of a century earlier.

Likewise, in his liner notes to *Ballads of the True West*, Cash insists that the album debunks Hollywood myths about the Old West and that he tells "the cowboy's story" through "legends, songs, and stories" to get "a glimpse *beyond* the movies and television, back to when a few tales could show us *THE TRUE WEST*." As part of his inquiry, Cash documents his research into original and twentieth-century sources. In his liner notes, he also writes of reading everything from John Lomax to Carl Sandburg to every issue of *True West* magazine, and, finally, of consulting with Tex Ritter. Updating western classics, Cash argues that he adapted the spirit of the "true West" to a twentieth-century context: "We aren't sorry for the modern sounds and modern arrangements on classics like 'I Ride An Old Paint' or 'The Streets of Laredo'; after all, they were meant to be heard on twentieth-century record players and transistor radios! For today that same West wind is blowing, although buckboards and saddles are lying out there turning to dust or crumbling from dry rot."

Cash's insistence on the appropriateness of using modern media to deliver his incarnation of the Old West's structure of feeling is telling and speaks to one of the central contradictions in country music. As Malone notes, commercial country music, with its investment in rural origins, was originated in the 1920s by the decidedly urban forces of recording technology and radio.[29] Malone traces the genre's fascination with the cowboy to the same nineteenth-century sources that produced twentieth-century commercial country music—changes in American life after the Civil War such as industrialization and a developing market economy, urbanization, wage labor, migration, and dislocation. He locates the cowboy fascination that emerged in America during the 1880s to 1910 as a period of national nostalgia for a simpler society and the idea of freedom, manliness, and independence. He argues that the cowboy symbol has endured in country music because it can adapt to new social contexts and even generate counter-meanings (like 1970s Outlaw country). Here, the cowboy becomes a flexible symbol reflecting the concerns of different socio-historical contexts, just as Richard Slotkin has argued about such recurring American mythologies.[30]

Cash's attempt to reach lived experience beneath layers of mythology leads Jonny Whiteside, in liner notes for the 2002 reissue of the album, to contend, expectedly, that Cash's album reflects his "contradictory state of mind," here in reference to folk versus commercial music:

> The attempt to rectify myth with reality and genuine folk music with commercial Western song was a daunting one. 19th century historic fact, 1930s era Hollywood fantasy and contemporary folkloric ideology, only recently codified by an Eastern elite who spearheaded the late 1950s folk revival, had collided in the popular mind as a mass of themes and images from which the notion of the true West seemed inextricable.

Whiteside cites Tex Ritter as a good example of the countervailing practices: Ritter grew up in a modern-day version of the West, in Texas, and offered a "gruff, authentic delivery" and painstaking research in his singing, but he also became one of Hollywood's Singing Cowboys.

Throughout, Cash's insistence on his ability to access the material experiences and emotions of the cowboy way is striking. In his second autobiography, he admits that some of his obsession was fueled by amphetamines; he was energized by speed, trying to relive the cowboy life, carrying a loaded gun, running around in the desert, loaded himself. He observes that, in making the album, he "just about became a nineteenth-century cowboy," went on "amphetamine communions with the cowboy ghosts," and sometimes "might have gone a little too far, not such an uncommon trait in a person on amphetamines." He describes carrying over his newfound persona into concert performances: "I'd put on my cowboy clothes— real ones, antiques—and go out to the desert or an abandoned ranch somewhere, trying to feel how they felt back then, be how they were. I wore authentic Western clothes on the road and in concert, too. Sometimes I even strapped on my gun before I walked in through the backstage door. It would be loaded, naturally."[31] By sleeping on the plains, killing his dinner, sitting in Indian burial grounds, walking trails others had perished on, and generally trying to reenact a cowboy lifestyle, Cash argues in his liner notes that he "learned the ways of the West": "It's still there, and even though the people I sing about are gone, I saw something of what their life was like. Most of it I enjoyed. Some it was mean as hell. But it's the same West: it's wild and hot and unbelievable till you try it on foot. It was the true West." His poetic incitement to the listener is that he "breathed the West wind and heard the tales it tells only to those who listen."

In his second autobiography Cash links his own self-destructive behavior to his search for historical meaning in one particularly striking image involving his attempted suicide, prompted by desperation over drug addiction. Describing how he went to Nickajack Cave in 1967, on the Tennessee River north of Chattanooga, Cash discusses how he intended to join the very artifacts he searched for in the dust. Noting that he knew of the cave because he had been there before, looking for Civil War and Indian artifacts, Cash writes:

> Andrew Jackson and his army had slaughtered the Nickajack Indians there, men, women, and children, and soldiers from both sides of the War Between the States had taken shelter in the caves at various times during the conflict. The Indians left their bones in mounds. The soldiers left their names and affiliations and sometimes a message carved into the limestone of a chamber close to the entrance: *John Fox, C.S.A; Reuben Matthews, Union; Jeff Davis, Burn in Hell.* The remains of the dead among them were joined by the bones of the many

spelunkers and amateur adventurers who'd lost their lives in the caves over the years, usually by losing their way, and it was my hope and intention to join that company.[32]

Cash, before he decides to leave the cave and return to life, intends to lie down and make a grave, to make some degree of identification with them all. He joins together a tangled mix of the Indian burial ground, the remains of both Northern and Southern Civil War soldiers—a nation torn asunder but buried together—and modern-day explorers searching the landscape or the historical artifacts only to lose their way and join the dead. He imagines himself a latecomer to the historical drama, like the modern-day cave explorers, but he plans to join the same collected remains, an observer and participant. He does not follow through on his original plan to kill himself and join them but instead makes the story part of his narrative self-fashioning to be shared with audiences.

In his songs on *Ballads of the True West*, he combines accounts of historical figures with more poetic considerations of the cowboy lifestyle, implicitly framing his mythical oppositions via typical dichotomies of the western genre: a masculinized western frontier versus an eastern feminized civilization and domestication. Musically the album's ballads use both Cash's spoken word deliveries and his signature, sparse sound to convey a feeling of the desolate plains, while the occasional Carter Family female backing vocals offer angelic harmonies that seem like a distant, intermittent voice of feminized civilization or domestication. Thematically he writes about masculinized frontier violence and frontier justice in "Hardin Wouldn't Run," sings about Tombstone in "The Ballad of Boot Hill," and laments President Garfield getting shot on "Mister Garfield." He inhabits the point of view and moral ambiguity of prisoners and men about to be hanged. In the haunting "25 Minutes to Go," written by Shel Silverstein, Cash delivers the lyrical repetition in his hoarse, drug-dried voice to convey the desperation of a convict's last minutes of life before he feels himself slipping away as he is being hanged. In the traditional song "Sam Hall," here arranged by Tex Ritter, Cash portrays a man who famously faced his hanging while drunk and curses the crowd; Cash enacts with gusto the man's vicious, hissing, menacing verbal attacks on his listeners, creating high drama.

Balancing these selections, Cash includes songs yearning for an element of feminized domesticity or lamenting the absence of it. A notable example is Mother Maybelle's "A Letter from Home," about the Bible. Cash explains in his liner notes: "Since the Bible on the plains was as uncommon as a letter from home, many cowboys called it that." In this song, women symbolize family and are linked to Christianizing influences. The lyrics tell the story of a cowboy who is dejected to find that he has not received "a letter from home" from his mother; after he is shot that same day, the speaker gives him a Bible as his letter from home, and the young man wistfully replies: "If only I had just a little more time to read it." Sadly, we learn that "he died with his letter unread." The cowboy is bereft of family and kinship connections, as well as religious salvation. In some of Cash's other songs, not on this album, he criticizes this kind of stereotypical gendering—the Victorian "separate spheres" paradigm, the imagined gendered separation between the public and private spheres, a distinction historians have proved had more basis in ideology than in fact, as the two spheres were less historically separate and more fluid than scholars first thought.[33] In his well-known song "Don't Take Your Guns to Town," Cash sings of a mother who opposes gun fights but whose son is shot because he ignores her titular warning. The lament criticizes versions of hard-bodied, violent masculinity. On "My Cowboy's Last Ride," a "cowboy's lady" shoots him for running around on her, justifying her actions by saying, "I will no longer be hobbled and tied," as she turns the tables on a masculinized ethic of death-dealing frontier justice.

As for the album's vision of the West and what the cowboy has to say about Manifest Destiny or American Indian–white race relations, Cash opens *Ballads of the True West* with white romanticizing of Indians in his spoken word adaptation of Longfellow's "The Song of Hiawatha." He follows with "The Road to Kaintuck," a song June Carter wrote about one of the first western roads, blazed by Daniel Boone while "Indian wars were raging." It applauds Boone's heroism and warns of attacking Indians who have killed Boone's son. As the Statler Brothers and the Carter Family alternate his-and-hers harmony backing vocals, the Statlers sing, "Every Injun in these hills has gone berserk" and "you're never going to make it to Kaintuck," while Cash defiantly replies as the song's hardy pioneer persona: "I bet I'm going to make it to Kaintuck." For all of Cash's insistence on updating the cowboy way for 1965 and on seeing history as a story with multiple viewpoints, the album nevertheless seems wedded to some persistent historical mythologies.

In contrast, *Bitter Tears*, from the year before, mines similar historical material and mythology but insists on an oppositional political message, addressed forcefully to the 1960s. Instead of relegating American Indians to history, the album keeps them in the present, a critical move. In so doing, Cash differs from the antebellum American practice of romanticizing American Indians precisely because they were displaced, "vanishing," and no longer perceived as much of a military or political threat (even though Indian resistance to the Indian Removal Act of 1830 and U.S. encroachment continued during that period). Many critics have noted the "Vanishing American trope," which portrayed Indians as noble savages destined to die as white civilization overtook them. This trope was most popular in 1820s and 1830s literature. As Lora Romero points out, it coincided with Indian Removal—the forced military removal of eastern tribes to west of the Mississippi, codified in the Indian Removal Act.[34] As Leslie Fiedler and Brian Dippie have shown, the American obsession with Indians involves a search for a distinctive indigenous American culture that could be defined against English or European culture.[35] In a fantasy of cultural miscegenation, the Indian could be banished from the face of America, but Indian culture could live on in white men on the frontier. This dynamic is evident in cultural expression ranging from the Indian imitation in the Boston Tea party to America's long-running love affair with Pocahontas. Cooper, for example, paradigmatically sympathizes with American Indians yet romanticizes them and presents their vanishing as ineluctable. His frontier hero, Natty Bumppo, adopts and values parts of American Indian culture in order to survive on the frontier but pathologically insists there is "no cross" in his "blood"; Cooper's fantasy hero maintains white racial purity while symbolically incorporating Indians into an Anglo-American subjectivity. As Roy Harvey Pearce has argued, it is because Indians were placed in the past or distanced nonthreateningly in the present that they were able to be portrayed as "noble savages."[36]

To flesh out the deep history of this trope, scholars have shown us how race became firmly and explicitly connected to nationalism in the nineteenth century during an era of U.S. expansionism.[37] During the first half of the nineteenth century, the U.S. doubled its landmass through such means as the Louisiana Purchase (1803), the Indian Removal Act, and the rapid expansionism of the 1840s, when the nation annexed Texas in 1845. The U.S. gained possession of Oregon from Britain (south of the 49th Parallel) in 1846 and, as a result of the Mexican War (1846–48), acquired California and New Mexico in 1848. At the same time national rhetoric was becoming racialized. Political, scientific, and popular discourses converged by mid-century to form a vision of an Anglo-American United States with a Manifest Destiny to populate the continent and either subordinate or exterminate nonwhite races already in the annexed areas. A link between whiteness and the U.S. nation permeated the cultural discourse of Manifest Destiny and the rhetoric of expansionism, juridical history, legislation, domesticity, and citizenship.[38]

Although his cowboy album includes strains of this rhetoric, his American Indian album breaks with the legacy of this long tradition, as his cultural expression in that album is more oppositional. "The Ballad of Ira Hayes" is a key example of his insistence that listeners see American Indians in the present tense, not only as part of the past. Written by his collaborator, LaFarge (who wrote half the songs on the album), the lyrics glorify the real-life Hayes as a World War II marine who heroically served his country and helped raise the flag at Iwo Jima despite the mistreatment that he and his fellow Pima Indians suffered at the hands of the U.S. government. After returning home and again having to face American racism, Hayes, drunk at the time, fell into an irrigation ditch and froze to death. Ironically the ditch where he died was the single source of water that was provided to the Pima Indians on their Arizona reservation by the same government Hayes had proudly served. As the song describes this injustice, it notes the long history of prior Indian claims to the water until the whites stole the water supply. The song opens and closes with "Taps"—on flute in the beginning and snare drum at the end—honoring Hayes's patriotism and heroism for choosing to serve in the U.S. military despite the government's hypocrisies.

The song uses the European ballad form to launch a stinging political diatribe against the U.S. government and its official discourse, articulating an American Indian protest. The song's storytelling includes an incitement to the audience to respond sympathetically to this story about a brave Indian who deserves to be remembered. It also centers on the continuing government abuses that cannot be relegated to the past or deflected by romanticizing the American Indians. The final stanza powerfully brings the narrative into the present tense, visualizing Hayes as a ghost still haunting the dry land in the ditch where he died.[39] LaFarge's chorus, repeated five times in the song, offers a summary image of how Hayes is, tragically, both brave marine and drunken, dead Indian: "Call him drunken Ira Hayes / He won't answer anymore, / Not the whiskey-drinking Indian / Nor the Marine who went to war."[40] In describing this song, Cash avers that Hayes went from being a part of this "great symbolic moment of American victory, hope, and sacrifice" to someone who "drowned in two inches of water in a ditch on the reservation, another no-hope, forgotten Indian."[41]

Cash's performance here echoes the liner notes by Hugh Cherry, who observes that the government had recently broken a treaty signed by George Washington giving land to the Senecas in New York State; the land was taken away in the 1960s to build a dam, flooding Indian homes and burial grounds. Cash sings about the conflict in "As Long as the Grass Shall Grow" written by LaFarge. The lyrics complain that Washington promised them the land forever, and while Kennedy's government was busy breaking that treaty, Congress turned down an alternative plan the tribe presented to them for building the dam. In response, the Senecas renamed the dam "Lake Perfidy." Cash sings of treaties signed by

Washington, Adams, and Kennedy only to be broken, the poisoned water from this figurative lake of lies flooding the Indians' fields. Though rebuking Kennedy the most, the song reclaims Washington for the Indian cause and castigates the current government for dehumanizing them: "But the Government of the U.S.A. has corrected George's vow / The father of our country must be wrong, what's an Indian anyhow."

Cash's expression was unusual at the time, particularly in the extent to which he harnesses U.S. patriotism to further American Indian causes. He overcame the objections of Columbia Records to doing the album at all. When country radio balked at playing the album, Cash took out a full-page ad in *Billboard* castigating them for their cowardice, slamming industry categories and insisting on his adaptability: "Classify me, categorize me—STIFLE me, but it won't work. . . . I am fighting no particular cause. If I did, it would soon make me a sluggard. For as time changes, I change." He argued that the single "Ira Hayes" "is not a country song" and that the audiences that stations believe would tune it out might care about it (teenage girls, avid Beatles listeners, might be drawn to its tragedy since they "always go to sad movies to cry"). Saying that he "had to fight back" when he realized "so many stations are afraid of 'Ira Hayes'," Cash linked his pro-Indian sentiment to the Civil Rights movement and the Vietnam War protests: "'Ballad of Ira Hayes' is strong medicine. So is Rochester—Harlem—Birmingham and Vietnam." In the face of Cash's social criticism, Columbia Records tried to turn the ad into a marketing ploy by running their tag line at the bottom: "Nobody but nobody more original than Johnny Cash," and the album sold more than one hundred thousand copies at the time.[42] However, Cash's antiwar, antiracist sentiments became a troubled commodity.

The album itself has elements of appropriation, but it is mostly social protest, articulated through the folk vernacular of music. In his autobiography Cash describes his approach to the album's material, a mixture of political advocacy and emotional response:

> I dove into primary and secondary sources, immersing myself in the tragic stories of the Cherokee and the Apache, among others, until I was almost as raw as Peter. By the time I actually recorded the album I carried a heavy load of sadness and outrage; I felt every word of those songs, particularly "Apache Tears" and "The Ballad of Ira Hayes." I meant every word, too. I was long past the point of pulling my punches.[43]

Here Cash expresses his identification with American Indian rights and causes, and fights the music establishment to have his message heard. But, again, he dresses up like an American Indian, with a sad look in his eye, a white man playing Indian in his marketing campaign and on his album cover, a problematic moment of appropriation.

Yet, on this album, Cash makes his own mixture of European and American Indian cultural forms and critiques. He merges European ballad forms with the oral storytelling of American Indians, Euro-American folk song traditions with American Indian chanting styles. Although romanticized nostalgia is evident to some degree, the lyrics emphasize social protest. In "Apache Tears," Cash describes an Indian burial ground and Indians dying as a result of white injustice, which the speaker is bound to memorialize: "Petrified but justified / Are these Apache tears" and "They're sleeping in my keeping / Are these Apache tears."[44] In this song, although the Indian's grief is romanticized and elegized, the lyrics decry war, arguing that no armed conflict mastered the land itself and thus passers-by should tread lightly.

Other themes are more critical. "White Girl" condemns anti-miscegenation sentiment, white appropriation, and any attempts to romanticize Indians, although it also invokes misogyny and displaces racial anger onto a gender hierarchy. Here, the male Indian speaker dates a white woman, but she uses him as a trophy—a captive artifact or museum piece—to parade at parties. When he proposes marriage, she laughs at him, saying she cannot marry an Indian; the tragic legacy she leaves him is the alcoholism that he learned from her. The song is distinctive in country music, however, because it reverses the more common "frontier marriage" scenario where white men practice their sexual prerogative to couple with American Indian women. Stephen I. Thompson points out that very few country songs imagine an interracial romance between a white woman and an American Indian man, and that the criticism of racial prejudice in Cash's song is unusual.[45] Such a coupling would incite greater anti-miscegenation sentiment based on race and gender hierarchies. White male interracial mixing has always been seen as more acceptable than the threat to white racial purity caused by white women straying.

The song "Drums" replicates American Indian drumming sounds, the general thumping sounds heard on folk albums of the period. It complains about forced assimilation from the viewpoint of an American Indian speaker. Cash sings that white wars with Indians have not been successful, because "fighting never made one Indian turn white" and that Indians taught whites the history of this land first. In "Custer," Cash uses his standard sound (his voice backed by the sparse "boom-chicka-boom" electric guitar and rhythm section) in the service of a highly oppositional message: he sings that "us Indians" celebrate the defeat of Custer and laughingly offers the refrain: "the General he don't ride well anymore." In "The Talking Leaves," Cash imagines "Sequoia" as a young Indian teen, starting his quest to write down the Cherokee alphabet as an act of resistance in order to compete with the white man's written texts. The song teaches believers "That the Indian's thoughts could be written down. / And he left us these talking leaves."[46] The concluding song of Bitter Tears, "The Vanishing Race," bemoans the "vanishing Navajo." In a good example of the album's musical mixture, the song begins with Cash chanting to American Indian drums and then adds a guitar that lightly echoes the drums. In "As Long as the Grass Shall Grow," the "forever" claim refers to the treaties the United States broke, but it can also be seen as an implicit reference to the theme of endurance in American Indian literature, implying that the Indians will live on long after white conquest and an eventual white downfall. This theme also appears in the Cash-penned "Navajo" (not on this album), where he rebuts tropes like the "Cult of the Vanishing American" or Anglo-American rhetoric that naturalizes American Indian genocide. Instead, Cash sings that "the Indian sun is rising instead of going down."

The singing persona on these songs is slippery, sometimes echoing white ro-manticist narratives (complicated by Cash's false identity claim in the liner notes) but mostly enacting forceful American Indian protest messages. Elsewhere, Cash delivers a similar sentiment but takes on a white speaking persona addressing a white audience. In "The Flint Arrowhead," Cash recites a story about finding an arrowhead; the discovery "left in his trust" makes him admire the "master trade" behind its creation and prompts him to question his own property claims: "That I inherited this ground is denied / By this stone that I found." He incites his listeners to join him in an attempt to recover the past and to treat the relic with deference, to look back with respect through the "veil" of time. While his pedagogy is poetic and unclear rather than practical, Cash's account turns the speaker's ambivalence into a political criticism of land rights.

The 1969 documentary The Man, His World, and His Music includes concert footage that encodes how what Cash is doing is dense, thorny, and ambivalent. The concert is Cash's performance of songs from Bitter Tears at a 1968 Sioux In-dian reservation concert in South Dakota. At the concert, one of many where he sang to raise money for tribes, Cash smoked a peace pipe, Sioux men and women performed traditional dances and songs, and he told his audience, "Let's have the house lights turned up so we can look each other in the eye and tell it like it really was."[47] Here Cash clearly compels emotional responses from some of his American Indian audience members. But there is obviously an unequal power relationship—they do not have his degree of agency and cultural access to be able to "tell it like it really was." The documentary covers Cash's trip to Wounded Knee, where a Sioux chief asked him to write a song about the 1890 massacre; the film shows him composing the song "Big Foot," decrying the slaughter. He tries to speak for the Sioux chief in order to condemn the Wounded Knee massacre, but the ventriloquism is troublesome, made more so because the song he composes then becomes part of his money-making catalogue of music sold to predominantly white audiences. Indeed, the song appeared on his album *America—A 200-Year Salute in Story and Song* (1972), incongruously taking its place alongside lauda-tory songs about the American folk heroes Daniel Boone and Andrew Jackson (both famous as "Indian fighters," and Jackson the infamous proponent of Indian Removal). Hence, Cash's social critique exists in tension with his commodity practices and his significantly greater economic, political, and social power than the American Indian subjects of his songs.

Cash's own identity claims and projected identity likewise muddy this picture. His false claim of "Cherokee blood," an attempt to establish his authenticity as a speaking subject, does not, of course, make sense in terms of traditional American Indian tribal kinships and affiliations, which were not based on ideas of "blood" or race until the U.S. government imposed the idea of "blood quantum" onto American Indian tribes to determine who would have rights and protections.[48]

But whereas a writer like Cooper represents white guilt that still romanticizes American Indians as noble savages, Cash is more complicated in this instance. In terms of American intellectual history, Cooper is what the postcolonial theorist Mary Louise Pratt might term "anti-conquest," the European who tries to claim innocence but at the same time asserts hegemony and, perhaps, apologizes for colonialism or imperialism but keeps those power hierarchies in place.[49]

Cash's work, meanwhile, gestures toward (though fails to enact fully) some-thing closer to the model imagined by Sherman Alexie in his novel *Reservation Blues* (1995).[50] Alexie's articulation fits a more specific model of hybridity around cultural contact, adapted to American studies from postcolonial theory—a mix-ture that critiques the colonial or imperial power; here the United States is a spe-cial case, in that it is a former colony that becomes an imperial power demanding the "internal colonization" of Indian reservations.[51] Alexie's novel envisions the extensive syncretism of American popular music itself as a resource for productive struggle with the legacy of colonialism and imperialism. In the novel the blues legend Robert Johnson, far from dead, arrives at the Spokane Indian Reservation in the 1990s, becomes a member of the tribe, and inspires an Indian rock band that mixes blues, rock, and Indian forms into a culturally hybrid music. Rather than a space of appropriation, this collaboration makes music a liberating space for cultural preservation and spiritual survival, one that speaks to a deeply hybrid-ized material existence. Alexie's "Reservation Blues" is based on shared under-standings of suffering, power, and political history, an act of what Pratt might term "transculturation" in the contact zone between cultures, where the margin appropriates the center's culture and changes it, generating intersubjective forma-tions that include a political critique of the dominant colonial or imperial power. Alexie includes the white artists Hank Williams and Janis Joplin in his panoply of greats who create positive cultural mixing. His idea of a utopian musical space is akin to what Josh Kun describes as "audiotopias," or sonic spaces that bring heterogeneous cultural sites together, necessarily making difference audible and imagining America as multicultural rather than monocultural. Kun describes such utopian musical visions as "identificatory 'contact zones,'" or "both sonic and social spaces where disparate identity-formations, cultures, and geographies historically kept and mapped separately are allowed to interact with each other as well as enter into relationships whose consequences for cultural identification are never predetermined."[52]

Cash's *Bitter Tears* does not enact that degree of cultural syncretism, and thus I would not argue that his work in that album should be understood as transcultura-tion. But although this case shows signs of appropriation similar to his Jamaica case, at the same time Cash's "both/and" paradigm of cultural ambivalence can sometimes be seen, as in the *Bitter Tears* album, as a source of potentially produc-tive critique, moving somewhat closer to transcultural syncretism than simply reinscribing U.S. frontier mythology. But I do not make a strong claim for this case; it is more a matter of nuance. More clearly, Cash's texts voice the contradic-tions in the American nationalist consensus, even while his songs and images are ambivalent and conflicted. Such themes illustrate the intricacy of Cash's equivo-cations and how his work can shed light on deep American ideological issues and hold them in dynamic tension.

5

MAN IN BLACK

Class and National Mythologies

Cash's representations of Southern working-class tribulations critique national mythologies, pointing up exceptions to the supposed freedom and equality in the country's foundational narratives. On another level, however, Cash's oeuvre also reinforces other aspects of America's core fictions, such as upholding patriotism, the flag as a symbol of pride, the valor of American soldiers fighting for liberty, and the idea that freedom defines America, even when it requires conquering or displacing others. His corpus thus does both things: it both critiques and reinforces national mythologies. It voices the incongruities at the heart of America's "official narratives" of democracy founded on ideals of Enlightenment rationalism and egalitarianism. It expresses the exclusions involved in this rhetoric, as many Americans are left out of a promised fraternity of equality. Taken together, Cash's oeuvre yearns for the American ideal of freedom even while it points up its shortcomings. His texts illuminate how these contradictions constitute national identity, even as they underscore the incoherence and ruptures in the American narrative of nation.

Cash's workers cannot afford to purchase the goods they produce. They build cars they cannot buy, and grow and harvest food they cannot eat. His sharecroppers toil all their lives, but if their crops fail, they must leave the land they do not own, carrying only the clothes on their backs (as in his song "Come and Ride This Train"). Cash's corpus specifically isolates the tension between free democracy versus the expansion of capitalism and its exploitation of labor (whether of black slaves or impoverished rural whites). By capturing their frustrations with class stratification and the economic system, Cash's songs decry the marginalization of his Southern white working-class men (and women, although his work primarily focuses on men). At the same time, his texts enshrine them as the "commonfolk" bedrock of America.

Cash's critiques of class are elaborately joined to his advocacy for American Indians, with both poor Southern whites and American Indians appearing as fellow marginalized "Others" who, paradoxically, are sometimes used to represent American distinctiveness and exceptionalism.[1] As detailed earlier, Cash's texts speak to an identification between the two groups (and an American Indian investment in country music);[2] his songs celebrate both cowboy frontier mythology and American Indian rights, yet his advocacy moves beyond simple romanticism. His two contrary impulses remain in painful conflict, counterbalancing each other in ways that elucidate American incongruities, such as "free" land gained through violent dispossession of the original inhabitants.

Cash commonly specifies the South as the setting for his class critiques, conveying throughout his work an ideology of place and a sense of communal identity grounded in the region's characteristics. The South itself joins the roster of abject Others rejected by and yet constitutive of official national narratives (another link in the chain of concepts: low, popular, mass, Gothic). As Teresa Goddu points out, fantasy images of the South in American mythology often depict it as "the nation's other." It serves as a repository for problems the nation wishes to displace or purge, such as institutionalized racism, the hypocrisies of democracy founded on race slavery, or the fitful movement into industrialization and the conditions of modernity.[3] Through a similar chain of associations, country music is also sometimes conceived of as a low Other and, at the same time, as a vehicle for conveying American ideals. Barbara Ching, for example, views "hard country" as the abject, the kind of "low other" defined by Peter Stallybrass and Allon White as constituting dominant cultural discourses (in European-derived cultures that depend on hierarchies).[4] Elsewhere Ching makes a similar argument about the rural as Other.[5] Jock Mackay offers a metropole/periphery argument: the periphery generates country music (and other popular music) in response to the structural dislocation caused by the political and economic dominance of the metropole.[6]

My reading of polyvalence and multivocality in Cash's texts is meant to show how his irresolvable, competing themes illuminate core American ideological contradictions. He taps into these conflicts in ways that engender passionate responses, and, as I suggested earlier, Cash's music has the potential to urge audiences into active contemplation of these problems. In the case of the protesters who marched on the 2004 Republican National Convention in New York, defending their vision of Cash and sparking heated debates, this hypothesis seems to hold true.

In this chapter I extend my case by further considering those student protesters. In examining Cash's themes of class, I undertake close readings of several key texts in this context and of Cash's lyrical content more broadly. Focusing first on an exemplar, I inspect Cash's representation of class issues on his labor concept album, *Blood, Sweat and Tears* (1963), and then connect it to his larger lyrical trends. Connecting class to his depictions of American mythologies, I investigate his three concept albums about the nation (and its music), *Songs of Our Soil* (1959), *America* (1972), and *Ragged Old Flag* (1974), and conclude with his overall lyrical treatment of this topic.

The Politics of Country Music

Cash's contrarian political stances, emerging through his blue-collar patriotism, engage with long percolating trends in country music. It can be difficult to untangle the genre's politics. Although it has historically been associated with populism, because it is bound to Southern rural folk cultures, country music's political affiliations have fluctuated, and it has often been seen as apolitical. When it does address political content, it is commonly seen as staunchly conservative: the traditional "medium for the transmission of rural conservatism" and the more recent mouthpiece for angry urban NASCAR dads.[7] Certainly the stereotype of the genre as the bastion of conservative, white, patriarchal family values has been rampant at least since Nixon courted the support of country music in the 1970s. Bill Malone argues that this conservative trend began in the Cold War 1950s, although he maintains that the politics of country music is so varied that one could not categorize it as either right-wing or left-wing, conservative or liberal.[8] The journalist Chris Willman, meanwhile, contends that the shift of country music to conservatism is part of the larger political transformation of the South into a Republican stronghold over the last two generations. However, he asserts that the common perception of country music conservatism does not always hold true. As he notes, some industry insiders swear the stereotype of conservatism is accurate (he quotes John Grady, head of Sony Nashville), but others dispute that characterization and insist that the genre cannot be pigeonholed. Willman cites the prominent country journalist Chet Flippo, who maintains that country music is populist, nonpartisan, and allows for a range of views.[9]

For critics who agree that country music is political, that it reflects the status of populism and working-class politics at any given moment in American history, the key disagreement is how it articulates its varying politics. Is it wholly escapist or does it retain some structural social critiques? Some scholars claim that the genre hews to escapism. Malone argues, for example, that Southern working-class individualism and fatalism offset class anger, leading to the focus on individual rather than collective response, which he calls "the most tragic consequence of union decline" in the South.[10] Perhaps leaving more room for expressions of discontent, Paul DiMaggio, Richard Peterson, and Jack Esco see a combination of fatalism and "primitive rebellion" that reflects a "populism in retreat."[11]

Other scholars find more resistant dynamics in the genre. Aaron Fox, in his ethnographic study of country music fandom in working-class Texas, argues that the genre represents, in a tenuous age of globalization, a nostalgia for the era of the postwar class compromise, which he describes as "the era of an advanced industrial political economy in which manual workers enjoyed both dignity and economic power unprecedented in the history of capitalist society."[12] In a new era of increased dislocation and undermined wages and status for these manual workers, country music, Fox contends, offers a cultural site for social identification that helps the working class grapple with these large-scale changes by referring back to communal and local cultural lineages. Fox insists that country music has also become a globally popular genre among other "victims of progress," including native North and South Americans, Aboriginal Australians, and many black Africans.[13]

Likewise, Mackay compares country music (what he calls the genre of the "classical industrial proletariat") to populism as "responsive cousins," maintaining that although no consistent political message is heard in country music, this inconsistency should not be read as mere political and thematic ambiguity.[14] Rather, it reflects the multiple tensions inhering in working-class life. He finds the same tension between "people's power" and "reactionary redneck conservatism" in both country music and in the history of populism in America.[15] For Mackay, country music will only reflect social realities, not spark social movements; thus the genre rarely hints at structural critiques but imagines resistance by way of thwarting authority or undermining the system, which, he thinks, moves beyond individual escapism. He also locates more resistant strains in country music, such as instances where local cultures translate and syncretize country songs across regional and ethnic barriers as working-class anthems. Here, he cites Quebecois translations of country songs, such as Willie Lamothe's "Le Mur d'Acier" (Steel Wall), which is an adaptation of Cash's "Folsom Prison Blues."[16]

Willman, meanwhile, tries to resolve the question of country music's politics by turning it into a debate within the genre. In his book *Rednecks and Bluenecks* (2005), he contends that, although mainstream country is dominated by conservative strains, it is also joined by the dissenting voices of progressive "outsider" subgenres like "alternative country" and Americana, making country music as a whole the most vibrant space for political debate of any American cultural genre. When noting country's folk roots and continuing relationship to folk music, he asserts of the two that the "chief point of divergence is whether the solution to social problems could be found in coming together in groups for reform or by pulling up one's own bootstraps, as it were."[17] In response, he argues that the redneck and the hippie strains have always coexisted in country music, most obviously in the Outlaw Country movement of the 1970s. In his telling, ornery "bluenecks" like Steve Earle and the Dixie Chicks are the "loyal opposition," and conservative "rednecks" like Toby Keith rule the mainstream (although Keith dubs himself a conservative Democrat, to which his sometime duet partner, the famously liberal Willie Nelson, has replied, "kind of").[18] Unpacking the convolution of such political affiliations, Willman argues that the shift from Democrat to Republican in the South was not only a result of Nixon's effort to lure racist Dixiecrats or Reagan's appeal to the white working class through family-values appeals, but also through the alienation of 1970s conservative Democrats who felt that liberal elites did not care to understand their regional culture.

Cash takes his place in these larger socio-historical trends through his structural social critiques, specifically through his multilayered combinations of seemingly opposed views and stances. He does not always reflect trends in country music more generally, but Cash as a case study does offer an argument that a greater sense of protest is possible in the country music genre.

Noting Cash's well-known political iconoclasm, Willman groups him with Merle Haggard, dubbing them both "omnipoliticians." He argues that both are ambiguous enough for all political sides to claim them, as they are either maverick independents who defy categories or deeply confused and conflicted patriotic souls.[19] Willman concurs with the reading that Ching and others have offered of Haggard. Although his signature song, "Okie from Muskogee," has been interpreted as a reactionary pro-war, conservative, blue-collar anthem, it is actually multivalent and also includes a satire of the attitudes of Middle America from an outsider's perspective.[20] While Willman quotes the liberal Malone as saying that Haggard disappoints him because there is nothing "politically activist" in him and that liberals keep hoping for some working-class advocacy that Haggard will never deliver, he also cites opposing views from leftist songwriters. Rodney

Crowell contends that Haggard is a "common-man Democrat" who reflects fluctuating working-class positions, and Kris Kristofferson and Steve Earle see him
as someone whose views have evolved over time, from more reactionary to more
progressive (witness his recent song indicting the war machine, "That's the News"
[2003]).[21] Such debates about Haggard offer a sense of his depth as an artist. Yet,
whereas Willman wants to group Cash and Haggard together because of this
iconoclasm, I argue that Cash is best understood as his own original case.

   I agree with Willman's understanding of Cash as an artist like Haggard who offers multivalent political messages. However, I also see Cash as distinctive. Again,
he is striking for his consistency in refusing to resolve binary tensions, in the depth
and longevity of his exploration of those binaries in a range of American themes,
and in the degree and longevity of his incorporation of that irresolvable tension
into his media image. After all, for the hundreds of protesters marching on the
2004 Republican National Convention, their investment in his work and image
had prompted them to insist that the Republicans could not claim Cash as their
own (I know of no such social protest action to protect Merle Haggard from false
appropriations). These marchers dressed in black, brought along guitars, sported
pompadours, and sang their favorite of Cash's political lyrics. Part of a larger bloc
of progressive activists, the students used Cash as a site around which to coalesce
their action. The organizer Erin Siegal, a twenty-two-year-old art student from
Brooklyn, in her press release playfully encouraged marchers to bring their "singing voice" and "dancing shoes," but also their "decentralized action schemes" and
"creative resistance"—those hallmarks of larger progressive protest movements.[22]
In fact, as discussed below, she was explicitly disputing any attempt to use Cash
for partisan politics. The students insisted that he was not affiliated with any party,
Republican or Democratic. Instead they saw him as a progressive voice for the
poor. For them, his lack of partisanship strengthened his progressive advocacy
for the working class.

   In my reading of Cash, here again I disagree with Malone. He argues that
Cash's contrary investment in progressive social protest versus conservative patriotism (he supported Vietnam protesters but also the office of the president) is
resolved into one side of the binary. For Malone, Cash's social protest is super-
ficial, and so the conservative patriotism side wins out.[23] While admiring the
spirit of Malone's argument, I hope that my previous discussions in this book
have shown the depth of Cash's investment in social protest and how his music
creates structural social critiques rather than retreating into the kind of escapism
where Malone consigns it. The assessments of Cash's collaborators speak to how

his equivocations remain open. Kris Kristofferson insists that although he and Cash agreed on some issues and disagreed on others (Cash would sometimes hold more right-wing opinions), Cash always fought for Kristofferson's right to voice his opinions. Kristofferson embraces Cash for being "a very concerned guy who always spoke the truth as he saw it, and he believed in fighting for the under-dog."[24] Rosanne Cash, similarly arguing that Cash was "an honest guy who was seeking out his own truth and living his own pain and his own life and his own joy," emphasizes that he was an iconoclast but "definitely was liberal in his social and political views."[25] Rodney Crowell, meanwhile, discussing Cash's anti-Bush sentiments, posits Cash as "an eloquent conservative individual who was socially liberal."[26]

Man-and-Woman-in-Black Bloc

What does the polyvalent sign "Johnny Cash" signify? Whose interests are served by its different meanings? What is its cultural work? The student protest offers a cogent example of how one group interpreted "Johnny Cash" as text and the purposes he served it.

My analysis of narrative themes and rhetorics in relation to specific socio-historical contexts, as I have been arguing, is particularly helpful for interpreting country music as a lyrics-focused genre, just as Ching has maintained.[27] As a liter-ary critic, my method of interpretation is to analyze thoroughly the polyvalence of cultural texts and to place them in relevant socio-historical and theoretical contexts. Thus, so far I have necessarily been concentrating primarily on text and context.

In discussing media and audience reception in general, I have not offered a deep analysis of audiences and their specific uses of Cash as a text. In this section I briefly discuss a specific case of audience reception in a way not meant to be exhaustive but only suggestive of how Cash might be relevant to discussions of consumption and reception, and as a sample of further possible research ques-tions beyond the scope of this book. My analysis of the cultural politics of Cash's reception in the specific instance of the student protesters is meant to exemplify how listening groups circulate mythologies about the musician and at the same time generate identity and meaning from popular music. Here I focus on the ideological meanings that this group ascribes to Cash, and thus I am isolating only one part of a much more complex reception process. Popular music theorists debate various models for understanding how musical meaning is made, and there is no single, commonly accepted, standardized method or theory. The field of ethnomusicology, of course, is the area traditionally dealing most extensively with issues of reception and how audiences use cultural texts. However, popular music studies as a field has also used media studies models to grapple with meaning in reception (Marx's "production in use," or what Michel de Certeau calls "secondary production"), by drawing on cultural studies models that posit complicated circuits of production, text, and reception as the elements producing meaning (models like those elaborated by Stuart Hall).[28] Here, I analyze a case of audience reception along the lines of such media studies approaches and not through specific ethnomusicology methods.

Erin Siegal, the organizer of the 2004 protest at the Republican National Convention (RNC), explicitly imagined her protest as a dispute over Cash's cultural meaning. In her "call to action" press release, she decries the RNC reception sponsored by the American Gas Association honoring Cash and Lamar Alexander at Sotheby's, the auction house where many of Cash's possessions were soon to be sold by his family in order to pay estate taxes. Siegal writes:

> On Tuesday, August 31, the Republicans who will invade our city have planned an exclusive "celebration" of Johnny Cash inside the famous high-art auction house Sotheby's for Tennessee delegates. This past July, Sotheby's locked out 54 union workers, Teamster Local 814 Movers, including some who had been employed for over thirty years. The people of New York will stand strong to voice our opposition to the current Republican administration and to remind the G.O.P that Johnny Cash was a working-class hero.[29]

Her description outlines how she thinks the Republicans are trying to pose Cash: as an entertainment icon for a clubby establishment of business people and union busters using the political system to further their enrichment at the expense of the working class. In contrast, she interprets Cash as a "working-class hero" and urges other activists to stage a protest at Sotheby's that would "make Johnny proud." She quotes his lyrics from "Man in Black" as evidence of his sympathies.

Siegal insistently places Cash in the context of labor unions. As she offers her counter-interpretation of him, she implicitly frames him as an organic intellectual for the working class, a sincere singer advocating proletarian causes. She goes so far as to imagine his stance on specific policy issues (antiwar, anti–drug laws, and anti–Bush economic policies):

> The songs of Johnny Cash were beacons of light for those who were unjustly locked up, kicked down, and knocked around. He sang for the poor, the imprisoned, and the oppressed. He sang from his heart. How dare the Republicans

think of using the memory of a true people's hero to promote their greedy causes and war-criminal president? Would Johnny support the president's economic policies? NO! Would Johnny support the Iraq war? NO! Would Johnny support the draconian Rockefeller drug laws? HELL NO![30]

Cash did make comments critical of the Iraq war, and Siegal draws parallels with Vietnam when she encourages protesters to bring the lyrics to Cash's songs questioning Vietnam ("Singin' in Viet Nam Talkin' Blues," "What Is Truth?"). As part of the spark driving her to action, Siegal says she turned to these songs to process her own feelings about the Iraq war when a relative returned from military duty there.[31] Siegal reads Cash's songs as arguments against the military-industrial complex (and she spins his record of drug use as more fodder to fight government control). Cash's questioning of Vietnam could be seen as counter to the prevailing trends in country music at the time. Most mainstream artists voiced support for the traditional American values of the "silent majority," which involved a pro-war stance and an irritation with war protesters.[32] However, in her firm interpretation of Cash, Siegal does not account for some of his ambivalences. She might have been surprised to hear Cash's commercials for American Oil in the 1970s or the hawkish comments that disillusioned an earlier generation of progressive activists back then. As demonstrated earlier, Cash often refused to be pinned down to specific political positions.

Siegal makes cultural use of her version of Cash by deploying him symbolically as part of a protest in the context of a leftist progressive network—part of larger activist movements protesting issues such as globalization, the Iraq war, and neoliberal economic policies. Her affiliation with that movement is evident through her method of organizing through the Internet and in her mode of address. She learned of the reception on an activist Web site (RNCnotwelcome.org) and advertised her protest on like-minded sites (such as PRWeb), her own Web sites (maninblack@riseup.net and defendjohnnycash.org), and via four thousand fliers.[33] She uses Cash as an occasion to form a political protest bloc, calling it the "Man-and-Woman-in-Black Bloc." Its members are united through their interpretation of Cash as a progressive working-class hero. Siegal emphasizes a sense of social responsibility in her symbolic protest: "We're passionate. We won't let the G.O.P. get away with this . . . we're painting and talking and doing everything we can to let people know about this. The city is with us; we just have an enormous responsibility to let everyone know."[34] In her press release, she clearly reads Cash's class-protest songs to mean he would be against the kind of neoliberal policies that have further widened the gap between rich and poor in America:

Well, Johnny sure wouldn't be too keen on this if he were still around, especially given the brutal stomping the current Republican administration has been doing on our nation's poor and working class. Actually, Johnny would be downright pissed. Just like we are. Over the past four years, conditions for the poor and working class have worsened. There are now over 31 million Americans living in poverty. 12.2 million children in our nation are poor, with over 1.35 million of them homeless. Over 43 million Americans have no health care and there are currently almost 10 million unemployed Americans. (Poor People's Economic Rights Campaign)

Siegal uses a fight over Cash's symbolic meaning as an occasion to use statistics to substantiate anti-poverty arguments. She goes on to cite the Cash memorabilia auction as a marker of class privilege (even though Cash himself requested the auction).[35] She insists that it is incongruous that the personal items of a "people's hero" would be "auctioned off to the rich bidder with the biggest wallet."[36]

When I contacted Siegal to learn more about the inspiration and goals of her protest, she stressed that she would speak out against any effort to co-opt Cash for one political party: "We are protesting the way RNC has affiliated itself with Johnny Cash. If the Democrats did it, rest assured, we'd still be protesting. We love Johnny Cash and are offended by the exploitation of his memory for any political gain. Johnny Cash was an independent, and an American hero. We will be singing his most political songs to remind the G.O.P that his songs belong to the people, not any political party, especially not theirs given the current Bush administration's politics."[37] She also said that members of the Cash family had contacted her privately to assure her that Cash would have supported her stance, even though publicly they could only say that Cash did not have a political party affiliation.

Siegal goes so far as to frame the content of her protest as a "platform," and her rhetoric emphasizes activist terminology. She made her specific case out of her interpretation of Cash and what he signifies, and she asked protesters to sign onto this platform (of political action based on cultural interpretation) by joining the demonstration. Siegal wrote that more than six hundred people felt summoned by her "platform" and took to the streets to protest with her.[38] Another activist, Kirsten Anderberg, writing on the Web in support of Siegal, emphasizes the humorous nature of the protest as well as the underlying seriousness, attributes she also finds in Cash:

Can we expect to see bands of roving Pompadour-and-Guitar Blocs at more pro-tests in the future, such as anti-war and free trade protests? I sure hope so. . . .

Not only is it fun for the participants, as well as the media, and observers, it is also pertinent and very serious in nature, really. Johnny Cash had a really serious political message. He understood poverty. He understood prison. He understood the working people. He is a good beacon for protest activity. And he also was really funny. Which is why this bloc has so much potential. Because Johnny Cash, himself, was so funny, intense, political, and honest. The bloc has endless material to work with.[39]

Her interpretation of Cash (funny and serious, politically committed and truthful) seems to be shared by many of the protesters who felt compelled to demonstrate publicly in support of it.

The protest sparked a debate in the press and on the Web that focused on competing views of Cash. Again, most striking here is that Cash's equivocations provide ammunition for both sides. In the national and international press coverage of the protest and the responses it provoked, some accounts misinterpret Cash as a Democrat, whereas others underscore the undecidable nature of the debate. One article quotes a participant speaking about the sense of working-class solidarity he felt with Cash, which led him to join the protest:

> John McCarthy, a Metro worker from Brooklyn, expressed outrage at what demonstrators considered the Republicans' use of Cash's image and possessions. "I am a working-class person so I can identify with him," McCarthy said. "He stood up for the poor and native Americans. Now the man's dead and the Republicans are using his name for something he would be very much against. Cash would be against the current war in Iraq, the economic problems in the U.S., and the U.S. exploitation of the Third World."[40]

His heated comments touch on the same themes as Siegal's platform, evidence that the rank-and-file members of the protest subscribe to the larger message and its sense of outrage.

Other press accounts emphasized the competing interpretive claims made by the RNC group and frame the event as a rather surprising and torrid debate whose nature is not made any clearer by the Cash family's responses. A BBC article quoted Tennessee Republican Party chairwoman Beth Harwell, who said the event was "a way for us to honour a great Tennessean" and that "a lot of the Tennessee delegates love Johnny Cash's music." The article goes on to cite another personal connection justifying the event, namely, that the reception was also designed to honor Tennessee Senator Lamar Alexander, a friend of Cash and June Carter Cash.[41] The Associated Press story, meanwhile, focuses on the debate generated by the event and asks, "Was the Man in Black a Democrat or a

Republican?" The article cites both son John Carter ("He wouldn't say if he had any political affiliation") and daughter Rosanne as saying that Cash did not have a political affiliation, as they each toe the Cash party line of evasion. However, Rosanne also emphasizes the degree to which she believes Cash would not have supported the Republican agenda. According to the article, "Cash's daughter, Rosanne Cash, who has been linked to Democratic causes, released a statement saying the Cash estate did not object to the Sotheby's party. She said the party was approved based on the 'personal relationship between our family and (Sen. Alexander), NOT as a show of support for the Republican agenda.'"[42] Her equivocation is actually closer to what Cash does in his autobiography on the Nixon White House issue. She denies a positive tie between Cash and a conservative political position; she leaves open the possibility of a progressive position but does not embrace it; and thus she rests on ambiguity.

On an activist Web site advertising the event, one respondent attempted to resolve the opposing perceptions of Cash. Angrily dismissing the protest as silly and reductive, the poster tries to unify Cash's vacillations through his Christianity. However, any effort to explain Cash that mends his competing tendencies into one coherent vision itself risks the failures of reduction. The poster reads:

> So the Republicans are using Johnny Cash's name and music—so what? Was Johnny Cash against everything Republican? No. Don't be silly. He had liberal tendencies and conservative tendencies. He was against the death penalty, yet he was pro-life. He believed in welfare, but not socialism. He founded his beliefs on Christian principles and nothing else. Every individual is deserving of respect—rich poor free slaved prisoned happy sad—because they were created in God's image. I think you'll find most of his politics grew out of this principle. He was essentially a moderate—taking the good points from both political persuasions—and promoting them. . . . Cash wasn't an extreme leftist, nor was he a right winger; he was a moderate. And protesting the GOP's using of Cash's name is silly.[43]

Although this discussant insists that the protest group had misinterpreted Cash, his effort to make Cash out to be a political moderate based on Cash's "Christian principles" fails when faced with the actual complexity of Cash's depictions of religion (as I detail in the next chapter).

Willman notes that, in addition to the 2004 RNC controversy, another example of conservatives trying to associate themselves with Cash after his death is a right-wing video parody of Cash's "The Man Comes Around," a song about the second coming of Christ. The video circulated on the right-wing Free Republic

Web site using the song over images of Bush and the Iraq war, posing Bush as "the man" coming to level righteous judgment. Willman observes that, in both cases, lawyers representing Cash's estate stepped in, making the RNC group stop circulating invitations using Cash's image and forcing the removal of the "Man" video from Web sites.[44] These competing responses and appropriations, taken together, indicate the strength of the contrary impulses in Cash's corpus.

The New York protest is a measure of only one segment of Cash's fan reception. As we know, different audience communities make various uses of their popular music, fashioning their own visions of the artists with whom they identify. The protest group is a particularly striking example of using the identification with Cash's image and music as a basis for social action.

Other fan groups are organized around different goals and beliefs. Cash's official fan club, "The Johnny & June Carter Cash International Fan Club," formed in 1971, the longest-running Cash fan club in the U.S., defines itself largely as an appreciation society. Comments in its publications emphasize the members' love of Cash's music, his family and religious values, and his sympathy for the downtrodden. Bonding enthusiastically through the written word, group members trade information about Cash and engage seriously in amassing archives and collections. It is a member of the largest umbrella of country fan groups, the International Fan Club Organization, which was launched in 1966. The club traditionally sponsored a table each year at the huge annual country music Fan Fair in Nashville, with themes ranging from All-American patriotism to Cash's American Indian causes. Cash's sister, Reba Hancock, coordinated a fan club for him in the mid-1960s, "The Johnny Cash Appreciation Society," but it was disbanded in 1968 because Hancock was busy managing Cash's "House of Cash" operations. Fan Virginia Stohler launched her club with Hancock's support, and began publishing newsletters and annual yearbooks called *The Legend*. The enterprising dynamo Bill Miller took the fan club online eleven years ago and runs it as "The Official Johnny Cash Web Site" at JohnnyCash.com. The site includes newsletters, biographical materials and cultural histories, chat and forum spaces, and an extensive commercial area for the sale of Miller's Cash memorabilia. It also sponsors gatherings that feature concerts such as a "Cash Bash" in Memphis in 2005 and a gathering at the Carter Family Fold performance space in Maces Spring, Virginia, in 2007. In 2007 it launched a streaming weekly broadcast featuring interviews with Cash family members, friends, and fans. Miller states that the site has hundreds of thousands of visitors each month.[45] Indeed, there are more than eleven thousand officially registered members.

The group's print publications (prior to the Web site) include reprints of newspaper articles sent in by members. Some are about Cash's patriotism such as a story about Cash being honored in 1989 by the Veterans of Foreign Wars for his support of the POW/MIA cause. Others concern his social protests, including an article about Cash supporting a local Teamster chapter of trade show workers on strike against the Trump Castle in Atlantic City in 1993.[46] One issue reprinted a 1989 article about Cash's AIDS activism. Cash was under fire in the press for an album compilation of his songs, 'Til Things Are Brighter, performed by Michelle Shocked and The Mekons, among other artists, with proceeds benefiting an AIDS research fund. Cash notes in an interview that his fans defended him for the album when others, because of homophobia, denigrated it as an anti-Christian cause. Cash responds: "How can you not support AIDS research if you're a man of God?"[47] In a personal letter from Cash to Waylon Jennings, dated 1 June 1987, currently in the archives at the Country Music Foundation, Cash expresses his concerns about the epidemic, citing statistics, and enlists Jennings to set up a foundation with him, Music Business Foundation for AIDS Research. Although he says, "I am not trying to be a modern-day prophet Jeremiah," he goes on to write that "I think we should all do everything within our power as 'we the people' to aid the medical establishment in finding a cure or a vaccine against AIDS."[48] Cash expresses outrage and conviction over the need for research funding. The official fan club has frequently noted such activist causes that Cash pursued.

This club does not share the activism found in the New York protest group, but it does attend to Cash's convolutions, patriotism, and protest. Building a pictorial memorial to him, Bill Miller published a book of Cash pictures, Cash: An American Man, where he enshrines the Man in Black as "the quintessential American Man." In Miller's account of his close dealings with Cash (who became the godfather of one of Miller's children), he testifies that Cash "treated everyone equally," that he "went out of his way to touch the common man," and that "there are hundreds of stories about him reaching out to the downtrodden and less fortunate."[49] Here, Cash's advocacy for the impoverished forms a core part of his American iconicity for this fan group.

Blood, Sweat, and Tears

A lively example of Cash's depiction of class tension in his work is his concept album, Blood, Sweat and Tears (1963). An LP that can be interpreted in the context of the folk revival movement, it includes his revision of well-known folk ballads about working men such as his variation on "John Henry." The album commiserates with admirable laboring men brought low by poverty, failed crops, dropping prices for their agricultural goods, lack of work, and the need to feed their families. It emphasizes pride and self-respect in response to class abjection (a common working-class response to class frustration).[50] Cash later starred in a film that dealt centrally with these themes, *The Pride of Jesse Hallam* (1981). There, Cash plays the role of a coal miner and widower who must move with his children from their Kentucky farm to the city in search of work; the character struggles in the city because he is illiterate, but he perseveres through recourse to his pride, learning to read and to support his family in an urban space. Similarly, this much earlier album focuses on how working men are heroically ethical and moral, insisting that they should be able to provide for their families and succeed (implicitly, they should be included in the mythology of the American Dream of freedom and opportunity). Yet they are marginalized, and structural conditions prevent them from reaching this American Dream.

As part of this class pride and criticism of how some are denied opportunities, Cash's songs on *Blood, Sweat and Tears* focus on masculine prowess and self-respect in response to oppression. But even when Cash's songs focus on personal pride, they also register the degree to which the troubles of the heroic male speaker stem from the process of industrialization or the inequities in the economic system. Two such songs on the album empathize with laboring men being displaced by mechanization or suffering from its effects. As discussed earlier, Cash's version of "John Henry" glorifies the train worker as a martyr who died to prove that men are better than machines. Some critics read that song as an example of anti-technological, Luddite sentiment in country music, but most focus on it as an example of admiration for the strong-bodied worker.[51] In Cash's version, he asserts that the lives of working men have value, and that these men should not be exploited and discarded. Also included here is Cash's adaptation of the ballad "Casey Jones," concerning the real-life train engineer who died in 1906 when his train, rushing in flood conditions to be on time, hit the back of a passenger train. Cash emphasizes Jones's aggression as the engineer leans out the window, ready to take his "trip to the Promised Land." Cash's musical elements help highlight these themes: communal despair over Jones's fate is signified by backup singers joining Cash in his chorus, while Cash uses a train whistle and a rhythmic snare drum to mime the sounds of a train.

Other Cash songs that empathize with the plight of working men's struggles to survive also underscore the structural conditions causing problems for these men. Desperate men who are not criminals nevertheless consider crime under conditions of extreme poverty when they need to provide for their families; they pray to God to give them alternatives (Harlan Howard's "Busted"). Even if these men do not turn to crime, they can be arrested simply for being poor. Howard's "Chain Gang" decries the fact that the male speaker was arrested for vagrancy because he was rambling around and had no money; the song relates that the shame of being on the chain gang and the harsh, inhumane conditions are worse than death. Another song that empathizes with men facing troubles because of poverty is Cash's cover of Jimmie Rodgers's classic song, "Waiting for a Train." It tells the story of a poor man kicked off a train by a brakeman because he has no money; he finds himself stranded in Texas, trying to return home to the South all the way from San Francisco. He is left broke and broken-hearted, with no one caring about his fate or offering help. Lack of money bars his mobility and his attempted return home. Ostracized as a hard-luck "bum," he is soundly rejected by those with money, leaving him isolated and alone.

Cash also turns to the cycle of poverty. Just as poor farmers, prisoners, and bums suffer the effects of structural conditions involving the accumulation of wealth by the few, these conditions can continue for generations. One Cash cover song here accentuates the abject nature of an impoverished existence, as men pinned in the cycle are ashamed of their condition. Sheb Wooley's "Roughneck" follows the speaker's father, a driller on a wildcat crew, into a pattern of deprivation coupled with masculine pride. He begins work as a child, never crying or questioning his fate, telling himself (as others tell him) that he was "born to be" a roughneck and therefore he will never "amount to anything." Humor provides a release valve in the lyrics. The boisterous hell-raiser learned to curse at age two, to fight at age three. Cash languorously drawls out the words "hard labor" when he sings of the speaker's existence, and the song exaggerates the man's condition for humorous purposes. Nevertheless, the tune bemoans the man's situation and sadly witnesses the cycle of poverty.

This sympathy with working-class men extends across racial lines. "John Henry" is an example of cross-racial class solidarity, although, as discussed earlier, Cash's treatment of racial hierarchies is generally complex and problematic. As he "plays" the part of John Henry, his rendition of this song also evinces the problematic dynamics of mixture and appropriation, love and theft that critics have found in blackface minstrelsy.[52] Two other songs on the *Blood, Sweat and Tears* album explicitly refer to African American musical traditions, and both are about men working on prison chain gangs; one of the men escapes from his work captain's abuse, and the other is caught escaping and is hanged in front of his children. In "Tell Him I'm Gone," Cash's arrangement features the blues alongside Cash's boom-chicka-boom sound. Cash ad-libs rockabilly-style yelps when recounting how the prisoner instructs his fellows to tell the captain "I'm gone." When the captain calls him a "hard-headed devil," the man defiantly replies "that ain't my name." The song applauds his brave resistance. On the next tune, "Another Man Done Gone," a traditional lament collected by John Lomax and attributed to him and Vera Hall, Cash sings it as a blues a capella in a call-and-response format; the male voice sings the first line and a woman's voice echoes in reply.

The album as a whole deploys musical elements in service of the key themes, among them sympathy for the working man. Another undercurrent in the LP is the conflict between the self and a society in which a subculture responds communally to the suffering of poor men but the larger society rejects them. Throughout, Cash uses sounds to signify labor (providing further sympathy for the men he sings about), such as the clanging of bells, train whistles, the clacking of trains, and hammers hitting steel. The female voices of the Carter Family sometimes join in angelically on the choruses, representing the sorrowful reaction of a community or the hope for God's help. Some of the songs also draw attention to a mixture of musical genres, implicitly signifying a cultural mixture and perhaps pointing to themes of cross-racial class bonding. In its instrumentation, the album relies on Cash's signature Tennessee Three boom-chicka-boom sound, which also mimics train sounds here, but some songs also combine that sound with more explicit genre references such as the blues (on "Tell Him I'm Gone"). Flashingly quick hillbilly or bluegrass-style banjos also make appearances, for example, on Cash's cover of Merle Travis's 1947 song, "Nine Pound Hammer." The bluegrass inflection connects "Nine Pound Hammer" to folk traditions. The lyrics describe a frustrated, yearning train worker who wishes his work crew would move faster because he wants to leave his labor behind to go see his woman "on the mountain" and never return. When the speaker says, "You can make my tombstone out of number nine coal," the lyrics starkly spell out the idea that the man's difficult toil will cause his death.

More generally, these topics are frequently the focus of the lyrics Cash wrote. As he advocates for ex-cons, coal miners, cotton pickers, sharecroppers, truckers, and gas station owners, all struggling to survive economically, Cash emblazons their pride in work and honor. Even the town drunk has great dignity ("Abner Brown"), because, even as a "bum," he had more friends and did more good than the "fine fancy people" in town, and this made him as good as all the "mighty men" in existence. He told the town youths tall tales and made them feel "ten feet tall," treating them like his own children, helping them dream about their own futures. Cash celebrates the sacrifices working men and ex-cons make for their families ("Call Daddy from the Mine," "Give My Love to Rose") and for God (as in the stonecutter who dies carving a stone to honor God, in "The Masterpiece"). Other songs underline the desolation and hardship caused by a life of hard work and poverty. In "Face of Despair," Cash writes poetically of "September country" in which one can look back on a life "as rough as a grand road" and question how "much of it can you bear." The heavy burden of hard toil, old age, and isolation (with no one left to care about such a person's plight) means that the young should be allowed to "seize the day" because "you can't show them better days" ahead. Cash's sympathy for the working class extends to justifying a life of hard partying on Saturday nights as a way for exhausted farmers to cope ("Saturday Night in Hickman County"). As he sides with the outsider and the underdog, Cash also castigates the rich for their psychological need to patronize others ("The Little Man").

Cash's structural critiques of poverty and economic inequity include his urges to political leaders to stand up for justice and peace ("Man in Black," "The World's Gonna Fall on You," and "What Is Truth?"). Part of Cash's structural critique also addresses larger-scale migration patterns and the human cost when children leave rural areas to seek work in cities, leaving an older generation behind. In "Mountain Lady," a son who has left for the city and his "Appalachian lady" mother who has remained in the mountains each sadly wonder if the other ever thinks of them. Cash's nostalgia for country life ("Country Boy") is tempered by a realistic portrayal of its hardships. Cash captures agricultural biorhythms when he considers the farmer's dependence on cotton-picking time to see how much food and clothing he can afford for his family; the ritual of harvest time is like his lodestar, leading him to believe that all his hard work will pay off ("Pickin' Time"). Meanwhile, Cash ponders the threat natural disasters pose to the very existence of farming families in "Five Feet High and Rising," his song about the Mississippi River flood that threatened his Dyess family home when he was a child.

Some of Cash's characters upend the meaning of slurs against their class status and reclaim them. "Cotton-Pickin' Hands," which he wrote with June Carter, portrays a married couple who are partners in their labor, each working to keep their farm functioning and both showing signs of wear and tear. The male speaker takes a class insult, "cotton-pickin' hands," and turns it into a love token: "Her face is pretty though it's tan / And I love those cotton-pickin' hands." He describes her matching reclamation, that she will only demand one thing, which is "to hold these cotton-pickin' hands." Another song that uses a gendered narrative where the speaker honors a life of hard labor is "Don't Step on Mother's Roses." The song's speaker and siblings have been called home for their mother's funeral.

Their father seizes on a symbol of the natural growth and life cycle of human mortality when he implores them to honor their mother's roses and not trample on them; she planted them on their wedding day, and they will remind him of her as they grow. The song's final verse brings this symbol into a new generation: the father has died and now the children carry on the tradition, since the roses may outlast them all.

Cash's many religious songs also feature class advocacy. He insists that whereas society denies freedom to sharecroppers and prisoners, God would give them that freedom, and so he urges his listeners to advocate for social change. One strong statement of this class advocacy comes in his version of "Jesus Was a Carpenter." The lyrics use the idea of Jesus as a worker to make a class and anti-modern critique, questioning how Jesus would be treated were he to return today. In a bit of class bonding, the song's speaker argues that Jesus saved the poor and dying and that he and his audience are the same "folks" as the kind whom Jesus saved and built his kingdom for. He goes on to question, if Jesus were here today, would he be turned away as a vagrant, would "we" reject him or lock him out, would he face animosity and be shunned as a hobo? He once walked the "burning highway" and people followed him, but would they now, since his modern-day correlate would be a travel-worn hitchhiker? The speaker uses the interrogative to hail his listeners, asking if they would turn the worker Jesus away, and the lyrics implicitly point to the dangers of class bias even within the "folk." In an anti-modern critique, the song decries monster churches, wealth, mansions, and the hubris of "screaming cities," arguing that some churches are dedicated to discontent and sorrow, and urging Jesus to return to "build a house on rock again." Elsewhere, Cash songs emphasize the role of workers in the biblical stories. Cash celebrates the agricultural workers who gave farm animals as gifts to Jesus ("The Gifts They Gave"), and he represents his listeners as part of the communal group of working shepherds who came to see Jesus ("We Are the Shepherds").

Even as some of Cash's speakers look to religious faith as a comfort, they still maintain their social criticisms. In "All God's Children Ain't Free," Cash makes an autobiographical link, identifying himself as the speaker: "I'd sing more about more of this land / But all God's children ain't free." Because a sharecropper "held out his hand" to Cash the speaker, Cash becomes a surrogate voice for working men whose necessities for survival are taken from them by society, whether they have lost their freedom by not owning their own land or because they are prisoners. In "Lead Me Father," Cash explicitly appeals to God to give him strength to sing in order to help others, specifically in his working-class advocacy. He implores God to help him with his own failures, so those weaknesses won't prevent him from assisting others: "pick me up when I stumble," "so the world won't know" (although listeners to his song are privy to this dynamic). He asks God to guide him ("Show me work that I should / Carry on for Thee"), and he specifically asks for the fortitude to write songs that will help workers: "And give me the strength for a song / That the words I sing" might give strength to and help poor workers. As discussed further in the next chapter, many of Cash's lyrics imagine his music as a ministry, and here his mission is explicitly one of class uplift.

Cash's speakers frequently use religion to comment on social injustice. Noting that poor workers are ill-treated, some songs argue that all people will be equal in heaven, despite the pretensions of the rich ("Country Trash"). Building on this theme, in "The Man on the Hill," a son asks his father if the owner on the hill will help the sharecroppers as their crops fail and they risk starvation. Even when they die, the ones left behind will have to pay a death tax and fees. In its final verse, however, the song shifts its hope from the rich to God, saying it is the "man in the sky" not the one on the hill who will help them. Although they will all be equal in heaven, the song nevertheless critiques earthly concerns such as the "dyin' bills" that outlast their departure.

Other songs condemn people who claim to be believers but do not help others in society ("What on Earth Will You Do [For Heaven's Sake]," "No Earthly Good"). Elsewhere Cash's lyrics imagine that a poor man's social status will not bar him from heaven. "I Call Him" argues that, although the speaker may have ragged and worn clothes, his religious faith has made him a "wealthy boy" since birth because, he asserts, "He always pulls me through my troubles some way." The speaker's religious beliefs give him cause for optimism. In Cash, such joining of working-class and religious themes is often bound tightly to his imaginings of America.

American Mythologies

In discussing the convolutions in Cash's work and image, Rodney Crowell insists on a version of Cash's patriotism as critical, and he highlights the connection between Cash's ideals for America and his social protest on behalf of the poor and disenfranchised:

> His patriotism was informed. He wore black as a political statement. He was critical of the American government for what it did to the American Indian, and his Christianity was compassionate and forgiving, not the ideology of the Church. Billy Graham endorsed him, and therefore he had credibility during what was,

for my tastes, a more enlightened Christian era. Through several traditional forms or archetypes—Christianity, patriotism—he filtered enlightenment, and in doing so therefore he resonated with conservative and liberal alike. Show me somebody who does that now, who has the audience's attention. Bono is the only one I can put my finger on immediately, in entertainment. Bruce Springsteen, maybe, although he doesn't introduce Christianity into it.[53]

For Crowell, Cash's patriotism is necessarily linked both to his social protest and his religious persona as it channels American archetypes. Through these relations, Cash appeals to both political poles.

In his lyrical content, Cash often links his class critiques to American ideals, effectively trying to reclaim American mythologies of freedom for the working class. He makes this link explicit in his early concept album, *Songs of Our Soil* (1959), a significant work because long-playing albums were still not as common during this time. Colin Escott, in his history of the genre, *Lost Highway*, argues that country music was driven by singles until the 1970s, and that Cash was one of the first to generate substantive and critically acclaimed LPs.[54] On this album, the songs that define America are folk ballad standards such as "Clementine" and "I Want to Go Home," famous gospel numbers such as "The Great Speckled Bird" (made famous by Roy Acuff), and Cash's songs about working people ("Five Feet High and Rising," "The Man on the Hill," "Don't Step on Mother's Roses"). He includes a romanticized version of American Indians in "Old Apache Squaw," a tune that sympathizes with the suffering she has seen, but this song is similar to the one before it, "The Caretaker," which empathizes with a working-class man disillusioned by social corruption. In this song an old, lonely cemetery caretaker ponders his own mortality as he faces dying alone, and he puts his hope in God, but his disillusionment stems, in part, from watching even people in mourning become consumed with "hate and greed and jealousy."

I have been arguing that Cash's work both critiques and reinforces American national narratives. These two dynamics exist in tension in his work, resisting easy resolution. I have already discussed how his work balances an investment in frontier mythology with American Indian advocacy and the censure of government policies. Here I examine how his texts reinforce American fictions of nation, but I also show how, even in moments when they do so, they also point out and criticize the exclusions those narratives make.

His bicentennial tribute, the concept album *America: A 200-Year Salute in Story and Song* (1972), is idealistic regarding democracy and freedom. The songs value freedom most highly and defy those who would deny American freedom (as in Jimmy Driftwood's "The Battle of New Orleans," which buoyantly baits the Redcoats). Cash includes a connecting monologue which he wrote that, in broad strokes, traces the history of America up to the bicentennial. Cash's emphasis in this narrative is on an America defined by freedom and the bravery of its "forefathers." He praises the original thirteen colonies because they "broke away from British rule and took a stand." Elsewhere in his oeuvre, Cash is continually drawn to historical narratives such as overviews of the evolution of America, labor in the United States, and rural and urban life, and he insists that listeners make up their own minds about history. They must move beneath the layers of story and myth, and depend on their own self-reliance rather than rely on the word of authorities. Cash makes this argument about the history of the West in his cowboy concept album, and he does the same in his American Indian one. He emphasizes that same theme of independent thinking when he addresses religion, while decrying the hypocrisies of many church leaders and of inhumane or self-serving orthodoxies.

In this narrative of America, Cash balances his discussion of American patriots (Paul Revere, Abraham Lincoln) by drawing attention to the "tragedy" of U.S.–American Indian history. He includes his song "Big Foot" (about Wounded Knee) on the album, and as he introduces it, he underscores that "free" land for westward expansion was previously occupied by Indian tribes. He describes how the West was won in the sense of giving settlers access to the land, but also how "the land was already claimed by a people when the cowboy came and when the soldiers came," and "the story of the American Indian is in a lot of ways a story of tragedy, like that day at Wounded Knee, South Dakota." By the same token, Cash unquestioningly upholds the Alamo as a symbol of American bravery (in Jane Bowers's "Remember the Alamo"). Likewise, as Cash introduces the album, his list of heroic Founding Fathers includes all the European explorers who helped start this violent process of displacing indigenous peoples: "We the people of the United States in order to form a more perfect union had to have men like Columbus, De Soto, Lewis and Clark, Kit Carson, Sam Colt, Thomas Edison, Henry Ford, Orville and Wilber Wright, My Grandpa, and Paul Revere." By including his grandfather alongside Wild West heroes and inventors who made technological advances, Cash builds a personal link to national history, just as he insists that he "belongs" to this land and vice versa because his forefathers shed their blood for its freedom.

Cash also monumentalizes the "common man" status of those forefathers, who are equally as heroic as presidents and famous men. He underscores the role of the common man and the folk in larger historical events. As he delivers the Gettysburg Address (whose authorship on the album liner notes is amusingly listed as "Abraham Lincoln; Arranged by Johnny Cash"), he does so in a conversational tone, personalizing it and landing heavily on the line "democracy must not perish from the earth." He covers Jack Elliot's "Mister Garfield," in which a working man travels to the White House to learn the fate of President Garfield after the president has been shot (he goes to "see about him" at the house where he lives). Similarly, in Cash's monologue, "the West," the daring, hard-riding cowboy, not the patrician, epitomizes American freedom.

In his song "These Are My People," Cash details these themes in his version of a Woody Guthrie–style folk ballad, in which the working class, the farmers, and the soldiers are the heart of the country. His people are the farmers who lived on the land and the men who built cities through their own hard labor. Cash is included in their "creed" of brotherhood—"This is my land / And these are my people"—by virtue of his loved ones dying for the sake of the land ("by loved ones' blood stains"). His treatment of the working-class base of America is optimistic in this song, for he concludes that these people have dreams of hope and they are the "light of the earth" as they "reach for the stars."

Strikingly, throughout his monologue, Cash also emphasizes the role of cultural expression, specifically literature and music, in defining national identity. He looks to the songs from the Civil War era to explain the "heartbreak" and "sadness" of that time. As he discusses stories of cowboys and westward expansion, he argues that "for the first time it seems that the nation was really conscious of itself as a nation," as communication and "public opinion" and "great ideas" crossed the country through "telegraph wires" but also through stories, such as tales about pulp-fiction cowboys. Here, Cash's comments almost suggest an imagined community of the kind Benedict Anderson has described as beginning in the eighteenth century, where citizens began to conceive of themselves as part of a nation-state through newspapers and literature.[55] Cash also refers to an American literary nationalism. In the section in which he describes the country's progress after the Civil War and the solidification of the Union, he crows that "great American novelists and poets were comin' into their own" and that "people were expressin' their love for America in song and poem." He later notes that songs he sings that are modeled on different eras of American history are meant to reflect the ethos of those periods. For example, in his re-creation of a song he said his mother used to sing in the 1910s, "Come Take a Trip on My Airship," Cash ponders hopeful technological developments like air travel. Here, Cash implies that popular music can reflect the beliefs and dreams of a group of people, or their structures of feeling, in particular socio-historical contexts.

In *Ragged Old Flag* (1974), the first album on which Cash wrote all the songs, he articulates staunch patriotism but also excoriates corruption and highlights the plight of the working man. In the title song, Cash condemns flag burning, infuriated by the way "she" has been "burned, dishonored, denied, and refused," and concluding that the government is "scandalized" by it. The lyrics contend that the American flag has suffered through wars and can take the flag burning now because she has survived much worse. Here the flag is a gendered symbol for America in much the same way women have been abstract symbols for liberty and freedom throughout the history of public art and representation in the United States.[56] Cash personalizes this history by telling an individual story: the speaker visits a town and speaks to an old man on a park bench, questioning why their flag and courthouse are so decayed. The old man replies that they are proud of their flag because it reflects a proud history, insisting that Washington took it across the Delaware and that it survived the Alamo, both world wars, Korea, and Vietnam. The man and his small town become a model for how to treat the flag correctly, as he says they "don't let her touch the ground" and they "fold her up right." In the live performance of this song included on the album, Cash incorporates patriotic American tunes in the background (such as a sprightly "Yankee Doodle Dandy" played on a banjo), and the audience erupts in approval with loud applause at the end.

This blue-collar patriotism is, however, joined by some insistent structural critiques. The next track, "Don't Go Near the Water," links pollution to the corrupt ways of big business that would poison all the mountains and streams. The speaker, fishing with his son on the lake by their home, warns him to stay away from the water and not to eat the fish, because "the water isn't water anymore." They cannot provide for themselves from the land because corporations have made it toxic. Cash also portrays the tribulations of factory workers slowly being killed by their dead-end jobs. In "Southern Comfort," the speaker works in a Nashville factory grinding tobacco leaves to make snuff. He is worn out by the snuff fumes, the traffic, and the hard labor. As the tobacco suffuses his clothes, "his woman" leaves him because she has grown weary of all the tobacco, or at least the "regular kind" (implying that she did not want to suffer through his poverty). As the fumes char his lungs, the speaker is left "sniffing and dipping and livin' alone"; the chorus rings out: "Southern comfort is killing me / I'm slowly choking in Tennessee." Cash offers one of his odder soundscapes here, because he embellishes the song by including sniffing noises. In a similarly tragic account of factory labor, "King of the Hill," the Oak Ridge Boys join him on the chorus to intone that one cannot become rich and powerful by working at a cotton mill.

Several songs also capture the emotional state of men made anxious, fearful, or resigned by their plight. In "All I Do Is Drive," Cash demolishes any attempt to romanticize working-class life. He places himself in the song, as his lyrics discuss how he talks to truckers at rest stops in his travels. He cheerfully asks them about how their life on the road must be full of adventure and freedom, music, and exploring new places. One trucker solemnly says that it is simply about survival: they have no time to think about freedom, they have nothing in common with people working 9:00 to 5:00 jobs, and they have to worry about even getting gas during the fuel crisis of the time. In his lyrics Cash speaks directly to his audience in the form of this trucker, recounting that he promised the man he will write this trucking song and sing it on the Grand Ole Opry for him Saturday night. Cash's song fits a common country music pattern of celebrating the importance of work while also rejecting it as tedious and alienating, but it is also innovative in its treatment of truckers. Country music has been seen as a genre that romanticizes the trucker as nouveau cowboy, the latest symbol of freedom and self-reliance. Cash departs from that broader thematic trend when he deromanticizes truckers by letting them "speak."[57] Elsewhere on the album, Cash sings of the fear of working men who cannot get resources for their family ("Worried Man") and of prisoners scared to leave prison because it is all they know and they fear being rejected by the world outside ("Please Don't Let Me Out"). He also uses religious ideologies to urge his listeners to help people who are impoverished, homeless, and imprisoned, and to fight to improve their conditions ("What on Earth Will You Do [For Heaven's Sake]").

These albums point to larger trends in Cash's corpus of lyrics, the blue-collar patriotism alongside the social critiques and a refusal to glorify war. "Sold Out of Flagpoles" asserts that although American society keeps changing over time, the one encouraging constant is that "good people" will always fly flags. While Cash's lyrics glorify soldiers as fighting for U.S. freedom, they also insist that war is hell, not the heroic epic of many Hollywood movies. In "Drive On," Cash's speaker remembers his Vietnam War buddies, some who are now, twenty-five years later, alcoholics, or suffering from flashbacks of the war, or feeling alienated because their country never welcomed them back. Describing the battle, the speaker says: "It was a slow walk in a sad rain / And nobody tried to be John Wayne." The chorus, "Drive on / It don't mean nothin'," represents a phrase the soldiers used to get them through battle, and now they must invoke it to get them through the distress of their lives back home. Likewise, "Singin' in Viet Nam Talkin' Blues" describes Cash's concerts for the troops in Vietnam and focuses on the welfare of the soldiers, arguing that apart from whether America should be there, one must support the soldiers and hope they can return home and "stay in peace."

As the RNC protest indicates, Cash's discussions of patriotism, war, and the working class have been seen as particularly relevant to current politics. In an article on the circulation of country music, such as the *O Brother Where Art Thou?* (2000) soundtrack, post 9/11, Aaron Fox notes Anthony DeCurtis's observation that a reissue of Cash's *Ragged Old Flag* (1974) album was rushed to be released in time for the three-month anniversary of the 9/11 attacks.[58] Fox argues that the saliency of country music at this time owed to a return to the American worker as a symbol in a way that quickly became commodified and the subject of "hegemonic appropriation." Fox writes that "'country music' came to stand for 'working-class' (and 'white') identity, which was in turn a metonym for 'American' identity, in ways that obscured and misrepresented quite complex fields of social conflict in the service of particular class ideologies and political ambitions."[59] Fox reads Cash's marketing as "alternative country," and his American Recordings albums as a renewal of Cash's "outsider" image, while still maintaining his mainstream image. Fox and DeCurtis suggest that Cash's appeal in the post-9/11 context is his merger of traditional values with his "alternative" political stances; Fox writes that "Cash's defiant, rebellious posture *and* his God-and-family patriotism have both become relevant simultaneously in the present moment."[60] Fox argues that the combination connects working-class traditions with alternative movements.

I agree with these arguments, but I also see Cash's competing images as less either/or and more intricately bound together than Fox does. For example, one image Fox reads as Cash's tribute to family values can, arguably, only be read as part of his saint-sinner dichotomy. In Fox's readings of album covers as representative of Cash's political valence, he contends that the cover art of the Johnny Cash and June Carter duet album, *Carryin' on with Johnny Cash and June Carter* (1967), pictures "his happy family life with wife June Carter Cash," and thus represents his image of respectable married life (as part of a coherent mainstream image for Cash).[61] But the album cover, one of Cash's most incongruous because of the real-life circumstances, is in fact an example of Cash's contradictions, not least because he appears strikingly gaunt and drug-addled. The 1967 cover makes it appear that the two are in a playful scene of marital bliss, as they sit under a tree leaning against each other. Other pictures in the original liner notes have him holding Carter's hand while he mischievously climbs a tree. However, Cash was not married to Carter at the time; he was still married to Vivian Liberto. He was officially divorced from Liberto on 3 January 1968, and he married Carter on 1 March 1968. His affair with June Carter prior to that time was an open secret that sparked social disapproval. The album cover is really a memento of that time. Thus the images on the cover and in the liner notes are actually much less straightforward than a "happily family" symbol—they combine the family man with the open secret of his infidelity.

The idea of a dialogue between mainstream and alternative of the kind Will-man sees in country music and in Cash remains a helpful explanatory rubric. Recent developments concerning the Dixie Chicks controversy perhaps provide further evidence. After lead singer Natalie Maines made her infamous 2003 onstage comment critical of President George W. Bush, her remark became a lightning rod in the highly charged political atmosphere in the wake of 9/11. Although she made her remarks before the U.S. invasion of Iraq, and the artists initially rebuking her did the same, the debate soon came to be seen in the context of Iraq. The group went from a top-selling country act to a target for boycotts and death threats. As chronicled in Barbara Kopple's documentary *Shut Up and Sing* (2006), the three women found themselves on an odyssey in search of free speech in an age of institutionalized censorship. They fought for the idea that their social protest was also an act of patriotism. Country radio programmers and many fans seemed to side with Toby Keith in his denigration of them (the band's airplay, record sales, and concert ticket sales plummeted). But after the release of their 2006 album, *Taking the Long Way* (notably, produced by Rick Rubin), with its defiant hit single "Not Ready to Make Nice," the Dixie Chicks enjoyed cross-over success with rock audiences. They were also embraced anew by mainstream country music radio, fans, and television, winning Grammy but also Country Music Television (CMT) recognition. This seesaw dynamic perhaps reflects the country's changing attitudes about the Iraq war, but it also indicates the complexity of country music's politics.

Escott, in *Lost Highway*, invokes a similar rubric of mainstream versus alternative. In his map of the country world, outsiders, such as leftist songwriter Kris Kristofferson, reinvigorate the genre as they present beneficial musical and ideological challenges to the more conservative mainstream, maintaining the vitality of the genre as a whole. CMT, as a significant player in the industry itself, often deploys such rhetoric in its programming (in its taste-making lists of top performers like "Greatest Outlaws"). It also aired the documentary version of Escott's history. Speaking there, Hank Williams III, whose mixture of country and punk is alt-country while his covers of his grandfather's songs secure his traditional country credentials, describes his sense of country's enduring appeal: "You need to pay respects to what made country music what it is today, and all these guys in business suits and all these lawyers that outsmarted all the musicians, they're not the ones that really made this whole thing happen. It's definitely a passion that you feel inside, you've got to eat it, breathe it, live it."[62] Throughout his commentary for the documentary, he argues, in effect, that despite all the corporations that are intent on generating big business out of country artists, the genre will always persevere. It will not die at the hands of country-pop mainstreaming, because folk roots will always bring audiences looking for their fantasies of authenticity in the face of an alienating modernity. Williams's commentary, as marketed on CMT, also speaks to Fox's point about the ease with which folk roots can be commodified and appropriated. Insistently dwelling in both worlds, Cash has played the dual role of mainstream figure and outsider, commodifier and purist. As the next chapter will make clear, Cash's combination of the mainstream and the alternative includes religious themes that offer a particularly provocative case in point.

6

THE GOSPEL ROAD
Cash as Saint and Sinner

You know, I used to sing, "Were You There When They Crucified My Lord?" while I was stoned on amphetamines. I used to sing all those gospel songs, but I really never felt them. And maybe I was a little bit ashamed of myself at the time because of the hypocrisy of it all: there I was, singing the praises of the Lord and singing about the beauty and the peace you can find in Him—and I was stoned.

—Johnny Cash[1]

There's nothing hypocritical about it. There is a spiritual side to me that goes real deep, but I confess right up front that I'm the biggest sinner of them all.

—Johnny Cash[2]

My father was raised a Baptist, but he has the soul of a mystic. He's a profoundly spiritual man, but he readily admits to a continual attraction for all seven deadly sins.

—Rosanne Cash[3]

Johnny Cash's themes of contradiction run strongly throughout his texts addressing religion. Depictions of Cash emphasize his saint-sinner dichotomy. He was
the devout Christian who took Bible classes, evangelized on the Billy Graham
crusades, and made his own self-financed film of Jesus' life long before Mel
Gibson did it so controversially. Yet Cash often bucked organized religion and
encoded serious intellectual interrogations of Christianity in his texts. He is the
godly man who nonetheless sees himself in lawbreakers, calls himself a serious
sinner, and is in constant communication with the ungodly side of himself.

This chapter analyzes how the binaries of saint and sinner, sacred and profane, structure Cash's lyrics, identity construction, and marketing. His religious
evocations always play alongside his self-identification as a sinner. This dynamic
is evident in his music and visual imagery in performance, in media accounts of
him, and in his biographical and autobiographical narratives. As scholars have
shown, the saint-sinner binary is common in country music and speaks to the
piety-hedonism duality in Southern white working-class life. As Bill C. Malone
has demonstrated, the Saturday night/Sunday morning conflict in artists ranging from Hank Williams to Ira Louvin forms a key part of their appeal.[4] Cash
follows such traditions, but he also proffers an idiosyncratic version of this common tension that is deeply multilayered. Unlike Williams, who sang "I Saw the
Light" but famously worried to Minnie Pearl that "there is no light,"[5] Cash does
not waver in his expression of religious faith. However, it is a faith of opposing
forces where the sacred and the profane sometimes emerge as mirror images of
each other.

Although it might seem that this obvious binary in his work and image would
be answered by redemption narratives, Cash's oeuvre, taken as a whole, does
not offer such a firm resolution. His work does emphasize the fallen man who,
nevertheless, is worthy of salvation and is redeemed. But the sinner side of the
dichotomy is never solved, demoted, or contained—it endures and retains great
currency. In his long-running examination of Christianity, Cash explores serious
intellectual issues about its historical and material bases, and he questions the role
of narrative and song in metaphorically expressing religious ideas. In a dynamic
that parallels larger trends in country music, he insists on an anti-authoritarian,
nondenominational, personalized version of his religion that rejects class bias
and, in a dynamic more distinctive to Cash, advocates for the downtrodden. As
his texts attempt to address religious complexity, they include an affirmation of
religious faith, although they emphasize not an easy resolution but, instead, constant opposing forces. This dynamic is detailed here in a discussion of Cash's song
lyrics as a whole, his autobiographical and biographical narratives, and key texts

that include his film, *The Gospel Road* (1973), and his novel, *The Man in White* (1986), based on St. Paul's life.

Religion, the South, and Country Music

Historians have detailed the long-running influence of Protestant evangelical religion in the Bible Belt South. As members of a rural Southern working class carried on Protestant religious practices, their religion offered solace in the face of economic hardship or social marginalization as well as a ritualized, shared cultural convention that spoke to nostalgia for home and tradition. Extensively delineating how country music's engagement with religion evolved over the twentieth century, Malone highlights the evangelical Protestant background of many performers and how the language and symbolism of that tradition still proffer a common cultural vocabulary for working- and middle-class Southern cultures. He argues that the region's music is the cultural site where this influence is most strongly displayed and expressed (whether gospel, the blues, or country music) and that even when popular music takes a song out of an explicitly religious context (or removes the religious content by turning a gospel song into a secularized country song), it crystallizes a broader shared cultural context.[6]

Other critics, in their assessment of the role of religion in country music, have emphasized the degree to which the genre's focus on individualism and a distrust of religious intermediaries in favor of a personal relationship to God reflects larger long-running value systems in Southern culture. Jimmie N. Rogers and Stephen A. Smith assert that whereas country music and Southern Protestant religion are symbiotic and grow from the same historical and cultural influences, country music often expresses an ambivalent critique of religion when the music departs from those Southern cultural values.[7] Some critics see country music as a vehicle for religious fundamentalism and others as a mode of "secular theology" expressed through popular music forms, but my view is that Rogers and Smith are correct in arguing that the genre is ambivalent.[8] They also see country music as exhibiting a lack of faith in institutions more generally (religious, political, and social); they see a marginalized Southern white working class both upholding the principles of institutions but often criticizing the "middle men" or agents of those institutions as out for their own gain.[9] Regarding the appeal of low-church Protestant denominations in the South, including small splinter churches, Donald G. Matthews writes: "Anyone who wished to be liberated from worldly standards which demeaned him or her would obviously be susceptible to a movement which honored the individual member."[10] Similarly, John Eighmy notes of the region: "the primary presuppositions and concerns of popular religion are individualistic, centering on the salvation of each soul. . . . Whether the issue is social responsibility, the nature of the church, basic theology, or the meaning of salvation, Southern Protestants think dominantly in individualistic terms."[11] Rogers and Smith show that many country songs criticize religion from the point of view of that individualism, as in the sentiment "you have to walk that lonesome valley by yourself." Tom T. Hall, the son of a Baptist minister, has a song titled "Me and Jesus" (1972), which insists that the speaker and Jesus "got our own thing going" and do not need "anybody to tell us what it's all about."[12] Cash fits such models in his focus on individualism and a personal relationship to religious faith, but he takes that model further because he also makes structural social critiques that move beyond the individual.

Some scholars have emphasized country music's gospel roots, but sometimes they read a contrast in the ideological content of country versus gospel. Don Cusic has argued that gospel music tends to emphasize a better life in heaven as opposed to calls for social change here on earth.[13] Tex Sample reads in country music an escapist protest response to the contradictions of Southern white working-class experience, although he asserts that the genre provides a venue for Protestant churches to adjust to this audience.[14] David Fillingim, meanwhile, interprets country music as carrying more social criticism than gospel offers; he traces theological content in a range of country music themes (even those not explicitly religious) to argue that country music often focuses on humanism or fatalism, not on gospel's heavenly dreams.[15]

Cash has such an intense, long-running involvement with religion, and such a wealth of songs that are specifically gospel or have explicitly religious themes, that he offers a clearer case of country's gospel roots compared to many other performers, with his recurring tropes cutting across both his gospel and country songs. Like other country singers, Cash includes gospel and religiously themed songs in his repertoire. Mary A. Bufwack and Robert K. Oermann note that many country music standards grew out of the music played at camp meetings. Hundreds of songs that have endured were generated at Southern religious revivals, beginning with the first "old-time Southern camp meeting" in 1801, when twenty thousand people spent six days in Cane Ridge, Kentucky, for a gathering of preaching and singing.[16] Malone cites the Carter Family as setting the pattern of a sacred-secular mix in country music in the twenties. He argues that country music in that decade hearkened back to evangelical Protestantism and to nineteenth-century values and beliefs in its moral didacticism and invective

against materialism or church corruption (in tropes reminiscent of revival meetings). By the thirties, country music focused on the pastoral retreat of Heaven
as a way of coping with the Great Depression (as in the Carter Family's version
of J. D. Vaughn's "There's No Depression in Heaven"). Regarding this period of
development, Malone notes the importance of shape-note singing schools and
the publication of paperback songbooks by composers such as Albert E. Brumley,
who wrote "He Set Me Free" (the inspiration for Williams's "I Saw the Light")
and "I'll Fly Away" (although, as with folk music, authorship was often ignored
and the songs treated as public domain).[17]

Bufwack and Oermann cite an explosion in gospel music in the decade from
1945 to 1955 sparked by a postwar religious movement, specifically a growth in
charismatic Christianity in response to Cold War nuclear age fears as well as
apprehension about looser social mores (in opposition to country's "good time"
honky-tonk music at the time).[18] Noting mid-century developments in country
music more generally, Malone asserts that although the Cold War 1950s witnessed
a thematic emphasis on millennialism, or the Second Coming, as a response to
fears about society becoming too secular, by the late 1950s and 1960s country music established a new, enduring pattern: it imagined a friendlier version of God,
with less fire and brimstone and more secularization of religious themes (even as
gospel backing sounds remained important to country music, as in Elvis's use of
gospel quartets like the Stamps Quartet). Malone notes that country television
variety shows from this period would include a gospel segment (such as Willie
Nelson singing "the gospel song of the day" on Ernest Tubb's television show, or
Lester Flatt and Earl Scruggs highlighting their "hymn time" segment on their
show).[19] Cash likewise included a closing gospel segment on his variety show,
and he devoted his final episode of the series entirely to gospel; as a guest on later
television variety shows, such as Barbara Mandrell's in the early 1980s, he would
frequently join in the closing group gospel sing at episode's end.

Cash's lyrical output includes songs fitting this more recent general trend of
a friendly vision of God or Jesus ("He'll Be a Friend," "The Greatest Cowboy of
Them All," and "Good Morning Friend"). But he also sustains a more residual
dynamic in songs with fire-and-brimstone messages and the warning of a Judgment Day. This theme is evident in songs such as "When He Comes" (in which
the speaker promises to be ready when Jesus will come to resurrect believers) and
the strikingly apocalyptic "The Man Comes Around" on *American IV: The Man
Comes Around* (2003).

This song and the marketing of it on this American Recordings album epito-
mize some of Cash's key religious themes. In his liner notes for *American IV* and

for *Unearthed* (2003), which includes a different version of the song, Cash notes that it is "based, loosely, on the book of Revelation, with a couple of lines, or a chorus, from other biblical sources." He explains that he originally wrote it as a poem in which he ponders interpretations of the book of Revelation: "I would go from one interpretation to another on this very complicated interpretation—or to me it's very complicated—until I finally found some lyrics that worked." Here, we see Cash's investment in using poetry and music to interpret religious belief systems, as well as his explicit model of drawing attention to multiple possible interpretations of Bible passages, his own included. In describing problems of meaning and interpretation, he observes that "'revelation' by its mere interpretation says that something 'is revealed.' I wish it were. The more I dug into the book the more I came to realize why it's such a puzzle, even to many theologians. Eventually I shuffled my papers, so to speak, drew out four or five pages, and wrote my lyrics." As he concentrates on multiple meanings and interpretive undecidability, Cash points out that his process of questioning and parsing generated forty or fifty more verses that he did not use.[20]

The song has a driving beat but the lyrics are bleak, offering an ominous fire-and-brimstone sermon concerning Judgment Day. Cash's singing voice shows signs of age, noticeably cracking at times, compared to his voice on his earlier albums. He is accompanied by acoustic guitars, and by piano and organ contributing occasional chords that crescendo in volume. In the version on *American IV*, the religious tone is amplified by the arrangement. Cash reads his opening and closing verses as if he were a preacher reciting from the Bible, that is, his adaptation of the Bible. The recording includes musical effects making Cash sound as if he is a preacher intoning a recitation that is playing on an old, crackling phonograph record. These opening and closing verses describe the speaker beholding Death riding in on a pale horse as "Hell followed with him." Among these foreboding images of the Apocalypse, Cash's lyrics describe how "everybody won't be treated all the same," all should remain as they are in order to be judged, and some will be saved and some will be damned. As the lyrics depict what will happen "when the man comes around," Cash admonishes: "Listen to the words long written down." He refers back to scriptural authority, but he has already taken his own liberties with scripture as he turns it into folk poetry.

In addition to his preaching recitations and the organ sounds, the album also foregrounds a religious context in its marketing elements. The liner notes emphasize that part of the album was recorded in an Episcopal church. A black-and-white picture of the church is included; Cash's recording microphone and music stand are arranged in front of an ornate wooden bench before the altar, as is a close-up picture of Cash's wrinkled hand grasping his lyric sheet, replete with his ring bearing a crucifixion image. In the alternate version of the song on *Unearthed*, Cash's voice is even more frail and we hear the occasional slurring caused by his jaw injury. In this other version, instead of a booming piano, an electric guitar with Cash's signature boom-chicka-boom sound occasionally joins the acoustic guitars accompanying Cash's vocal track. The phonograph recitation effect is not present, although Cash does use recitation for several verses. The overall effect is more personalized and less majestically sermonic.

Cash also describes in his liner notes his inspiration for the song. His account is typical of larger dynamics in his oeuvre in that Cash places equal emphasis on his far-ranging reading and study of intellectual questions alongside his belief in dreams and visions. He writes:

> The initial idea for the song came from a dream I had seven years ago. I was in Nottingham, England, and had bought a book called *Dreaming of the Queen*. The book talked about the great number of people in that country who dream that they are with Queen Elizabeth II. I dreamed that I walked into Buckingham Palace, and there she sat, knitting or sewing. She had a basket full of fabrics and lace. Another woman sat beside her, and they were talking and laughing. As I approached, the Queen looked up at me and said, "Johnny Cash! You're like a thorn tree in a whirlwind." Then of course, I awoke. I realized that "Thorn tree in a whirlwind" sounded familiar to me. Eventually I decided it was biblical, and I found it in the book of Job. From there it grew into a song, and I started lifting things from the book of Revelation.[21]

Cash responds to religious codes when he decides this dream is of some portent, and so it haunts him. Yet he claims the authority to inscribe his own personalized version of the Bible and of Christian stories and to circulate those imaginings in his music. Although his dream of Queen Elizabeth seems odd and idiosyncratic, it does have links to religion (the divine right of kings and queens?), and it is also prompted by his own study of the media and discussions of how individuals respond to larger institutions—how they personalize their relationship to a symbolic figure by dreaming of an individual interaction with that figure. Cash reflects on how his own Southern rural upbringing and religious training would have influenced his version of the common Queen dream. He pondered the "whirlwind" line for seven years before he realized it was from the Bible. In his *Unearthed* liner notes, he surmises: "My grandfather was a minister and I was brought up reading the scriptures, so I guess I did have it in there somewhere!"[22] He incorporates that line into his chorus ("And the whirlwind is in the thorn tree") to signify another element of confusion and mass upheaval occurring on Judgment Day. Cash would later call this song his "spiritual odyssey of the apocalypse."[23] Most significant about this song is how it both reflects his writerly combination of influences (sacred and secular, faith and intellectual debate) and illuminates Cash as a product of his culture.

Another album that reflects Cash's musical and cultural roots is *My Mother's Hymn Book*, his gospel album in the *Unearthed* box set. There he returns to the even earlier musical traditions that Malone describes, culling songs from the hymnbook *Heavenly Highway Hymns* which his mother carried all her life. This album also speaks to the profound mixture of cultural traditions that shaped Cash and that he passes on in his music. He sings Brumley's "I'll Fly Away," as well as his "If We Never Meet Again This Side of Heaven." Cash also includes songs that were sung at his brother Jack's funeral in 1944, noting that he and his family repeatedly sang those specific gospel songs throughout their lives, such as the standards included on this album, "When the Roll Is Called up Yonder" and "In the Sweet By and By"; the other standards Cash cites as songs from Jack's funeral they returned to include "I Am Bound for the Promised Land," "Shall We Gather at the River," "Peace in the Valley," "I'll Fly Away," and "How Beautiful Heaven Must Be."[24] The album is a synthesis of what Cash terms, in the liner notes, "old church songs, country gospel songs, and black gospel songs," and he argues that this cultural mixture reflects the array of music he heard on the radio growing up, ranging from The Louvin Brothers to the Carter Family to Sister Rosetta Tharpe.[25] In her vibrant biography that posits Tharpe as a primary influence in black gospel and rock 'n' roll, Gayle Wald quotes Rosanne Cash as saying that Tharpe was Cash's favorite performer.[26] Regarding his investment in black gospel music, Cash had expressed a desire to make a future album of black gospel songs, and he did record some here, such as "I Shall Not Be Moved," a version of "We Shall Not Be Moved"; in his liner notes Cash describes the song as a rural white church version of a rural black church song. He includes "Just As I Am," the hymn that was playing when Cash responded to an altar call at age twelve in his Baptist church, inspired here by Mahalia Jackson's rendition (Jackson was also a guest on Cash's variety show).[27] Elsewhere his repertoire included songs from the pioneering black gospel composer Thomas A. Dorsey, such as "Peace in the Valley."

A significant portion of Cash's lyrics centers on religion. Many songs praise Jesus and his deeds for the "common man," for example "It Was Jesus," "Nazarene," "Praise the Lord," and "He Turned the Water into Wine"; some celebrate born-again Christianity, such as "I'm a Newborn Man," and several focus on specific historical sites as material grounding or "proof" for the religious beliefs they advocate, for instance, "Land of Israel," "Come to the Wailing Wall," and much of the *Gospel Road* soundtrack. Still others focus on travails in the speaker's faith and raise religious problems.

A number of Cash's songs resist resolving the saint-sinner dichotomy through redemption, in that they retain uncertainty about salvation in the face of constant temptation. Certainly Cash's songs affirm a Christian faith and propose to follow it, but many frequently return to the enticements of the devil. On one level the devil, the speaker's "old friend," defines the human condition of a Christian life fraught with traps and even tries to undermine great preachers, as in the song "Billy & Rex & Oral & Bob." On another level, the focus on temptation in the lyrics offers some degree of questioning within that religious framework. Cash's songs often address the complexity of his religion and the issues within it, and they do so as a reaffirmation of religious faith; the emphasis, however, is on the struggle between opposing forces.

The speaker expresses uncertainty in some songs by saying that "if" the miracles described in the Bible are true, then he hopes that he, too, will be saved ("I See Men Walking as Trees"). In "My Children Walk in Truth," the speaker prays to "know more joy" in his "salvation" and is reassured by the thought that his children have faith, as this idea makes him project confidence because "a frightened child won't hold a trembling hand." The speaker's performance of religious faith is, implicitly, a role he plays to inspire certainty in others. In "Welcome Back Jesus" the speaker worries that he might be overlooked on Judgment Day, because "temptations come and I sure get tired"; although he tries to "stay upon the right track," he might not be saved. Cash addresses questions about Christian doctrine in "The Preacher Said, 'Jesus Said'," where the speaker empathizes with listeners who "wonder how you are to know whose word is true." He concludes that the longevity of the message makes it convincing, because preachers "from St. Paul to Billy Graham" have been repeating it for centuries. Aside from lionizing two of his religious idols, Cash also leaves room for religious doubt and questioning. Similarly, in his graphic song "Redemption," Cash writes that Jesus' blood on the cross brought freedom, with the "tree of life" growing from it. The speaker clings to that tree even though the Devil tempts him—his "old friend Lucifer," a familiar visitor who still has the power to lure him. Though the speaker claims to be "redeemed by the blood" of Jesus, the lyrics still express worry and uncertainty.

This constant battle between God and Satan reflects Southern Baptist teachings, but Cash's treatment of these issues also reflects his own emphatic themes.

Cash also expresses doubt about his own role in explicit autobiographical references. He asks for God's help in using him and his music as a vessel ("Lead Me Father"), but he insists elsewhere that he is not trying to be a role model but is simply expressing his beliefs; they are efficacious for him, but this does not mean they will be for his listeners ("You'll Get Yours, I'll Get Mine"). Thus Cash advocates personal witnessing but disavows it as an influence on others.

Cash's religious songs focus on class and gender in ways that underscore his continual address to Southern white working-class masculinity. Poor men are made wealthy by their religious faith ("I Call Him"). Both Jesus and other biblical figures are the same "common folk" as the working-class group Cash addresses (his version of "Jesus Was a Carpenter," "The Gifts They Gave," "We Are the Shepherds"). Other Cash songs urge listeners to work for social justice on earth—specifically aid for the impoverished and the imprisoned—based on their religious beliefs, not to defer these issues to heaven ("No Earthly Good," "All God's Children Ain't Free"). Cash's empathy with the fallen is often in the form of a criticism of class bias. Many songs argue that even people who think they are saved must still help others in need and not shun them. The lyrics urge his listeners not to look down on vagrants or hobos; to do so would make their religious faith hypocritical ("No Earthly Good"). Because his lyrics often frame convicts as working-class men trying to provide for their families in the face of an economic structure that thwarts their ability to do so, Cash's songs focus on religious support and the promise of salvation for prisoners.

In a related dynamic, several of Cash's songs imagine Jesus as a masculine role model ("The Greatest Cowboy of Them All," "He'll Be a Friend"). In "I'm Gonna Try to Be That Way," the speaker pledges to try to be like Jesus and "do the kind of things a man oughta do." Discussing his religious faith in an interview, Cash once insisted: "Being a Christian isn't for sissies. It takes a real man to live for God—a lot more man than to live for the devil, you know? If you really want to live right these days, you gotta be tough."[28] Cash's version of Protestant Christianity is thus strongly influenced by his formulation of Southern white working-class masculinity.

Life Narratives

Malone asserts that many country performers routinely testify about being saved, often by describing how they strayed for awhile but ultimately returned to the Christian faith of their youth. Beginning with Roy Rogers, performers published autobiographies professing their faith and conversion, and insisting that their performance was a form of religious ministry.[29] Cash fits this pattern but also departs from it, as his life narratives both assert a salvation story but also attest to never-ending temptations that Cash could not resist. Even though his narratives claim that he is saved in spite of his sins, the triumphant message of his first autobiography cannot be sustained in the face of the other narratives. The sacred and profane remain together, defying separation.

As discussed earlier, Cash's first autobiography, *Man in Black* (1975), invokes the conventions of spiritual autobiography to frame his life as a struggle between drugs and God, his inner demons and the angels of his better nature. It offers a triumphant pedagogical message: he bears witness to the steps he took to revelation, redemption, and spiritual salvation as he testifies to readers and models a story of Christian faith for them. In the preface he writes, "if only one person can be saved from the death of drugs, if only one person turns to God through the story which I tell, it will all have been worthwhile."[30]

In *Man in Black*, Cash discusses his own religious upbringing, when he attended both a Baptist and a Pentecostal church with his mother. When Cash was a child, the Baptist church at first left him fearful and the preacher "terrified" him, but he eventually felt more drawn to it, especially through the music. The Pentecostal church, Cash recalls, "allowed all kinds of musical instruments" (other stars, Dolly Parton, for example, have described getting their musical start in "Holy Roller" Pentecostal churches that encouraged everyone to sing and express themselves). Cash wrote: "It was the songs I was beginning to feel" and he "used the songs to communicate with God."[31] Cash describes deciding to make his "commitment" at age twelve in the Baptist church as he responded to an altar call, believing "there were two distinct ways to go in life" and he had to choose one path or the other, the righteous or the sinful.[32]

Following larger trends in country music, Cash was doggedly anti-denominational. He writes in his first autobiography that he feels it is "dangerous" when "this or that denomination begins to feel or, still worse, begins to teach that their particular interpretation of the Word opens the only door to heaven."[33] As an adult, Cash largely attended Baptist churches (when he attended), but for a time he was also a member of a Pentecostal Assembly of God church.[34] Thus organized religion did influence him through the Baptist and Pentecostal churches, as can be seen in his emphasis on religious expression and the culture of marginalized Southern rural groups. Bufwack and Oermann attest that the boom in the Pentecostal movement of the forties and fifties, located, for example, in Churches of God and Assemblies of God, represented a protest against modernity, technology, industrialization, and urbanization; seeing those developments as the roots of moral decay, Pentecostalism insisted on austere values, for example, the prohibition of dancing, drinking, and smoking. Yet the church services themselves focused on music as a key to charismatic rituals such as testimonies and emotional displays, speaking in tongues, and snake handling. Bufwack and Oermann note that anthropologists categorize this movement as "the vision of the disinherited," because the faithful members came from "the poor, the unschooled, the rural, the left-behind."[35] The Southern Baptist tradition, meanwhile, has had a broader impact on Southern culture through its notions of "congregational freedom," in which local churches have the right to live out the Gospel according to the needs of the specific local community, and "soul freedom," the idea that individuals have the right to read and interpret scripture as they choose because their individual relationship with God through Jesus is primary. Jack Weller observes that "the Baptist form of government, which set up the local church as the only authority and allowed no interference from regional or national bodies, was most compatible with the leveling philosophy" of southern Appalachia.[36] Cash's insistence on individual, personalized interpretations of religion reflects the impact of this Baptist tradition.

Cash's autobiographical narrative in *Man in Black* combines his deep investment in personal witnessing (a dynamic common in country music) with his own existential questioning (much less common in country music). In his story Cash highlights two major turning points in his religious life: the first was the tragic death of his older brother Jack in an accident involving a saw, when Cash was twelve, and the second was his (temporary) recovery from drugs in 1967. Citing Jack as a godly person who was to become a preacher, Cash writes that Jack's death prompted his own existential questioning of God and faith. He wondered if everyone was expendable, as it seemed Jack was, and this trauma left him nearly silent for a year afterward. Yet Jack, on his deathbed, spoke glowingly of seeing a "fire on one side and heaven on the other," and he told his family that he was going with the angels to a "beautiful city"; his last words were: "Oh, mama, I wish you could hear the angels singing." Cash writes that his brother's "vision of heaven" and his godly life and faith were Cash's deepest inspiration in life (also inspiring his song "Meet Me in Heaven").[37] He also described a dream he had that Jack was going to die—two weeks before it happened—and later dreams that Jack returned to him throughout his life, his best friend comforting him in times of need.[38] Thus the legacy Cash took from this episode, as represented in his autobiographical narratives, is both renewed religious faith and existential angst. Regarding how Cash's self-taught intelligence functions as part of his heroic image, Rosanne Cash has remarked: "My dad definitely had heroic proportions. He wasn't a man you could sit down and talk to about like, what's going on in math class. He's sort of frightening. Incomprehensible. But he's also extremely literate and intelligent—that didn't come with his upbringing."[39]

When Cash discusses detoxifying from drugs in *Man in Black*, he views his transformation as a return to God, writing that "God had given me back my life," and the biopic *Walk the Line* hews closely to this narrative.[40] He describes hitting "rock bottom" with his drug abuse and then going through detox at his lake house in 1967 with the help of June Carter, her family, and Nat Winston (then Tennessee Commissioner of Mental Health). June Carter's father, Ezra "Eck" Carter, insisted at the time, "The Lord's got his hand on Johnny Cash and nothing's going to happen to him. The Lord's got greater things for him to do."[41] Some of the key events Cash cites that sent him into a spiral of self-hatred and finally a plea for help include his arrest for drugs in 1965, his overnight stay in a small-town jail in Georgia in 1967 where a sheriff said he was ashamed of Cash, and a subsequent incident where he drove a tractor into the water at his lake house.[42] In his second autobiography, *Cash* (1997), he fashions an even more dramatic transformation narrative, asserting that it was his 1967 suicide attempt that instigated his recovery. He adds an account of his effort to commit suicide by crawling into Nickajack Cave, because he "was as far from God" as he had ever been. Prompted by his religious beliefs, Cash decides to wend his way back out of the cave instead of dying there. Although he says he did not hear God speak to him, he believes God "put feelings" in his heart and "ideas" in his head that he was meant to live: "I hadn't prayed over my decision to seek death in the cave, but that hadn't stopped God from intervening."[43] Thus Cash frames in ever more dramatic terms his supposed redemption from drugs as coextensive with his religious redemption.

Cash's subsequent autobiographical statements and many of his recent biographies indicate, however, that he was never finally victorious over the drug abuse that sent him on his spiritual quest. While Cash's narratives emphasize his reaffirmation of faith, they nevertheless powerfully underscore the idea that his battles with his own polarities are unceasing: drugs and the devil are always with him. His second autobiography and many subsequent autobiographical statements he made in interviews highlight his continuing drug use. In *Cash*, he admits that his "liberation from drug addiction wasn't permanent," although he undersells the case by saying, "Though I never regressed to spending years at a time on amphetamines, I've used mood-altering drugs for periods of varying length at various times since 1967: amphetamines, sleeping pills, and prescription painkillers."[44] Cash's band mate Marshall Grant, in his own recent memoirs, and biographer Michael Streissguth, who set out to debunk Cash mythologies, both insist that Cash was only drug-free for a six-year period after 1970.[45] They assert that Cash was abusing drugs heavily for the rest of his life, more so than even his second autobiography admits. His son, John Carter Cash, concurs in his recent biography of his mother, and also points out, with great poignancy, that while June Carter Cash fought Cash's drug abuse and was credited with sparking his "recovery," not only was Cash's recovery temporary but Carter Cash herself fell into drug addiction for the final decade of her life (a development her son calls the "fall of Camelot," after his mother's habit of calling their lake home and its hub of activity "Camelot"). John Carter Cash observes that varying degrees of drug addiction afflicted most of their family (and resulted in the death of June Carter Cash's daughter, Rosey Nix).[46] In an interview after Carter Cash's death in 2003, Cash talks about being continually haunted by the demons of temptation, whether drugs or sex.[47]

Cash's religious themes in some ways become tied to his "authenticity effect," particularly in the way that he and his record labels incorporate his saint-sinner persona into their marketing and his media image. Malone notes that a public expression of faith by country singers often was also a commercial necessity, as it frequently translated into higher record sales. Cash fits this pattern, but he also insisted that when he professed his faith on his network television show to a more mainstream audience (1971), it actually harmed his career, contributing to his waning record sales in the 1970s.[48] However, he continued to use his pious/ hell-raiser image in marketing, as did his corporate partners, from Columbia to American Recordings, from Billy Graham's distribution company that released *The Gospel Road* to the smaller record companies that Cash relied on to release some of his gospel albums.

This image of him has wide enough circulation in popular culture to migrate into other media forms and to become the object of parody or ridicule. Cash produced a version of his *Man in Black* (1975) life story as a religious comic book, *Hello, I'm Johnny Cash*. There Cash uses religious terms to recount his need to recover from drugs ("I've got to get this devil off my back"), and when he turns to June and her parents for help, she says they will "call on God" for help. Cash worries about the struggle ahead ("every day's gonna be a brand-new mountain") but June offers him religious assurances ("I'll climb them with you Johnny! God will pull us to the top!").[49] The comic book seems to represent an evangelistic effort to tell a story of religious conversion to a youth audience, and it is Cash's dichotomous image that supports that kind of appeal. In a later foray into animated television, Cash famously provided the voice of God in a 1997 episode of

The Simpsons. After eating spicy chili, Homer Simpson hallucinates and imagines himself wandering through the desert, where he encounters a talking coyote that he believes is channeling the voice of God (Cash) but who is also a trickster figure.[50] Cash's distinctive voice and saint-sinner persona made him the best candidate for God's voice in the realm of satirical animated television.

Cash's religious guise has also been a target of ridicule by mainstream journalists, most memorably Nick Tosches in his ramshackle, speedballing account of country music's roots and its boom period of the 1970s, *Country: The Twisted Roots of Rock 'n' Roll.* Eager to excoriate country music's sacred cows, Tosches seizes on Cash: "There are several offensively pious men in country music. Johnny Cash and his God are a particularly tedious act. The strongest drink Cash serves at his parties is non-alcoholic fruit punch." Tosches takes on the role of a cosmopolitan observer impatient with sanctimony; he disdains Cash and finds that the only possible explanation for Cash's act is that it is hypocritical and phony rather than sincere. Tosches goes on to denounce Cash's understanding of the history of country music, calling it "surreal": "In the first show of his 'Johnny Cash' series, broadcast by CBS in August 1976, Cash referred to his mother-in-law, Maybelle Carter, as 'one of the most influential instrumentalists in country music.' Mother Maybelle Carter's influence as a country-music instrumentalist is equal to that of, say, Rudy Vallee." Tosches refers to the four Johnny Cash shows, taped at the Grand Ole Opry House and Opryland in Nashville, that were broadcast in August and September of 1976 and featured a typical Cash concert lineup: Cash, June Carter Cash, Carl Perkins, the Statler Brothers, the Carter Family, and the Tennessee Three. As we have seen, musicians widely credit Maybelle Carter with popularizing the Carter Scratch guitar technique, and her place in the Country Music Hall of Fame speaks to the industry-wide recognition of her contributions as an instrumentalist. That Tosches is so wildly inaccurate in his critique of Cash's version of country music history, and so shockingly dismissive of the impact of Maybelle Carter's career, indicates the zeal with which he approached his task of attempting to debunk icons—but it may also be related to the scorn that Cash's religiosity provoked among mainstream journalists.

Finally, completing an unholy triumvirate of themes (God, country music, and the country itself), Tosches reviles Cash for his patriot act as well: "Each year, Johnny Cash's mind seems to grow more monomaniacal. His 1976 hit 'Sold Out of Flagpoles' was an absurd mess of godly patriotism, a song berserk with blandness and as dumb as any in the 1975 film *Nashville.*"[51] Here, Tosches tries to position himself as a satirist on the order of Robert Altman in the director's famous film attacking country music's parochialism. Tosches is finely attuned to the hypocrisies involved in marketing "godly patriotism," and his comments perhaps point to moments when Cash's persona becomes particularly obvious in its manipulations or, from the point of view of journalistic aesthetic criticism, when Cash peddles pablum in order to make a profit. Again, however, the bile of Tosches's account perhaps speaks more to an irritation with a religious focus in the culture of country music.

Bufwack and Oermann discuss the complexity in the marketing of religious imagery and music. They claim that Mother Maybelle and the Carter Sisters turned to gospel when they came to Nashville and the Grand Ole Opry in 1950 because of its popularity; Maybelle had composed mostly religious songs for their first songbook in 1949. They were careful to emulate the old-fashioned "country sweetheart" pious and proper image during this time, replete with modest gingham dresses. Bufwack and Oermann argue that the degree to which June Carter and her sister Anita departed from traditional gender and moral codes at that time likely prevented the group from pursuing superstardom in the gospel genre alone. Both sisters had multiple divorces between them; June had married honky-tonk star Carl Smith in 1952 and policeman, contractor, and racecar driver Rip Nix in 1960, before she married Cash in 1968. The *Walk the Line* biopic focuses, in particular, on the social disapproval she faced at the time because of her divorces.

Malone observes that some country stars even became preachers or closely affiliated with evangelical ministers, which, again, impacted their marketing. Cash joined other singers like Kris Kristofferson in becoming publicly associated with Jimmie Rodgers Snow (the son of country star Hank Snow) and his evangelical Pentecostal Assembly of God congregation, Evangel Temple, outside Nashville; in a much publicized act, Cash even walked up to respond to an altar call in the church in 1971. After doing so, he professed that he saw his career as a ministry: "I don't have a career anymore. What I have now is a ministry. Everything I have, and everything I do, is given completely to Jesus Christ now. I've lived all my life for the devil up 'til now, and from here on I'm going to live it for the Lord."[52] Snow baptized Cash in the Jordan River. Cash later departed that church, but he worked with other ministers such as the California preacher Floyd Gressett on his prison concerts, and he was also associated with Will Campbell, a religious guru affiliated with the Outlaw Country movement (Kristofferson would later quote Campbell as saying that there was "no explanation" for the depth of Cash's saint-sinner conflicts).[53] A minister even traveled with Cash on tour.

Cash's affiliation with Billy Graham is similarly related to other dualities in Cash's image, such as the Man in Black protester alongside the establishment conservative, because Graham, more than his contemporary evangelists, maintained a social justice imperative alongside his fundamentalist bent. Although he insisted that he and Billy Graham had decided that Cash "wasn't an evangelist," Cash often performed on Graham's crusades and was closely associated with him.[54] Graham's theological emphasis is on personal salvation, as he calls listeners to have an individual relationship with Jesus and thus to achieve salvation. Compared to some of the more right-wing evangelists such as Pat Robertson, Graham may be seen as somewhat more moderate because he was a stronger advocate for the marginalized and was invested in social justice. Graham, therefore, compared to other televangelists, might more closely fit the model of "prophetic" Christianity, described by Cornel West, that challenges dominant social structures—a point, of course, that is highly debatable.[55] Graham thought that Cash could draw more young people back to the church with his music and urged him to keep singing his popular songs about prisoners and fallen men.[56] Cash recalls: "[Graham] said the kids were not going to church, that they were losing interest in religion, and he thought that the music had a lot to do with it, because there was nothing in the church house that they heard that they liked."[57] Based on Cash's religious output and gospel albums, especially in the late sixties and early seventies, including *Gospel Road*, the journalist Dave Urbanski insists that Cash provided a "blueprint" for the emergence of contemporary Christian music.[58] Just as the marketing of country music stars and religion is complex, so, too, is the marketing of evangelical leaders like Graham (whose son Franklin has sparked controversy with greater corporatization of his father's empire) and of evangelical culture in the media.[59] Heather Hendershot has shown that the marketing of the evangelical subculture in the United States, especially since the seventies, exhibits the kinds of tensions between "authenticity" and the market that we have seen in the historical evolution of country music, and also speaks to its impact on American culture in the late twentieth century.[60]

Ultimately Cash offers a series of equivocating autobiographical narratives in which a devout path is always spectacularly joined by a sinful one. For example, he uses the *Unearthed* liner notes for this gospel album as an occasion to assess himself as a "C-minus Christian":

> I don't think my concept of God is much different from anybody else's. God to men has always been a friend that I can call on, that was always there, ready to listen, and it was always my fault if I didn't call on him enough. I'm not all

that much of a praying person, and I'm definitely not a religious person, but I do consider myself a spiritual person and a Christian. I guess I might be a C-minus Christian, but I am one. I'm very happy with my relationship with God. I think God leaves it up to me for the most part to handle my own affairs. He puts walking-shoes on my prayers to make me do it myself, which suits me fine.[61]

Cash takes this stance against organized religion and focuses on a personalized relationship with God, again mirroring larger trends in country music, by pointing to his own personal agency and responsibility. Cash is against proselytizing as well as imposing his vision on others.[62]

Cash's discussions in his autobiographies and in interviews regarding his own physical ailments and suffering similarly underscore a personal faith and insistence on stoicism. Near the end of his life, when interviewed by Larry King, Cash said that he did not believe in giving up: "I don't give up . . . and it's not out of frustration and desperation that I say 'I don't give up.' I don't give up because I don't give up. I don't believe in it."[63] Cash famously went back to the recording studio to work very soon after June Carter Cash's death, at her earlier request. In his many brushes with death, Cash invoked his religious paradigms for understanding his experiences. June Carter Cash insisted that the prayer circle she started through the Internet brought Cash out of a twelve-day coma in 1997. Cash recounted a near-death experience after his emergency heart bypass surgery in 1988: he had been angry when he was awakened because he had been going toward a peaceful "light." When discussing his ailments he also emphasized his belief in God's will and in heaven: "I just don't have any fear of death . . . I'm very much at peace with myself and with God . . . And when he sees fit to take me from this world, I'll be reunited with some good people I haven't seen for a while."[64] Cash outlined his sense of religious salvation with his "light" symbolism: "That great light is a light that now leads me on and directs me and guides me. That great light is the light of this world. That great light is the light out of this world, and into that better world. And I'm lookin' forward to walkin' into it with that great light."[65]

Some commentators who have noted Cash's equivocations in press accounts of him attribute Cash's complexity to the vicissitudes of personality. The journalist Dave Urbanski, in *The Man Comes Around: The Spiritual Journey of Johnny Cash*, compiled an overview of the religious events in Cash's biographical narratives, including quotations from his autobiographies and press interviews. He cites many of Cash's contradictory quotations, such as his line "please don't tell anybody how I feel about anything . . . unless I told you in the last few days." Attributing

Cash's enigmatic statements to his "puzzling personality," Urbanski then asserts that, instead of trying to explain Cash's confusing nature, the book simply focuses on the "incredible ups and downs of Cash's spiritual journey" as a "chronicle of his highs and lows."[66] However, as I have been arguing, Cash's contradictions are deeper than mere personality quirks, and they reflect the complexity of the evolution of country music and the Southern white working class in twentieth-century America and earlier.

The Gospel Road

Perhaps Cash's most extensive artistic expression of his spiritual beliefs comes in his film *The Gospel Road* (1973). The movie amplifies and deepens the themes evident in his music. A film he financed, co-authored, and co-produced, Cash's "labor of love" was re-released on DVD by Twentieth Century Fox in 2005 to coincide with the theatrical release of *Walk the Line* (2005).[67] Unlike Mel Gibson's *The Passion of the Christ* (2004), Cash's filmic vanity project about the life of Jesus does not focus on sensationalized scenes of torture and suffering in service of a certain kind of fundamentalism. Instead, it emphasizes Cash's personalized story of Jesus of Nazareth, a material connection to the historical sites in Israel where it was filmed, and a version of Jesus as fighting for the underdog against the political and religious authorities of his day.

Cash narrates the story, quoting scripture and his own retelling of events, and intersperses songs throughout the film conveying key events or ideas. We see shots of him standing on a mountaintop or walking along the sea, speaking directly to the camera, intercut with reenactments of the events. Robert Elfstrom, who earlier made the direct cinema documentary of Cash's life, *The Man, His World, and His Music* (1969), directed the film and also stars as Jesus, and his son plays Jesus as a youth. Originally they had intended only to portray Jesus in disparate shots—a figure walking or hands moving—but later they decided, on location, to have an actor play the role of Jesus, and Elfstrom stepped in; his hippie, long-haired, aesthetic look makes the film seem slightly akin to the countercultural Jesus movement of the 1960s, with which Cash sympathized and which spawned the *Jesus Christ Superstar* rock opera in 1972.[68] June Carter Cash plays Mary Magdalene and hers are the only scenes with dialogue, as she talks of her love for and devotion to Jesus. The film's other reenactment scenes are accompanied by the film's soundtrack, and they often feature slow-motion shots, close-up reaction shots, and repetitive cuts. The film incorporates symbolic images such as doves flying as well as extensive landscape shots of the Jordan River and the Sea of Galilee. Elfstrom employs a mixture of documentary styles, with Cash either addressing the camera directly or narrating the voice-over for the more realistic scenes, the camera following Jesus of Nazareth from a "fly on the wall" perspective.

As part of his effort with Graham to compel more popular musicians to record religious songs that would appeal to younger audiences, in the film Cash draws on a cohort of fellow musicians for songs and performances. Tracks include Carter Cash's rendition of John Denver's "Follow Me," Kris Kristofferson's version of Larry Gatlin's "Help Me" (a song included on the American V [2006] album to poignant effect), Cash's renditions of Kristofferson's "Burden of Freedom" and Gatlin's "Last Supper," and biographer Christopher Wren's "Gospel Road" and "Jesus Was a Carpenter." Cash released the soundtrack to the film, including his narration, as well as his original songs such as "I See Men as Trees Walking" (describing a blind man made to see) and "He Turned the Water into Wine."

In the marketing of the film, which was distributed to movie theaters by Billy Graham's company and was also screened in churches, Cash did radio advertisements (included in the DVD extras) emphasizing the idea that the project is "a very personal film." He explains that the idea for the film came to him six years prior to its making, when June Carter told him she had dreamed that Cash, with a book in hand, was "on a mountaintop talking about Jesus." He continues to underscore the personal when describing his motivations for making the film: "There comes a time in every man's life where he says to himself I've got to do something worthwhile in this world. That time came recently in my life, and the result is this film, Gospel Road."[69] Cash's insistence on the personal resonates with the broader country music dynamic where audiences prefer personal messages regarding religion. Rogers and Smith offer an overview of how Southern audiences distrusted mass media distribution of religious messages, particularly on TV but less so on radio, as radio in rural areas encouraged listeners to experience broadcasts as a "local" source much like a local minister. That they find lyrical evidence of such media distrust in mass-distributed country songs is ironic.[70]

The film also casts Cash as an individual on a personal journey for religious belief and tries to use his cult of personality to market his faith. The DVD tag line is "one man's journey on the road to truth," as it pictures Cash in black holding his guitar, sitting on a rock on the shore of the Sea of Galilee. The film itself opens with Cash singing a simple rendition of his song "Praise the Lord," and accompanying himself on acoustic guitar with a straightforward alternating bass line, as an image of the sun rising appears. In the next shot Cash is holding the Bible, talking about why people have religious faith, as he says "come along with me in the footsteps of Jesus and I'll show you why they do." The camera then pans out to circle around him as he stands on the top of a mountain flashing a peace sign. As the film intercuts scenes with Cash directly addressing the camera, he walks through historical sites, describing his understanding of his religion and quoting from the Bible.

Cash's film frames Jesus as an advocate for the poor even as it draws attention to the idea of multiple interpretations of the Bible. In his narration of events Cash follows Jesus' early years, and then his emergence as a radical religious leader, his crucifixion, and stories of his resurrection. Cash's discussion underlines the idea that Jesus ignored class and privilege: "Jesus addresses men as men, and not as members of any particular class or any particular culture. The differences which divide men such as wealth, position, education and so forth, he knew were strictly on the surface." He highlights the idea of Jesus raising the fallen. Cash argues that although interpretations differ on Mary Magdalene's status and Scripture tells little about her, Jesus embraced those with "questionable character" and taught that no one is sinless or capable of judging others. Describing the disciples as the camera focuses on actors playing each disciple, Cash intones that "some of them were roughly educated" but they had a "strong inner life." Asserting Jesus' particular appeal to the poor, Cash emphasizes his aid for them and his excoriation of hypocrites. Maintaining that Jesus performed miracles, Cash narrates them as "parable[s] of his teachings" and acts of "kindness, love, and charity for his neighbors," which caused people to follow him: "the mass of the people, especially the poor and underprivileged, followed him in such numbers that they walked on top of each other."

In addition to linking his version of religion to class advocacy, Cash includes other elements that stress the personal or attempt to put audiences into the viewpoint of the historical people pictured. Elfstrom stages a blurry shot that gradually sharpens from the perspective of the blind man who suddenly can see while Cash sings "I See Men as Trees Walking," which describes the odd experience of regaining vision. Elsewhere in the film Cash sings "Children" (with the Carter Family) describing how all believers are like "children" before Jesus, while Elfstrom films shots of children playing on the beach beside Jesus intercut by shots of Jesus as a child himself. Similarly, in imagining how Jesus faced his own death, Cash's voice-over insists, "you know we can't forget the fact that Jesus was human" and focuses on Jesus' feelings of being "completely alone," with Cash then singing "Burden of Freedom" about Jesus' sacrificial death. Cash proclaims that "Jesus was 33 years old now and had a little less than four months to live" and that "this thought alone would make most men say what's the use, you know." He then sings

"Help Me," an appeal to God to bolster faith, but as Elfstrom intercuts shots of Jesus walking in the desert, the film associates the song with Jesus' point of view, with him as the subject asking for help. Along with using Cash's direct address to the camera to appeal to the viewer, the film also uses one scene where it intercuts a shot of these historical sites with modern cities, implicating the audience. In the crucifixion scene, the camera does a 360-degree pan of Jesus on the cross, and when it returns to the front view of him, the backdrop suddenly shifts to scenes of different modern cities with skyscrapers and neon signs. Thus, if Cash positions himself as a sinner eager to be saved, the film summons his audience into this vantage point as well. It employs familiar tropes for doing so, such as a personal, individualized version of Christianity; yet it also incorporates Cash's more distinctive elements, for example, his intellectual questioning of religious bases and interpretations.

The Man in White

Cash not only used the film medium to convey religious messages, he also turned to the novel. In *The Man in White* (1986), Cash offers his version of St. Paul's narrative, limited to six years in Paul's life, beginning with his persecution of Christians and highlighting his conversion on the road to Damascus. Cash observes in his substantial introduction that he "started writing about Paul in a kind of documentary way" but realized that scriptural and historical accounts of him were sparse.[71] Commenting on the novel form itself, Cash argues that he chose this literary form because he wanted to convey the "character and personality" of the people involved in this biblical story. He defends his imagined version of Paul—and his right to engage in that imagining:

> Someone said a religious novelist can be "God's liar"; that is, by novelization of the activity and reality surrounding a tiny grain of truth, great truths can be illuminated and activated. I have not and do not claim to be a novelist, but I suppose that is the form my writing about Paul has taken. I found a story to tell in those few verses and the story I tell around those verses is my own.[72]

Cash insists on the truth of his fiction, as he links historical accounts and narratives, imagined stories and religious beliefs as two sides of the same coin. Cash also implies that he turns to literature in an effort to hint at his version of the ineffable and sublime: "What exactly was Paul seeing and hearing that instant he went blind on the Damascus road? I suppose I was trying to see beyond the great void, to perceive just a flicker of the divine brilliance that struck him down."[73]

In his introduction Cash compares autobiographical tropes in his life to Paul's, and his framing narrative underscores key themes that Cash infuses into his writings on religion. As in *The Gospel Road*, Cash emphasizes a material, historical, and personal relationship with his religion. He cites his extensive travels in Israel as a motivating factor in encouraging his artistic output on religion. His introduction is notable for how it grounds Cash's novel in historical accounts and Cash's own reading of interpretive debates about the Bible. He remarks that June Carter Cash's father, Eck Carter, left Cash his "religious-historical library" when he died, and before his death he prompted Cash and Carter Cash's interest in biblical studies and early Jewish and Roman history (by writers such as Josephus, Pliny, Seutonius, Gibbons, and Tacitus). Cash describes traveling with a saddlebag full of religious and historical books for five years as he began working on the novel (and as he asked people he met in his travels about their knowledge of the period). He writes that his interest in Paul was sparked by a correspondence Bible course that he and Carter Cash took for three years starting in 1974 from the Christian International School of Theology (from which he earned an associate degree of theology in 1977) through their Evangel Temple Church. Noting the wide differences of opinion about Paul in biblical commentaries, Cash argues, ironically, that "the Bible can shed a lot of light on commentaries," and then he asserts that he has the right to join commentators and do his own speculating about Paul: "Well, I decided, if theologians can do so much speculating and make it interesting, I might throw in my two cents worth."[74] Cash displays humor, irony, and word play in much of his religious output—characteristics that Rogers and Smith read in country lyrics more generally.[75]

Cash also insists on his narrative (and himself) as being nondoctrinal, and he emphasizes his familiar trope of eschewing categorization. He recounts how reporters would question him about his novel, wanting to know if it was from a Baptist or Jewish perspective. Cash would insist: "I'm a Christian, don't put me in another box."[76]

The most obvious connecting trope that Cash points to between himself and Paul as his role model is the saint-sinner dichotomy. His analogies between himself and Paul offer a prime example of the complexity of this trope in Cash. Like the accounts in many religious studies of Paul, Cash sees Paul as a troubled speaker, appearing arrogant and yet humble and deeply flawed in his own writings, a historical figure who talked ceaselessly about his own struggles with an ambiguous "thorn in his side" and approached his religious beliefs with a willing spirit but weak flesh. In his novel Cash emphasizes Paul's uncertainty and fear, and then later his confidence in the vision he has seen and in his own mission.

Cash embodies Paul's story in song lyrics included in the text of his novel. Saul (before his name change to Paul) "became enraged" by Jesus of Nazareth's followers and "led a slaughter zealously," but then the Man in White appeared to him "in such a blinding light" that it "took away" his sight; he was blinded so he "might see," as the Man in White spoke to him in "gentle loving tones." In his introduction Cash explains why he saw Paul as his "hero":

> He was invincible! He made it his life's mission to conquer and convert the idolatrous, pagan world over to Jesus Christ. And he did everything he planned that he lived long enough to do.
>
> He smiled at his persecutions. He was beaten with rods, with the lash, with stones; he was insulted, attacked by mobs, and imprisoned; his own people hated him. Yet he said, because of Jesus Christ, he had learned to be content in whatever state he was in. (5)

Even though Cash does not draw a strong analogy in this passage between himself and Paul, he expresses his admiration for Paul as a religious figure who persevered, despite constant suffering, through his dedication to Jesus. He also accentuates Paul as an individualistic hero who achieves his personal religious goals and refuses to be defined by his society, preferring to define himself through his interaction with religion.

Part of what interested Cash about Paul was his drastic shift, in biblical accounts, from persecuting Christians to becoming one of the chief spokespersons for Christianity. Cash writes that he is fascinated by Paul's "amazing transformation," specifically "how he turned that zeal for persecution and slaughter around and immediately went forth with the same zeal for Christ" (8). Cash argues in his introduction that he wrote his novel because Paul insisted that Jesus spoke to him, transformed him, and told him to spread Jesus' teachings; Cash calculates from Bible verses that it was a one-minute conversation, but Cash sees it as "one great paramount minute in the history of humankind" (7). Because Paul's transformation happens over only a few verses in the Bible, Cash writes that he was left fascinated by what happened, by what the historical Paul felt and thought. He emphasizes that this transformation is important to his understanding of Christianity, as Paul went on to evangelize for Christianity and built the first Christian theologies. Paul was not one of the original twelve disciples, but he was central to Christian history because his accounts represent some of the earliest extant Christian writings, and he encoded the theology as he told his story and evangelized, underscoring a personal access to religious faith.

Elsewhere in the narrative, Cash makes more forceful analogies to Paul. In the introduction Cash compares his personal struggles to Paul's, particularly Paul's ambiguous "thorn in his side," and his own sources of inspirations to Paul's. Noting that it took ten years to write the novel, Cash emphasizes his ongoing struggles with drugs and the ill health that resulted, making his life difficult and preventing him from writing the novel that he wanted to write. When he heard Billy Graham tell audiences about his *Man in White* novel, describing it as "one of the best writings on Paul" Graham had ever read, Cash reacted with shame, because he was having such difficulty finishing it (9–10). Cash writes that when he married June Carter in 1968, he had just been through seven years of serious amphetamine and prescription drug addiction, and he describes himself as "a devastated, incoherent, unpredictable, self-destructive, raging terror at times during those years" (4). He argues that his trip to the Betty Ford Center for rehabilitation in 1983, after more drug relapses, prompted him to work on the novel and finish it. His bizarre tangle with the ostrich on his farm sent him back into a painkiller-initiated drug haze (he writes that when he was attacked he was thinking about Paul on the road to Damascus, but the "Light" that struck him down was the ostrich), just as another accident (a broken kneecap) and round of painkillers later caused internal bleeding and landed him in intensive care, and then on to the Betty Ford Center (8–9). Finally, Cash explains that he needs some vision akin to Paul's to inspire his writing, and he finds it in dreams such as his dream that his brother Jack was going to die, or his dream on the day of his father's funeral that his father came back to say he was in heaven. He wanted some personal revelation that would help him finish the novel, and he found it again in yet another round of drug recovery.

In the text of the novel itself, Cash writes of Paul's suffering and his questioning of his own beliefs as he persecutes Christians, which is later balanced by his trust in a consoling version of the Man in White. Thinking of the Christians that he ordered killed, Saul recalls: "Their apparent expression of love lingered until their last breath. Was God trying to tell him something through these people? Should he abandon his mission? How many would die in Damascus in the fulfillment of his task? The thought of the dying men, women, and children overwhelmed him, and he was almost sick to his stomach" (118). In Cash's account, Saul, after he is blinded by his vision of the Man in White, hears Jesus of Nazareth as a kindly, friendly voice: "It was a stern, but kind voice, piercing yet consoling. It was a friendly voice of love, of familiarity, of brotherhood and compassion. A voice as ageless and endless as creation, coming all the way from the divine dwelling place, through the gulf, bridging the eternal with the temporal, came to the ears on the persecutor" (120–121). As Cash attempts to imagine Paul's conversion in novel form, he emphasizes a personal relationship to this body of religious belief just as he underscores a sense of suffering and questioning alongside faith. Cash's songs, as we have seen, express his ceaseless tensions and religious questioning, just as his forays into film and literature do. Joining with his saint-sinner touchstone, these tropes combine in Cash's work to voice the contradictions of religion in Southern white working-class culture, and some of its tensions in American culture more generally.

CONCLUSION
"God's Gonna Cut You Down":
Cultural Legacies

Throughout his corpus Johnny Cash generates strong contradictory currents around the theme of Southern white working-class masculinity. As he leaves the sinner-saint, the rambler-homebody, the Saturday night–Sunday morning binaries in productive tension, his work voices larger contradictions in American culture. From his uncertainties about masculinity to his fraught representations of race—especially of whites and American Indians—Cash illuminates core national paradoxes. In so doing, his work challenges and yet reinforces nationalism, although its tensions insistently raise questions of difference, power, and appropriation in ways that leave America never coherently monocultural. The way that texts such as the *Hurt* video sell Cash further epitomizes how formulations of his authenticity are exploited to market that very idea of contradiction, drawing on the necessary overlapping of opposed ideas in American culture, such as the market versus art or individualism versus community. His image sheds light on how these kinds of competing social forces shape the contested idea of the American character.

Drawing on the previous discussion of religious binaries, a brief case study of a posthumous text offers signs of how Cash's image might continue to circulate after his death. I analyze the framing of him in the posthumous video for his song "God's Gonna Cut You Down," from *American V: A Hundred Highways* (2006). In this instance, the text encapsulates Cash's equivocating image and refers to how that image relates to a Southern white working-class culture. But at the same time that the video turns Cash into a media icon, it also accentuates the commodity nature of its endeavor and introduces a new level of appropriation—Cash the media image can seemingly be appropriated for different ideological causes. The text points toward a process of flattening him, making him one-dimensional, so that he is primarily an icon in a way that moves afield from the content of his work. This detachment and superficiality, though worrisome, also indicates how Cash as a symbol can be incorporated into new wrinkles of American cultural ambivalences.

In the celebrity-laden video for Cash's version of this traditional folk song, which appeared on his posthumous release, *American V: A Hundred Highways* (2006), we get a clear sense of the degree to which Cash's saint-sinner persona is both iconic and marketable, and of the extent to which it circulates in media images after his death. This chart-topping album notably includes, in addition to Cash's last composition, "Like the 309," an updated version of the song Larry Gatlin wrote for Cash's *Gospel Road* movie in 1973, "Help Me," and another religious song that Cash wrote, "I Came to Believe." A contemplative album that unflinchingly addresses death, it also includes tunes that point to a departure, an afterlife, or the aftereffects of an individual's presence (Lou Herscher and Saul Klein's "I'm Free from the Chain Gang Now," Bruce Springsteen's "Further on Up the Road").

"God's Gonna Cut You Down" has been released by other artists such as Elvis Presley under the title "Run On," and has often been performed as a gospel song (released by Odetta on *Odetta Sings Ballads and Blues* in 1956). Cash's version has a stomp-clap rhythm driving it forward alongside his sparse vocals, emphasizing the lyrical content in which God has final judgment over all sinners, no matter how they might try to escape him. Cash's version includes lyrics that describe how God spoke to the song's speaker, calling his name and telling him to do His will. Cash emphasizes a compassionate God here in the speaker's exchange with Him, but the message that God instructs the speaker to spread is all fire and brimstone: "Go tell that long tongue liar" the message "that God's gonna cut 'em down." The speaker then warns others that they can "run on for a long time" but eventually God will catch them and reveal their sins if they have sinned against others.

The video, meanwhile, takes Cash and his message of religious warning and fetishizes him in a way that illuminates how Cash's saint-sinner persona is a core part of what others frame as "authentic" in their constructions of the man. Prompted by Justin Timberlake (who famously called it a "travesty" when his video for "Cry Me a River" beat Cash's *Hurt* for Video of the Year at the 2003

MTV Video Music Awards), the director Tony Kaye filmed a black-and-white video with various stars and musicians lip-synching to Cash's song while making somber faces, praying, or flashing various vague religious symbols. The video opens with a speaker intoning, "You know, Johnny always wore black, and he wore black because he identified with the poor and the downtrodden." The text thus frames Cash in terms of his Man in Black persona, linking the proletarian image to religious messages through the content of the song.

Bono's contribution to the video summarizes how it is informed by Cash's saint-sinner image. Early in the video we see "Redemption" painted onto the bed of a couch. Later, Bono paints "Sinners make the best saints, J.C. R.I.P." on a bank of newspapers on a wall. While Bono's graffiti testimony emphasizes the mythical rock star nature of Cash's pious hell-raiser image, other parts of the video are more vague or generic in using this trope.

The video includes brief moments of old footage of Cash playing guitar, but his image is largely absent. Instead, the constant stream of different celebrities and musicians appear to signify in some way their investment in Cash and this song. Moments in the video, such as the world-weary face of drug addict Keith Richards of the Rolling Stones staring at the camera, followed by a close-up shot of his skull-and-crossbones ring, highlight the lyrical idea of sinners who will face judgment. The video also implicitly draws on the cultural connotations associated with some of the performers, such as hard-living rock 'n' roll icons like Richards.

Using stop-motion photography, Kaye flashes quickly on the faces of the singers and musicians, who implicitly genuflect both to Cash and to God; the musicians pictured include Timberlake, Iggy Pop, Patti Smith, Sheryl Crow, Flea and Anthony Kiedis of the Red Hot Chili Peppers, Travis Barker, Tommy Lee, Billy Gibbons of ZZ Top, Keith Richards, Brian Wilson, and Lisa Marie Presley. Flea points to a crucifix and then stands in a sacrificial pose, Kanye West glares at the camera, Chris Martin claps and dances. Kris Kristofferson plays his guitar and sings along (all dressed in black), as the Dixie Chicks gaze somberly into the lens and country singer Shelby Lynne (who played Cash's mother in *Walk the Line*) cries. Kid Rock snarls and raises his arms, Jay-Z flashes his "Hova" (Jehova) symbol, and Graham Nash holds up a book of pictures of Cash. Woody Harrelson falls backward into a river as if he is being baptized by immersion, as Johnny Depp plays along on his guitar. The video also includes images of celebrities or actors, including Chris Rock, Terrence Howard, Kate Moss, and Owen Wilson. Some of these stars had a musical relationship of sorts with Cash, playing on a few of his albums (Kristofferson, the Red Hot Chili Peppers), appearing in tributes to him (Crow, Kid Rock), or acting in his earlier videos (Moss). Others seem to be there only because of their association with Rubin or for no clear reason (Adam Levine of Maroon 5, pop singer Corinne Bailey Rae).

On one level, the eclectic mix of popular culture figures perhaps indicates the range of Cash's fan base and his appeal to musicians from various genres. On another level, it could be seen as an effort to benefit from Cash's cultural capital. As these celebrities display for the camera the degree to which they see Cash as deep and meaningful, the video appears to fetishize the fire-and-brimstone, Southern Baptist, rural Southern working-class dimensions of Cash's image as some kind of "authenticity effect" that the celebrities try to emulate. As the drummer Tommy Lee claps his hands while sticking his head out of a sunroof or as Rick Rubin and Owen Wilson ride around in a limousine wearing black cowboy hats (a different kind of "hat act"), some parts of the video come across as a set of incongruous poses, jarring for their Hollywood tone. After a montage in which all the celebrity faces blur together in their lip-synched images, the video ends with Rick Rubin and Owen Wilson decamping from the limousine to throw flowers into the ocean. This parade of images might imply that all listeners are equally subject to God's judgment, including wealthy and famous artists and actors, but the video also underscores a markedly parasitic relationship to Cash and his image. In this video, Cash circulates posthumously as a reductive media image, a vague saint-sinner icon. The video does gesture toward the intricacy and historical base of Cash's work, but it also provides an object lesson in the degree to which one must return to Cash's work itself and to its contexts in order to grasp the depth of his complexity.

The difference between this posthumous Cash text and others is the lack of personal address from Cash. When Cash becomes a disconnected media image, or when an array of other media personas is substituted for him, his connection to Southern rural working-class culture lessens. Rubin comments that Cash could compel hipster audiences, who normally would not be interested in religion, to listen to his religious music, just as Rubin himself began celebrating communion with Cash every day over the phone.[1] But Rubin's more general point about Cash has to do with the complexity of Cash's personal address combined with his constructed authenticity and charismatic image. Rubin writes that Cash would deliver a blessing before dinner, and those with no interest in religion would feel moved by it: "You felt blessed. Because he comes from such a deep place of faith, that you know it's real. You don't have to believe; all you have to believe in is him, and if you believe in him, you go for the ride."[2]

Cash brings his spiritual and secular themes into the mass art forms that he inflects with his folk poetry, introducing layer upon layer of contradictions in his texts. The "God's Gonna Cut You Down" video, where Cash is largely absent (in images from his earlier career) and instead exists as a media effect, illustrates the difficulty in capturing and replicating his productive entanglements. Whether they have been turned into a pose or style to mimic and market (in the video) or appear as part of an arduous, deeply felt quest for meaning and multivalent interpretations in his own work (the film and novel), Cash's dichotomies (such as the saint-sinner binary) endure and resist resolution. Cash's oeuvre speaks to how regionally typed elements (such as Protestant evangelism) still shape Southern working-class culture and its music, and how other groups project nostalgia onto that culture as they consume it. As part of what Sut Jhally terms the "commodity-image system,"[3] Cash himself becomes a version of that culture offered up as a commodity for consumption.

Notes

Introduction

1. Noting the intensity of Cash's affect on some audiences, Marty Stuart says that while on tour with Cash, "I saw everything from a little boy coming backstage in Kansas and asking him to pull his tooth to a prisoner's mom getting down on her hands and knees, wrapping her arms around his calves, and begging him to get her boy off of death row." See Brian Mansfield, *Ring of Fire: A Tribute to Johnny Cash* (Nashville: Rutledge Hill, 2003), 64.

2. Of the extant academic discussions of Cash, some of the most significant or extensive include Michael Streissguth's detailed history of Cash's Folsom Prison concert (1968), where he places the concert in the historical context of Cash's career, that era's popular music, and California's prison system. See Streissguth, *Johnny Cash at Folsom Prison: The Making of a Masterpiece* (Cambridge, Mass.: Da Capo, 2004). Don Cusic has published an edition of his songs that includes a scholarly biographical introduction. See Cusic, *Johnny Cash: The Songs* (New York: Thunder's Mouth, 2004). Unless otherwise noted, all song lyric quotations are from Cusic. Some of the most recent citations include *Literary Cash*, a collection featuring several scholarly essays, including an article of mine, as well as some creative fiction inspired by Cash. See Bob Batchelor, ed., *Literary Cash: Writings Inspired by the Legendary Johnny Cash* (Dallas: Benbella Books, 2007). After my own book went into press, the Christian writer Rodney Clapp's book on Cash and religion appeared, in which he productively details how Cash illuminates issues in Christian theology. See Rodney Clapp, *Johnny Cash and the Great American Contradiction: Christianity and the Battle for the Soul of a Nation* (Santa Ana, Calif.: Westminster John Knox Press, 2008). See also a forthcoming edited collection on philosophy: John Huss and David Werther, eds., *Johnny Cash and Philosophy* (Chicago: Open Court Press, 2008). Aaron Fox includes a discussion of working-class responses

to Cash in a chapter of his ethnographic study of country music in rural, working-class Texas: *Real Country: Music and Language in Working-Class Culture* (Durham, N.C.: Duke University Press, 2004). Fox also discusses the circulation of Cash's image after 9/11 as part of his assessment of the uses of country music in that context. See Fox, "'Alternative' to What? *O Brother*, September 11, and the Politics of Country Music," in *Country Music Goes to War*, ed. Charles K. Wolfe and James E. Akenson (Lexington: University Press of Kentucky, 2005), 164–191. Frederick E. Danker's article on Cash analyzes his repertory and performance style for signs of country music's transition from traditional folk music to commercialized popular mass media form. See Danker, "The Repertory and Style of a Country Singer: Johnny Cash," *Journal of American Folklore* 85, no. 338 (October–December 1971): 309–329. All these studies speak to a vibrant ongoing interest in Cash.

3. The Cash popular biographies include Michael Streissguth, *Johnny Cash: The Biography* (New York: Da Capo, 2006); Steve Turner, *The Man Called Cash: The Life, Love, and Faith of an American Legend* (Nashville: Thomas Nelson, 2004); Stephen Miller, *Johnny Cash: The Life of an American Icon* (London: Omnibus, 2003); Garth Campbell, *Johnny Cash: He Walked the Line, 1932–2003* (London: John Blake, 2003); Dave Urbanski, *The Man Comes Around: The Spiritual Journey of Johnny Cash* (Lake Mary, Fla.: Relevant Books, 2003); Christopher S. Wren, *Winners Got Scars Too: The Life of Johnny Cash* (New York: Ballantine, 1971). See also Peter Lewry, *A Johnny Cash Chronicle: I've Been Everywhere* (London: Helter Skelter, 2001); John L. Smith, *The Johnny Cash Record Catalog* (Westport, Conn.: Greenwood, 1994); a Carter Family biography by Mark Zwonitzer, with Charles Hirshberg, *Will You Miss Me When I'm Gone? The Carter Family and Their Legacy in American Music* (New York: Simon and Schuster, 2002); Cash's band mate Marshall Grant's memoir, written with Chris Zar, *I Was There When It Happened: My Life with Johnny Cash* (Nashville: Cumberland House, 2006); and son John Carter Cash's biography of his mother, *Anchored in Love: An Intimate Portrait of June Carter Cash* (Nashville, Thomas Nelson: 2007). The collections of journalism about Cash include Michael Streissguth, ed., *Ring of Fire: The Johnny Cash Reader* (Cambridge, Mass.: Da Capo, 2002), and Jason Fine, ed., *Cash: By the Editors of Rolling Stone* (New York: Crown, 2004).

4. I use "America" as a placeholder but note that the term is contested in much American studies scholarship. Current "post-national" paradigms question American exceptionalism and challenge the nationalist consensus found earlier in American studies as a field. Jan Radway has noted the problems with using the "America" in "American Studies" in ways that would seek a false monocultural view of that "America" ("What's in a Name? Presidential Address to the American Studies Association, 20 November 1998," *American Quarterly* 51, no. 1 [March 1999]: 1–32). See John Carlos Rowe, *Post-Nationalist American Studies* (Berkeley: University of California Press, 2000), and Donald E. Pease, ed., *National Identities and Post-Americanist Narratives* (Durham, N.C.: Duke University Press, 1994).

5. Kris Kristofferson, "The Pilgrim; Chapter 33," Resaca Music, 1971. Because of fair use standards, I have had to limit my quotation of song lyrics throughout the book.

6. Fine, *Cash: By the Editors of Rolling Stone*, 43.

7. See Barbara Ching, *Wrong's What I Do Best: Hard Country Music and Contemporary Culture* (New York: Oxford University Press, 2001); Joli Jensen, *The Nashville Sound: Authenticity, Commercialization, and Country Music* (Nashville: Country Mu-

sic Foundation/Vanderbilt University Press, 1998); Richard Peterson, *Creating Country Music: Fabricating Authenticity* (Chicago: University of Chicago Press, 1997); Michael T. Bertrand, *Race, Rock and Elvis* (Urbana: University of Illinois Press, 2000); Cecelia Tichi, ed., *Reading Country Music: Steel Guitars, Opry Stars, and Honky-Tonk Bars* (Durham, N.C.: Duke University Press, 1998); and Kristine M. McCusker and Diane Pecknold, eds., *A Boy Named Sue: Gender and Country Music* (Jackson: University Press of Mississippi, 2004).

8. Ching, *Wrong's What I Do Best*, 3–4.

9. Geertz argues that close readings of texts can "open up the possibility of an analysis which attends to their substance rather than to reductive formulas professing to account for them," since "the culture of a people is an ensemble of texts, themselves ensembles" that can be "read over the shoulders of those to whom they properly belong." See Clifford Geertz, *The Interpretation of Cultures* (New York: Basic Books, 1973), 452.

10. Charles Wolfe, "Postlude," in *A Boy Named Sue: Gender and Country Music*, ed. Kristine M. McCusker and Diane Pecknold (Jackson: University Press of Mississippi, 2004), 196–198. I use the term "genre" to refer to country music as a category, although more specific musicology terminology would refer to it as a "style" of vernacular music. For an explanation of debates about defining these discursive categories, see William Echard, *Neil Young and the Poetics of Energy* (Bloomington: Indiana University Press, 2005), 43–45.

11. Vivian Cash, with Ann Sharpsteen, *I Walked the Line: My Life with Johnny* (New York: Scribner, 2007).

12. I use "American Indian" as the most commonly used term in current academic discussions, but I do so with the knowledge that the issue of naming for indigenous groups is a contested one because of the power dynamics of colonialism and imperialism.

13. Jensen details how Cline's image speaks to country music's constructions of femininity. See Joli Jensen, "Patsy Cline's Crossovers," in McCusker and Pecknold, *A Boy Named Sue*, 107–131.

14. David Brackett, *Interpreting Popular Music* (Berkeley: University of California Press, 2000 [1995]), 76.

15. Sacvan Bercovitch, *The Office of "The Scarlet Letter"* (Baltimore, Md.: Johns Hopkins University Press, 1991); idem, *The Rites of Assent: Transformations in the Symbolic Construction of America* (New York: Routledge, 1993).

16. For accounts of this kind of neo-Gramscian cultural studies model of popular culture as a site of negotiation and struggle, see Stuart Hall, *Stuart Hall: Cultural Dialogues in Cultural Studies*, ed. David Morley and Kuan-Hsing Chen (London: Routledge, 1996), and John Storey, *Inventing Popular Culture* (Oxford: Blackwell, 2003), 48–62. For discussions of how popular music exceeds the logic of the marketplace, see Michael Bertrand, "I Don't Think Hank Done It That Way: Elvis, Country Music, and the Reconstruction of Southern Masculinity," in McCusker and Pecknold, *A Boy Named Sue*, 63, and Barry Shank, *Dissonant Identities: The Rock 'n' Roll Scene in Austin, Texas* (Hanover, N.H.: University Press of New England, 1994), 251.

17. George Lipsitz, *Time Passages: Collective Memory and American Popular Culture* (Minneapolis: University of Minnesota Press, 1990), 22, 3.

18. For an "integrated approach" to media studies, see Julie D'Acci, "Gender, Representation and Television," in *Television Studies*, ed. Toby Miller (London: British Film

Institute, 2002), 91–94. Although D'Acci is concerned with television specifically, this "integrated approach" has become increasingly important in popular music studies as well.

19. Joli Jensen, "Patsy Cline's Crossovers," 107–131.

20. Angela McRobbie, *Postmodernism and Popular Culture* (London: Routledge, 1994); McRobbie, *The Uses of Cultural Studies* (London: Sage, 2005).

21. Shirley Halperin, "Music Man," *Entertainment Weekly* 935, 25 May 2007, 16.

22. Theodor Adorno, "On Popular Music," in *Cultural Theory and Popular Culture: A Reader*, ed. John Storey, 2nd ed. (Athens: University of Georgia Press, 1998), 197–209; Storey, "Rockin' Hegemony: West Coast Rock and Amerika's War in Vietnam," in *Cultural Theory and Popular Culture*, 225–235; Simon Frith, *Sound Effects: Youth, Leisure, and the Politics of Rock* (London: Constable, 1983).

23. Stuart Hall and Paddy Whannel, *The Popular Arts* (London: Hutchinson, 1964), 269–283.

24. Madison J. Gray, "3-Day Johnny Cash Auction in New York Rakes in Nearly $4 Million," *Associated Press State and Local Wire*, 16 September 2004; Erin Siegal, e-mail to author, 29 August 2004.

25. "Row over 'Political' Cash Tribute," BBC, 28 August 2004, available at http://news.bbc.co.uk/2/hi/entertainment/3608956.stm.

26. Chris Willman, *Rednecks & Bluenecks: The Politics of Country Music* (New York: New Press, 2005), 248.

27. Mansfield, *Ring of Fire*, 12.

28. *Controversy: Johnny Cash vs. Music Row*, Country Music Television, 16 July 2004.

29. Greil Marcus, *Mystery Train: Images of America in Rock 'n' Roll Music* (New York: Plume, 1997).

30. Timothy Parrish, *Walking Blues: Making Americans from Emerson to Elvis* (Amherst: University of Massachusetts Press, 2001).

31. Barry Shank, "'That Wild Mercury Sound': Bob Dylan and the Illusion of American Culture," *boundary* 2 29, no. 1 (2002): 97–123. Other examples of academic studies that see popular musicians as prisms for American contradictions include accounts of how Bruce Springsteen stages the conflicting evolution of the white working class or republican civic ideals. On Springsteen and the white working class, see Jefferson Cowie and Lauren Boehm, "Dead Man's Town: 'Born in the U.S.A.,' Social History, and Working-Class Identity," *American Quarterly* 58, no. 2 (June 2006): 353–378; and Bryan K. Garman, *Race of Singers: Whitman's Working-Class Hero from Guthrie to Springsteen* (Chapel Hill: University of North Carolina Press, 2000). On Springsteen and republican civic ideals, see Jim Cullen, *Born in the U.S.A.: Bruce Springsteen and the American Tradition* (Middletown, Conn.: Wesleyan University Press, 2005). William Echard has analyzed how Neil Young's inconsistent politics indicates his dedication to individualism, and comments on what Lawrence Grossberg calls the "utopian and disintegrative" binary of rock as a social formation. See Echard, *Neil Young and the Poetics of Energy*, 27, and Lawrence Grossberg, "Reflections of a Disappointed Popular Music Scholar," *Rock over the Edge: Transformations in Popular Music Culture*, ed. R Beebe, D. Fulbrook, and B. Saunders (Durham, N.C.: Duke University Press, 2002), 49.

32. Stuart Hall, "Notes on Deconstructing 'the Popular'," in *Cultural Theory and Popular Culture: A Reader*, ed. John Storey, 2nd ed. (Athens: University of Georgia Press,

1998), 442–443. See Storey's introduction for an explanation of how definitions of terms such as "popular," "folk," and "culture" are matters of scholarly debate.

33. Willman, *Rednecks & Bluenecks*, 6.

34. Cecelia Tichi, *High Lonesome: The American Culture of Country Music* (Chapel Hill: University of North Carolina Press, 1994), 1.

35. Peterson, *Creating Country Music*; Bill C. Malone, *Don't Get above Your Raisin': Country Music and the Southern Working Class* (Urbana: University of Illinois Press, 2002); George Lewis, "Tension, Conflict, and Contradiction in Country Music," in *All That Glitters: Country Music in America*, ed. George H. Lewis (Bowling Green, Ohio: Bowling Green State University Popular Press, 1993), 208–220.

36. Peterson, *Creating Country Music*, 178.

37. Peterson, *Creating Country Music*; Jensen, *The Nashville Sound*; Aaron Fox, "The Jukebox of History: Narratives of Loss and Desire in the Discourse of Country Music," *Popular Music* 11 (1992): 54.

38. Bill C. Malone, *Singing Cowboys and Musical Mountaineers: Southern Culture and the Roots of Country Music* (Athens: University of Georgia Press, 2003 [1993]), 68.

39. George Lipsitz, *Time Passages: Collective Memory and American Popular Culture* (Minneapolis: University of Minnesota Press, 1990), 22, 3. In her cogent account of commercialism and the country music industry, Diane Pecknold demonstrates that fans were aware of commercialism and often embraced it because the mass media (especially radio) is precisely what would allow them to engage with a national imagined community formed through appreciation of this music. The genre thus encodes a paradoxical merger of tradition and modernity (Pecknold, *The Selling Sound: The Rise of the Country Music Industry* [Durham, N.C.: Duke University Press, 2007]).

40. Jensen, *The Nashville Sound*, 15.

41. Malone, *Don't Get above Your Raisin'*, ix.

42. John Buckley, "Country Music and American Values," *Popular Music and Society* 6, no. 4 (1978): 293–301, reprinted in Lewis, ed., *All That Glitters*, 198, 205.

43. Lewis, "Tension, Conflict, and Contradiction in Country Music," 209.

44. Malone, *Don't Get above Your Raisin'*, ix.

45. Raymond Williams, *The Long Revolution* (Harmondsworth, U.K.: Penguin, 1965), 64.

46. See Diane Pecknold, "'I Wanna Play House': Configurations of Masculinity in the Nashville Sound Era," in McCusker and Pecknold, *A Boy Named Sue*, 86–106; Pecknold, *The Selling Sound*.

47. Wilber J. Cash, *The Mind of the South* (New York: Knopf, 1941), 44–47, 56–58.

48. Lewis, "Tension, Conflict, and Contradiction in Country Music," 217.

49. Malone, *Don't Get above Your Raisin'*, 137.

50. Ibid., 119.

51. Lewis notes the dearth of female ramblers in country music songs, observing that, although a few appeared in songs after the 1970s feminist movement, women generally do not have the same freedom as male ramblers ("Tension, Conflict, and Contradiction in Country Music," 218).

52. Malone's arguments are given substantial consideration here, since his histories of country music remain the most important accounts of the field.

53. Malone, *Don't Get above Your Raisin'*, 49.

54. Ibid., ix.

55. Michael Kimmel, *Manhood in America: A Cultural History*, 2nd ed. (New York: Oxford University Press, 2006), 231.

56. Quoted in Fine, *Cash: By the Editors of Rolling Stone*, 208.

57. Teresa Ortega, "'My Name Is Sue! How Do You Do?': Johnny Cash as Lesbian Icon," *South Atlantic Quarterly* 94 (winter 1995): 267.

58. Mary A. Bufwack and Robert K. Oermann, *Finding Her Voice: The Saga of Women in Country Music* (New York: Crown, 1993), 216; Michael Bertrand, "I Don't Think Hank Done It That Way: Elvis, Country Music, and the Reconstruction of Southern Masculinity," in McCusker and Pecknold, *A Boy Named Sue*, 62, 64.

59. Eric Lott, *Love and Theft: Blackface Minstrelsy and the American Working Class* (New York: Oxford University Press, 1993); W. T. Lhamon Jr., *Raising Cain: Blackface Performance from Jim Crow to Hip Hop* (Cambridge, Mass.: Harvard University Press, 1998); Michael Rogin, "The Two Declarations of American Independence," *Representations* 55 (summer 1996): 13–30.

60. Streissguth, *Johnny Cash: The Biography*, 44–45.

61. Johnny Cash, with Patrick Carr, *Cash: The Autobiography* (New York: Harper-Collins, 1997), 19.

62. Cash, *Cash: The Autobiography*, 72–73.

63. Streissguth, *Johnny Cash: The Biography*, 139, 87; Grant, *I Was There When It Happened*.

64. See also her two autobiographies: June Carter Cash, *From the Heart* (New York: Prentice Hall, 1987), and *Among My Klediments* (Grand Rapids, Mich.: Zondervan, 1979).

65. Streissguth, *Johnny Cash: The Biography*, 234.

66. *Controversy: Johnny Cash vs. Music Row*, Country Music Television, 11 September 2004.

67. Quoted in Dawidoff, *In the Country of Country: A Journey to the Roots of American Music* (New York: Vintage, 1998), 186.

68. The Million Dollar Quartet moniker was immortalized when Elvis, who had already left for RCA in 1955, visited Sun Studios and crashed Carl Perkins's recording session on 4 December 1956, joining Perkins, Lewis, and Cash in an impromptu jam session that Perkins recorded. Though some scholars have argued that Cash either came late or left early and only appeared in the famous photo, not in any of the tracks on the recording, Cash insists that he is there singing—just higher than usual and far away from the microphone, so his voice is less recognizable. A local Memphis reporter, Robert Johnson, dubbed them the "Million Dollar Quartet" when he wrote the story.

69. Johnny Cash, *Man in Black* (Grand Rapids, Mich.: Zondervan, 1975), 197.

70. *Controversy: Johnny Cash vs. Music Row*, Country Music Television, 16 July 2004.

71. Brian Mansfield, "Even in Death, Man in Black Looms Large," *USA Today*, 4–6 November 2005, national edition, A1.

72. Katie Hasty, "Cash Earns First No. 1 Album since 1969," *Billboard.com*, 12 July 2006, available at http://www.billboard.com/bbcom/news/article_display.jsp?vnu_content _id=1002837777.

73. "Johnny Cash Album Sales Soar," *Launch Radio Networks*, 18 November 2003, available at http://launch.yahoo.com/read/news.asp?contentID=214647.

74. Mansfield, "Even in Death."

75. "Johnny Cash: Fire at Cash's Former Home Still under Investigation," *CMT. com*, 17 April 2007, available at http://www.cmt.com/artists/news/1556874/20070411/cash _johnny.jhtml.

1. "What Is Truth?"

1. Barbara Ching, *Wrong's What I Do Best: Hard Country Music and Contemporary Culture* (New York: Oxford University Press, 2001), 5; Joli Jensen, *The Nashville Sound: Authenticity, Commercialization, and Country Music* (Nashville: Country Music Foundation/Vanderbilt University Press, 1998), 15.

2. See, for example, Shank's critical cultural studies ethnography of identity constructions involving ideas of "sincerity" in Austin music scenes, in his *Dissonant Identities: The Rock 'n' Roll Scene in Austin, Texas* (Hanover, N.H.: University Press of New England, 1994).

3. Ching, *Wrong's What I Do Best*; Jensen, *The Nashville Sound*; Richard Peterson, *Creating Country Music: Fabricating Authenticity* (Chicago: University of Chicago Press, 1997); Michael T. Bertrand, *Race, Rock and Elvis* (Urbana: University of Illinois Press, 2000).

4. Aaron Fox, "The Jukebox of History: Narratives of Loss and Desire in the Discourse of Country Music," *Popular Music* 11 (1992): 54.

5. Peterson, in *Creating Country Music*, has argued for "hard-core country" as the "roots of country" in the "raw" singing style, "rough" life experiences, and lack of artifice in artists like Hank Williams or Loretta Lynn. "Soft-shell country" is "sell-out" pop of the post–World War II Nashville Sound and its pop-country offspring, from Jim Reeves to Kenny Rogers and beyond. The problematic gendering of the "hard country" discourse has been examined by Ching, *Wrong's What I Do Best*; Richard Leppert and George Lipsitz, "Age, the Boy, and Experience in the Music of Hank Williams," in *All That Glitters: Country Music in America*, ed. George H. Lewis (Bowling Green, Ohio: Bowling Green State University Press, 1993), 22–37; and David Sanjek, foreword to *A Boy Named Sue: Gender and Country Music*, ed. Kristine M. McCusker and Diane Pecknold (Jackson: University Press of Mississippi, 2004), vii–xv.

6. Sanjek, foreword.

7. *Lost Highway: The Story of Country Music*, Part 1, Country Music Television, 22 February 2003.

8. Michael Streissguth, *Johnny Cash at Folsom Prison: The Making of a Masterpiece* (Cambridge, Mass.: Da Capo, 2004), 34.

9. Ching, *Wrong's What I Do Best*, 26, 139.

10. John R. Cash, "Country Trash," *Songs of Cash*, ASCAP, 2002.

11. John R. Cash, "I'll Say It's True," *House of Cash*, BMI, 1979.

12. Johnny Cash, with Patrick Carr, *Cash: The Autobiography* (New York: Harper-Collins, 1997), 17.

13. Barry Shank, "'That Wild Mercury Sound': Bob Dylan and the Illusion of American Culture," *boundary* 2 29, no. 1 (2002): 98–99.

14. John R. Cash, "Country Boy," *Songs of Cash*, ASCAP, 1957.

15. George Lipsitz, *Time Passages: Collective Memory and American Popular Culture* (Minneapolis: University of Minnesota Press, 1990), 22, 3.

16. David Brackett, *Interpreting Popular Music* (Berkeley: University of California Press, 2000 [1995]), 88.

17. Sylvie Simmons, "Cash Unearthed," liner notes, Johnny Cash, *Unearthed*, American Recordings (2003), 84.

18. Jason Fine, ed., *Cash: By the Editors of Rolling Stone* (New York: Crown, 2004), 153.

19. Ibid., 155.

20. Fabian Holt, *Genre in Popular Music* (Chicago: University of Chicago Press, 2007), 67.

21. Ibid.

22. Quoted in Michael Streissguth, *Johnny Cash: The Biography* (New York: Da Capo, 2006), 74–75.

23. Benjamin Filene, *Romancing the Folk: Public Memory and American Roots Music* (Chapel Hill: University of North Carolina Press, 2000); Ronald D. Cohen, *Rainbow Quest: The Folk Music Revival and American Society, 1940–1970* (Amherst: University of Massachusetts Press, 2002); Ronald D. Lankford Jr., *Folk Music USA: The Changing Voice of Protest* (New York: Schirmer Trade Books, 2005); Reebee Garofalo, ed., *Rockin' the Boat: Mass Music and Mass Movements* (Cambridge, Mass.: South End Press, 1992); Ian Peddie, ed., *The Resisting Muse: Popular Music and Social Protest* (Aldershot, Hampshire: Ashgate, 2006); Ron Eyerman and Andrew Jamison, eds., *Music and Social Movements: Mobilizing Traditions in the Twentieth Century* (Cambridge: Cambridge University Press, 1998).

24. See note 23, above.

25. Quoted in Peter Lewry, *A Johnny Cash Chronicle: I've Been Everywhere* (London: Helter Skelter, 2001), 49.

26. Jan Wenner, "The New Bob Dylan: A Little Like Johnny Cash?" *Rolling Stone*, 6 April 1968.

27. Peter Doggett, *Are You Ready for the Country: Elvis, Dylan, Parsons, and the Roots of Country Rock* (New York: Penguin, 2000).

28. Lewry, *A Johnny Cash Chronicle*, 46.

29. Don Cusic, *Johnny Cash: The Songs* (New York: Thunder's Mouth, 2004), xxiv, xxv.

30. Bill C. Malone, *Don't Get above Your Raisin': Country Music and the Southern Working Class* (Urbana: University of Illinois Press, 2002), 64.

31. *The Best of Hootenanny*, Shout Factory, DVD, 13 October 2006.

32. James C. Cobb, "Country Music and the 'Southernization' of America," in *All That Glitters: Country Music in America*, ed. George H. Lewis (Bowling Green, Ohio: Bowling Green State University Popular Press, 1993), 86; Streissguth, *Folsom*, 148.

33. Streissguth, *Folsom*, 148.

34. Streissguth, *Johnny Cash: The Biography*, 165.

35. Cobb, "Country Music and the 'Southernization' of America," 75.

36. *Controversy: Johnny Cash vs. Music Row*, Country Music Television, 16 July 2004.

37. Ibid.

38. Ibid.

39. Ibid.

40. Shirley Halperin, "Music Man," *Entertainment Weekly* 935, 25 May 2007, 16.

41. Holt, *Genre in Popular Music*, 46.

42. *Controversy: Johnny Cash vs. Music Row*, Country Music Television, 16 July 2004.

43. *Inside Fame: Johnny Cash*, Country Music Television, 28 March 2003.

44. Aaron A. Fox, *Real Country: Music and Language in Working-Class Culture* (Durham, N.C.: Duke University Press, 2004), 312–313.

45. *Controversy: Johnny Cash vs. Music Row*, Country Music Television, 16 July 2004.

46. William Echard, *Neil Young and the Poetics of Energy* (Bloomington: Indiana University Press, 2005), 192.

47. Fox, *Real Country*, 310–311.

48. Ibid.

49. Ibid., 315.

50. Denise Von Glahn, personal interview, 22 March 2006.

51. Brian Mansfield, *Ring of Fire: A Tribute to Johnny Cash* (Nashville: Rutledge Hill, 2003), 38.

52. Steve Turner, *The Man Called Cash: The Life, Love, and Faith of an American Legend* (Nashville: Thomas Nelson, 2004), 234.

53. Albin J. Zak III, *The Poetics of Rock: Cutting Tracks, Making Records* (Berkeley: University of California Press, 2001).

54. *Walk the Line*, dir. James Mangold, perf. Joaquin Phoenix and Reese Witherspoon, 20th Century Fox, 2005.

55. Fine, *Cash: By the Editors of Rolling Stone*, 77.

56. Colin Escott, liner notes, *Johnny Cash: The Complete Sun Recordings, 1955–1958*, Time/Life (2005).

57. Ibid.

58. *The Carter Family: Will the Circle Be Unbroken*, PBS, 2005.

59. Mansfield, *Ring of Fire*, 40.

60. Streissguth, *Johnny Cash: The Biography*, 77.

61. Pamela Fox analyzes class and gender-coded notions of authenticity and identity switching in autobiographies of female stars such as Dolly Parton, Loretta Lynn, and Reba McEntire. See Pamela Fox, "Recycled Trash: Gender and Authenticity in Country Music Autobiography," *American Quarterly* 50, no. 2 (June 1998): 234–266, 235.

62. John R. Cash, "Man in Black," House of Cash, 1971.

63. Cash, *Cash: The Autobiography*, 9.

64. Ibid.

65. Ibid., 146.

66. Turner, *The Man Called Cash*, 226–27.

67. Fine, *Cash: By the Editors of Rolling Stone*, 13–14.

68. Turner, *The Man Called Cash*, 194.

69. Quoted in Fine, *Cash: By the Editors of Rolling Stone*, 24.

70. Turner, *The Man Called Cash*, 225–235.

71. Cash, *Man in Black*, 13.

72. Cash, *Cash: The Autobiography*, 191.

73. Ibid., 232.

74. Streissguth, *Johnny Cash: The Biography*; Marshall Grant with Chris Zar, *I Was There When It Happened: My Life with Johnny Cash* (Nashville: Cumberland House, 2006).

75. Cash, *Cash: The Autobiography*, 76, 77, 84.

76. Streissguth, *Johnny Cash: The Biography*, 48–49.

77. Cash, *Cash: The Autobiography*, 76–77.

78. Cash, *Man in Black*, 73.

79. Cash, *Cash: The Autobiography*, 86.

80. Turner, *The Man Called Cash*, ix.

81. Mansfield, *Ring of Fire*, 12; Streissguth, *Johnny Cash: The Biography*, xiv.

82. Mansfield, *Ring of Fire*, 5–7.

83. Brian Mansfield, "Even in Death, Man in Black Looms Large," *USA Today*, 4–6 November 2005, national edition, A1.

84. Nicholas Dawidoff, *In the Country of Country: A Journey to the Roots of American Music* (New York: Vintage, 1998), 169–199.

85. Ibid., 169.

86. Ibid., 182.

87. Fine, *Cash: By the Editors of Rolling Stone*, 16, 159, 161.

88. Ibid., 43.

89. Ibid.

90. John R. Cash, "What Is Truth?" copyright John R. Cash, published by Songs of Cash, ASCAP, 1970.

91. Bill Miller, ed., *Cash: An American Man* (New York: CMT and Pocket Books, 2004), 168.

92. Cash, *Cash: The Autobiography*, 286; Fine, *Cash: By the Editors of Rolling Stone*, 102.

93. George Lewis, "Tension, Conflict, and Contradiction in Country Music," in *All That Glitters: Country Music in America*, ed. George H. Lewis (Bowling Green, Ohio: Bowling Green State University Popular Press, 1993), 208–220.

94. Antonio Gramsci, *Selections from Prison Notebooks*, ed. and trans. Quintin Hoare and Geoffrey Nowell-Smith (London: Lawrence and Wishart, 1971), 453. More specifically, Gramsci defines "organic intellectuals" as class organizers in the process of hegemony; each class creates its own intellectuals who provide cultural and ideological leadership.

95. Malone, *Don't Get above Your Raisin'*, 241.

96. Ibid., 243.

97. Christopher S. Wren, *Winners Got Scars Too: The Life of Johnny Cash* (New York: Ballantine, 1971), 6.

98. Robert Levine, "Cash Film's Missing Ingredient: Religion," *New York Times*, 4 March 2006, available at http://www.nytimes.com/2006/03/04/movies/MoviesFeatures/04cash.html.

99. Trent Reznor, "Hurt," Nothing Records/Interscope, 1994.

100. The Cash cover of Reznor's song itself went to number 3 on the country charts and number 33 on the modern rock charts. The album on which it first appeared, *American IV: The Man Comes Around* (2002), hit number 2 on the country charts and number 22 on *Billboard* 200.

101. Sut Jhally, "Image-Based Culture: Advertising and Popular Culture," in *Gender, Race, and Class in Media: A Text-Reader,* ed. Gail Dines and Jean M. Humez, 2nd ed. (Thousand Oaks, Calif.: Sage, 2003), 249–257.

102. John Caldwell, "Prime-Time Fiction Theorizes the Docu-Real," in *Reality Squared: Televisual Discourse on the Real,* ed. James Friedman (New Brunswick, N.J.: Rutgers University Press, 2002), 259–292.

103. Robert Elfstrom, dir., *Johnny Cash: The Man, His World, and His Music,* DVD, 1969, Sanctuary Records Group, 2002.

104. Bertrand, *Race, Rock and Elvis.* Marcus reads Elvis as a symbol of America's cultural mixture; see Greil Marcus, *Mystery Train: Images of America in Rock 'n' Roll Music* (New York: Plume, 1997).

105. Kurt Loder, "The Final Interview," in Miller, *Cash: An American Man,* 76–79.

106. Simon Frith, *Performing Rites: On the Value of Popular Music* (Cambridge, Mass.: Harvard University Press, 1996), 95.

2. "A Boy Named Sue"

1. "Johnny Cash: Original Gangsta," *MTVNews.com,* 2 February 2007, available at http://www.mtv.com/bands/c/cash_johnny/news_vma_feature/index4.hhtml.

2. Barbara Ching, *Wrong's What I Do Best: Hard Country Music and Contemporary Culture* (New York: Oxford University Press, 2001).

3. Sheila Whiteley, *Women and Popular Music: Sexuality, Identity and Subjectivity* (London: Routledge, 2000), 16–17.

4. Ibid., 157.

5. Notable studies include Michael T. Bertrand, *Race, Rock, and Elvis* (Urbana: University of Illinois Press, 2000); Richard Leppert and George Lipsitz, "Age, the Boy, and Experience in the Music of Hank Williams," in *All That Glitters: Country Music in America,* ed. George H. Lewis (Bowling Green, Ohio: Bowling Green State University Press, 1993), 22–37; and Ching, *Wrong's What I Do Best.*

6. Susan Bordo, *The Male Body: A New Look at Men in Public and in Private* (New York: Farrar, Straus and Giroux, 2000); Toby Miller, *Sportsex* (Philadelphia: Temple University Press, 2002); Sean Wilentz, *Chants Democratic: New York City and the Rise of the American Working Class, 1788–1850* (New York: Oxford University Press, 1984); Eric Lott, *Love and Theft: Blackface Minstrelsy and the American Working Class* (New York: Oxford University Press, 1993); David Roediger, *The Wages of Whiteness: Race and the Making of the American Working Class* (New York: Verso, 1991); Gail Bederman, *Manliness and Civilization: A Cultural History of Gender and Race in the United States, 1880–1917* (Chicago: University of Chicago Press, 1995).

7. Mary A. Bufwack and Robert K. Oermann, *Finding Her Voice: Women in Country Music, 1800–2000* (Nashville: Country Music Foundation/Vanderbilt University Press, 2003).

8. Bufwack and Oermann, *Finding Her Voice: Women in Country Music;* idem, *Finding Her Voice: The Illustrated History of Women in Country Music* (New York: Crown, 1993).

9. Pamela Fox, "Recycled Trash: Gender and Authenticity in Country Music Autobiography," *American Quarterly* 50, no. 2 (June 1998): 234–266, 235.

10. Sheila Whiteley, ed., *Sexing the Groove: Popular Music and Gender* (London: Routledge, 1997). Whiteley's collection as a whole examines the gendered dynamics of rock discourse, such as the stereotypical association of "rock" with authenticity and masculinity, and "pop" with artifice and femininity.

11. Rob Walser, *Running with the Devil: Power, Gender, and Madness in Heavy Metal Music* (Hanover, N.H.: University Press of New England, 1993). Whiteley argues that while Jagger popularized a highly aggressive version of masculinist rock, androgyny (a highly debated topic in popular music studies) in his performances also opened up definitions of gender in the early 1970s. See Whiteley, "Little Red Rooster v. The Honky Tonk Woman: Mick Jagger, Sexuality, Style, and Image," in *Sexing the Groove*, 67–99. Palmer argues that Springsteen maps the signifiers of the Western onto his contemporary blue-collar culture and performs his version of "authentic masculinity" in his labor-intensive stage shows. See Gareth Palmer, "Bruce Springsteen and Masculinity," in Whiteley, *Sexing the Groove*, 100–117. In the same collection Norma Coates analyzes the gendering of rock as a masculinist discourse. Drawing on well-known feminist theories such as Teresa De Lauretis's "technologies of gender" argument, in which social technologies like popular culture produce gender, and Judith Butler's gender-as-performativity arguments, Coates assesses how women in rock might break up the genre's masculinist discourse. See Norma Coates, "(R)evolution Now? Rock and the Political Potential of Gender," in Whiteley, *Sexing the Groove*, 50–64. See also Simon Frith and Angela McRobbie, "Rock and Sexuality," in *On Record: Rock, Pop, and the Written Word*, ed. Simon Frith and Angela Goodwin (London: Routledge, 1990), 375.

12. Ching, *Wrong's What I Do Best*; Leppert and Lipsitz, "Age, the Boy, and Experience in the Music of Hank Williams," 22–37. David Sanjek, foreword to *A Boy Named Sue: Gender and Country Music*, ed. Kristine M. McCusker and Diane Pecknold (Jackson: University Press of Mississippi, 2004), vii–xv.

13. Andreas Huyssen, *After the Great Divide: Modernism, Mass Culture, Postmodernism* (Bloomington: Indiana University Press, 1986).

14. Quoted in Michael Kimmel, *The Gendered Society* (New York: Oxford University Press, 2000), 11.

15. Ibid.

16. Antonio Gramsci, *Selections from Prison Notebooks*, ed. and trans. Quintin Hoare and Geoffrey Nowell-Smith (London: Lawrence and Wishart, 1971), 5. Hegemony is a contested process involving what Gramsci terms "negotiation" between dominant and subordinate groups and processes of both "resistance" and "incorporation." "Hegemonic masculinity" takes Gramsci's argument about class and applies it to gender, again isolating the form of masculinity that is most culturally privileged at any given moment.

17. Connell elaborates on the concept: "Hegemonic masculinity can be defined as the configuration of gender practices which embodies the currently accepted answer to the problem of legitimacy of patriarchy, which guarantees (or is taken to guarantee) the dominant position of men and the subordination of women." Connell identifies subordinated masculinities in Euro-American cultures, such as that of homosexual men, as well as "complicit" masculinities, that is, men who do not embody hegemonic ideals but who benefit from the "patriarchal dividend" of male supremacy. See R. W. Connell, *Masculinities*, 2nd ed. (Berkeley: University of California Press, 2005 [1995]), 75–77.

18. Ibid., passim.

19. Dana Nelson, *National Manhood: Capitalist Citizenship and the Imagined Fraternity of White Men* (Durham, N.C.: Duke University Press, 1998), ix.

20. In tracing how the ascendancy of the middle class translated into a focus on masculinity rather than class in American culture, Leverenz defines the emergent entrepreneurial manhood against what he terms "patrician manhood" as a paternalism of the upper bourgeoisie reflecting British aristocratic ideals which have, as he notes, endured longer in the South than in the North, and against an "artisan" manhood celebrating pride in hard work and independence. See David Leverenz, "Manhood, Class, and the American Renaissance," in *Background Readings for Teachers of American Literature*, ed. Venetria Patton (Boston: Bedford/St. Martin's, 2006), 261–262, and idem, *Manhood and the American Renaissance* (Ithaca, N.Y.: Cornell University Press, 1989). Similarly Kimmel attributes the emergence of the "Self-Made Man of American mythology" in the early nineteenth century to the effects of the Industrial Revolution and sees this model displacing "the Genteel Patriarch" landowner model and the "Heroic Artisan" independent farmer model. See Michael Kimmel, *Manhood in America: A Cultural History*, 2nd ed. (New York: Oxford University Press, 2006).

21. Connell notes, for example, that the nineteenth-century bourgeois concept of "separate spheres," in which women ruled the domestic sphere and men controlled the public sphere of economics and politics, emerged as a result of women's advocacy for their own roles (Connell, *Masculinities*, 195). Although feminist scholars have demonstrated that the separate spheres were more rigid in ideology than in actual social practice, this gender ideology has nonetheless had a lasting impact on gender ideals. See Cathy N. Davidson and Jessamyn Hatcher, eds., *No More Separate Spheres!* (Durham, N.C.: Duke University Press, 2002).

22. Connell, *Masculinities*, 194.

23. Kimmel, *Manhood in America*, 228.

24. Historians now question how far back to date the nuclear family. Many assert the need to nuance the long-held theory of a total family revolution from premodern to modern families between the 1780s and 1840s as a result of industrialization. Coontz argues that the conventional idea that industrialization ushered out the extended family does not hold true when one considers that the highest numbers of extended families occurred in the mid-nineteenth century. Most scholars do agree, however, that the white middle-class nuclear family model became idealized and codified in the Victorian period, even when the reality of people's lives differed drastically, and that it has been used to regulate ideas of family and behavior since that time. See Stephanie Coontz, *The Way We Never Were: American Families and the Nostalgia Trap* (New York: Basic Books, 1992), 12.

25. Two-parent households were the majority only from the 1920s to the 1970s, and the modern nuclear family represented only a minority of those households. See William H. Frey, Bill Abresch, and Jonathan Yeasting, *America by the Numbers: A Field Guide to the U.S. Population* (New York: New Press, 2001), 123–124.

26. Edward Shorter, *The Making of the Modern Family* (New York: Basic Books, 1975).

27. See Judith Stacey, *Brave New Families: Stories of Domestic Upheaval in Late Twentieth Century America* (New York: Basic Books, 1990), 3–19; Nancy F. Cott, *Public Vows: A History of Marriage and the Nation* (Cambridge, Mass.: Harvard University

Press, 2000). Stacey notes that more children now live with single mothers than in modern nuclear families; married couples with children comprise only a minority of U.S. households, and many of those couples are divorced and have remarried (Stacey, *In The Name of the Family: Rethinking Family Values in the Postmodern Age* [Boston: Beacon, 1996], 45).

28. Kimmel, *Manhood in America*, 217.

29. Quoted in ibid., 219.

30. Jefferson Cowie and Lauren Boehm, "Dead Man's Town: 'Born in the U.S.A.,' Social History, and Working-Class Identity," *American Quarterly* 58, no. 2 (June 2006): 353–378.

31. Kimmel, *Manhood in America*, 231.

32. Ibid.

33. *Ridin' the Rails: The Great American Train Story*, dir. Nicholas Webster, Webster/ Rivkin Productions, 1974.

34. Aaron A. Fox, *Real Country: Music and Language in Working-Class Culture* (Durham, N.C.: Duke University Press, 2004), 309.

35. Bill C. Malone, *Don't Get above Your Raisin': Country Music and the Southern Working Class* (Urbana: University of Illinois Press, 2002).

36. Ibid., 134.

37. For a full account of the factual basis for the narrative as well as the history of different performances of the song in different historical contexts, including as a protest song, see Scott Reynolds Nelson, *Steel Drivin' Man: John Henry, the Untold Story of an American Legend* (Oxford: Oxford University Press, 2006).

38. Connell, *Masculinities*, 45–66.

3. Gender and "The Beast in Me"

1. Mary A. Bufwack and Robert K. Oermann, *Finding Her Voice: The Saga of Women in Country Music* (New York: Crown, 1993).

2. Michael T. Bertrand, *Race, Rock and Elvis* (Urbana: University of Illinois Press, 2000).

3. Craig Morrison, *Go Cat Go! Rockabilly Music and Its Makers* (Urbana: University of Illinois Press, 1998); Billy Poore, *Rockabilly: A Forty-Year Journey* (Milwaukee, Wis.: Hal Leonard, 1998).

4. Michael Streissguth, *Johnny Cash: The Biography* (New York: Da Capo, 2006), 84.

5. Elaine Tyler May, *Homeward Bound: American Families in the Cold War Era* (New York: Basic Books, 1988).

6. Richard Leppert and George Lipsitz, "Age, the Boy, and Experience in the Music of Hank Williams," in *All That Glitters: Country Music in America*, ed. George H. Lewis (Bowling Green, Ohio: Bowling Green State University Press, 1993), 22–37.

7. Diane Pecknold, "'I Wanna Play House': Configurations of Masculinity in the Nashville Sound Era," in *A Boy Named Sue: Gender and Country Music*, ed. Kristine M. McCusker and Diane Pecknold (Jackson: University of Mississippi Press, 2004), 86.

8. Cecelia Tichi, *High Lonesome: The American Culture of Country Music* (Chapel Hill: University of North Carolina Press, 1994).

9. Wilber J. Cash, *The Mind of the South* (New York: Knopf, 1941), 44–47, 56–58.

10. Bill C. Malone, *Don't Get above Your Raisin': Country Music and the Southern Working Class* (Urbana: University of Illinois Press, 2002).

11. Ibid., 122.

12. Ibid., 121–123.

13. George Lewis, "Tension, Conflict, and Contradiction in Country Music," in Lewis, *All That Glitters*, 218.

14. David Brackett, *Interpreting Popular Music*, 2nd ed. (Berkeley: University of California Press, 2000 [1995]).

15. Nick Bromell, *Tomorrow Never Knows: Rock and Psychedelics in the 1960s* (Chicago: University of Chicago Press, 2000).

16. *Lost Highway*, Part Three, Country Music Television, 8 March 2003.

17. *Johnny Cash in San Quentin* (Sony/Legacy edition, 2006), liner notes 16.

18. Streissguth, *Johnny Cash: The Biography*, 160.

19. *Johnny Cash in San Quentin* (Sony/Legacy edition, 2006), liner notes 32, 33.

20. Michael Kimmel, *Manhood in America: A Cultural History*, 2nd ed. (New York: Oxford University Press, 2006), 231.

21. Teresa A. Goddu, *Gothic America: Narrative, History, and Nation* (New York: Columbia University Press, 1997), 3–4.

22. Ibid., 10.

23. *Controversy: Johnny Cash vs. Music Row*, Country Music Television, 16 July 2004.

24. Josh Kun, *Audiotopia: Music, Race, and America* (Berkeley: University of California Press, 2005), 20.

4. Race and Identity Politics

1. Vine Deloria Jr., *Custer Died for Your Sins* (New York: Avon, 1969), 11–12.

2. Quoted in Christopher S. Wren, *Winners Got Scars Too: The Life of Johnny Cash* (New York: Ballantine, 1971), 14.

3. Blake Green, "Johnny Cash—The Man, The Legend," reprinted in *The Legend I* (1972), 4–5. This publication is from Cash's fan club and is in the archives at the Country Music Foundation in Nashville.

4. Leslie A. Fiedler, *The Return of the Vanishing American* (New York: Stein and Day, 1968).

5. Frederick Jackson Turner, *History, Frontier, and Section: Three Essays* (Albuquerque: University of New Mexico Press, 1993).

6. Mary Louise Pratt, *Imperial Eyes: Travel Writing and Transculturation* (London: Routledge, 1992), 7.

7. Aaron A. Fox, *Real Country: Music and Language in Working-Class Culture* (Durham, N.C.: Duke University Press, 2004), 320.

8. Witness protests over songs such as Tim McGraw's "Indian Outlaw."

9. David W. Samuels, *Putting a Song on Top of It: Expression and Identity on the San Carlos Apache Reservation* (Tucson: University of Arizona Press, 2004).

10. Fiedler, *The Return of the Vanishing American*.

11. Specifically he notes that indigenous musicians in Australia, since Marley's tour there in 1979, have claimed reggae and blackness as a means of establishing solidarity with blacks globally and as a way to resist Australian governmental control of them. See

George Lipsitz, *Dangerous Crossroads: Popular Music, Postmodernism, and the Poetics of Place* (New York: Verso, 1994), 142–146.

12. Fox, *Real Country*, 320.

13. "Johnny Cash: Original Gangsta," *MTVNews.com*, 2 February 2007, available at http://www.mtv.com/bands/c/cash_johnny/news_vma_feature/index4.hhtml.

14. Johnny Cash, with Patrick Carr, *Cash: The Autobiography* (New York: Harper-Collins, 1997), 45.

15. Ibid., 13.

16. Ibid., 53.

17. Ibid., 55.

18. Ibid., 56.

19. Ibid., 57.

20. Ibid., 58.

21. Ibid., 48.

22. Timothy Brennan, *At Home in the World: Cosmopolitanism Now* (Cambridge, Mass.: Harvard University Press, 1997).

23. Sylvie Simmons, "The Gunslinger," *Mojo* (November 2004): 75; Peter Lewry, *A Johnny Cash Chronicle: I've Been Everywhere* (London: Helter Skelter, 2001), 45.

24. Cash, *Cash: The Autobiography*, 163.

25. Simmons, "The Gunslinger," 74.

26. Bill C. Malone, *Singing Cowboys and Musical Mountaineers: Southern Culture and the Roots of Country Music* (Athens: University of Georgia Press, 2003 [1993]), 68.

27. Raymond Williams, *The Long Revolution* (Harmondsworth: Penguin, 1965), 64–65.

28. Cash, "Reflections," *Johnny Cash Sings the Ballads of the True West*, Columbia/Sony Legacy (1965, 2002).

29. Malone, *Singing Cowboys*, 7.

30. Slotkin, *Regeneration through Violence: The Mythology of the American Frontier, 1600–1800* (Middletown, Conn.: Wesleyan University Press, 1973). Shank, meanwhile, has noted the stubborn nativism that still informs the cowboy imagery in more recent country music. See his *Dissonant Identities: The Rock 'n' Roll Scene in Austin, Texas* (Hanover, N.H.: University Press of New England, 1994).

31. Cash, *Cash: The Autobiography*, 263–264.

32. Ibid., 230–231.

33. Cathy N. Davidson and Jessamyn Hatcher, eds., *No More Separate Spheres!* (Durham, N.C.: Duke University Press, 2002).

34. Lora Romero, "Vanishing Americans: Gender, Empire, and New Historicism," *American Literature* 63 (1991): 386–404, 385. Romero cites the original use of the term "Vanishing American" in G. Harrison Orians, *The Cult of the Vanishing American: A Century View* (Toledo, Ohio: Chittenden, 1934). See also Brian W. Dippie, *The Vanishing American: White Attitudes and U.S. Indian Policy* (Middletown, Conn.: Wesleyan University Press, 1982), 2; Fiedler, *The Return of the Vanishing American*.

35. Fiedler, *The Return of the Vanishing American*; Dippie, *The Vanishing American*.

36. Roy Harvey Pearce, *Savagism and Civilization: A Study of the Indian and the American Mind* (Baltimore, Md.: Johns Hopkins University Press, 1967), 194–195. See also Dippie, *The Vanishing American*. Vine Deloria Jr. has noted that a problem facing the American Indian movement, beginning in the early 1970s, is to get Americans,

obsessed with a romanticized image of Indians of the past, to pay attention to the concerns of American Indians today. See Deloria, *God is Red* (New York: Grosset and Dunlap, 1973), 39–56.

37. I side with critics who argue that imperialism is an important historical context here, too. Most political theorists mark the beginnings of U.S. imperialism in the post-bellum era, when the U.S. embodies advanced stages of capitalism and clearly exhibits the kinds of international capitalist relations used to define imperialism. However, Michael Rogin and Wai-chee Dimock have studied America's nascent imperialism in the antebellum era, focusing on what Rogin terms "internal imperialism" or what Dimock calls the "domestic articulation" of empire (Michael Rogin, *Fathers and Children: Andrew Jackson and the Subjugation of the American Indian* [New York: Vintage, 1976], 167; and Wai-chee Dimock, *Empire for Liberty: Melville and the Poetics of Individualism* [Princeton, N.J.: Princeton University Press, 1989], 10). Thomas R. Hietala discusses how imperialist expansionism created ideological problems for a democratic nation trying to claim that it was not building an empire but rather expanding a federalist republic (*Manifest Design: Anxious Aggrandizement in Late Jacksonian America* [Ithaca, N.Y.: Cornell University Press, 1985], 173–214).

38. Amy Kaplan illustrates how this racial ideology permeates not just the purportedly male world of politics but also the female world of domesticity in domestic fiction ("Manifest Domesticity," *American Literature* 70, no. 3 [September 1998]: 581–606). Dana Nelson shows that what she terms "national manhood," an ideological link between a brotherhood of white men and civic identity, shaped national identity in this period (*National Manhood: Capitalist Citizenship and the Imagined Fraternity of White Men* [Durham, N.C.: Duke University Press, 1998]). Similarly, in terms of citizenship rhetoric, Priscilla Wald demonstrates how antebellum legislation such as the Fugitive Slave Act codified a possessive investment in whiteness, and Eric Sundquist details how postbellum legislation such as *Plessy v. Ferguson* illustrates a racialization of citizenship, especially in the 1890s (Priscilla Wald, *Constituting Americans: Cultural Anxiety and Narrative Form* [Durham, N.C.: Duke University Press, 1995]; and Eric Sundquist, *To Wake the Nations: Race in the Making of American Literature* [Cambridge, Mass.: Harvard University Press, 1993]).

39. For a discussion of how the trope of American Indians as ghosts haunts the U.S. national imaginary, see Renee Bergland, *The National Uncanny: Indian Ghosts and American Subjects* (Hanover, N.H.: University Press of New England, 2000).

40. Peter LaFarge, "The Ballad of Ira Hayes," Edward B. Marks Music Company, 1962.

41. Cash, *Cash: The Autobiography*, 294–95.

42. Lewry, *A Johnny Cash Chronicle*, 44–45.

43. Cash, *Cash: The Autobiography*, 264–265.

44. John R. Cash, "Apache Tears," Southwind Music, 1964.

45. Stephen I. Thompson, "Forbidden Fruit: Interracial Love Affairs in Country Music," in *All That Glitters: Country Music in America*, ed. George H. Lewis (Bowling Green, Ohio: Bowling Green State University Popular Press, 1993), 262.

46. John R. Cash, "The Talking Leaves," Southwind Music, 1964.

47. Lewry, *A Johnny Cash Chronicle*, 67.

48. Melissa Meyer, *Thicker Than Water: The Origins of Blood as Symbol . . . and Ritual* (London: Routledge, 2005).

49. Pratt, *Imperial Eyes*, 7.

50. Sherman Alexie, *Reservation Blues* (New York: Warner Books, 1995).

51. Homi Bhabha, *The Location of Culture* (London: Routledge, 1994).

52. Josh Kun, *Audiotopia: Music, Race, and America* (Berkeley: University of California Press, 2005), 16, 23.

5. Man in Black

1. Leslie A. Fiedler, *The Return of the Vanishing American* (New York: Stein and Day, 1968).

2. On American Indian investments in country music, see Aaron A. Fox, *Real Country: Music and Language in Working-Class Culture* (Durham, N.C.: Duke University Press, 2004), 320; David W. Samuels, *Putting a Song on Top of It: Expression and Identity on the San Carlos Apache Reservation* (Tucson: University of Arizona Press, 2004).

3. Teresa A. Goddu, *Gothic America: Narrative, History, and Nation* (New York: Columbia University Press, 1997), 76.

4. Barbara Ching, *Wrong's What I Do Best: Hard Country and Contemporary Culture* (Oxford: Oxford University Press, 2001), 33; Peter Stallybrass and Allon White, *The Politics and Poetics of Transgression* (Ithaca, N.Y.: Cornell University Press, 1986), 3.

5. Barbara Ching and Gerald W. Creeds, eds., *Knowing Your Place: Rural Identity and Cultural Hierarchy* (New York: Routledge, 1997).

6. Jock Mackay, "Populist Ideology and Country Music," in *All That Glitters: Country Music in America*, ed. George H. Lewis (Bowling Green, Ohio: Bowling Green State University Popular Press, 1993), 285–304.

7. John Buckley, "Country Music and American Values," *Popular Music and Society* 6, no. 4 (1978): 293–301, reprinted in Lewis, *All That Glitters*, quote at 198; Michael Kimmel, *Manhood in America: A Cultural History*, 2nd ed. (New York: Oxford University Press, 2006), 231; Stephen I. Thompson, "Forbidden Fruit: Interracial Love Affairs in Country Music," *Popular Music and Society* 13, no. 2 (summer 1989): 23–37, reprinted in Lewis, *All That Glitters*, quote at 260; Chris Willman, *Rednecks & Bluenecks: The Politics of Country Music* (New York: New Press, 2005), 3, 7.

8. Bill C. Malone, *Don't Get above Your Raisin': Country Music and the Southern Working Class* (Urbana: University of Illinois Press, 2002), 211.

9. Willman, *Rednecks & Bluenecks*, 8, 16.

10. Ibid., 12.

11. Paul DiMaggio, Richard A. Peterson, and Jack Esco Jr., "Country Music: Ballad of the Silent Majority," in *The Sounds of Social Change: Studies in Popular Culture*, ed. R. Serge Denisoff and Richard A. Peterson (Chicago: Rand McNally, 1972), 38–55, quote at 51.

12. Fox, *Real Country*, 319.

13. Ibid., 320.

14. Mackay, "Populist Ideology and Country Music," 289, 290, 298.

15. Ibid., 301.

16. Ibid., 298–300.

17. Willman, *Rednecks & Bluenecks*, 12.

18. Ibid., 79.

19. Ibid., 248.

20. Ching, *Wrong's What I Do Best*, 41–44.

21. Willman, *Rednecks & Bluenecks*, 250–255.

22. Erin Siegal, "No Cash for the Rich! NYC Man/Woman in Black Bloc Prepare for the Republicans," *PR Web*, 23 August 2004, available at http://www.prweb.com/releases/2004/8/prwebxm1151658.ph.

23. Willman, *Rednecks & Bluenecks*, 253.

24. Ibid., 250.

25. Ibid.

26. Ibid., 251.

27. Ching, *Wrong's What I Do Best*, 4.

28. Michel de Certeau, *The Practice of Everyday Life* (Berkeley: University of California Press, 1984); Stuart Hall, "Notes on Deconstructing the Popular," in *Cultural Theory and Popular Culture: A Reader*, ed. John Storey, 2nd ed. (Athens: University of Georgia Press, 1998), 442–453; David Morley and Kuan-Hsing Chen, eds., *Stuart Hall: Cultural Dialogues in Cultural Studies* (London: Routledge, 1996); Angela McRobbie, *Postmodernism and Popular Culture* (London: Routledge, 1994); idem, *The Uses of Cultural Studies* (London: Sage, 2005).

29. Siegal, "No Cash for the Rich!"

30. Ibid.

31. Kirsten Anderberg, "Pompadour-and-Guitar Bloc Celebrates Johnny Cash's Legacy at the RNC!" 23 August 2004, available at http://santacruz.indymedia.org/newswire/display/11031/index.php.

32. Buckley, "Country Music and American Values," 201, 204; Paul DiMaggio, Richard A. Peterson, and Jack Escoe Jr., "Country Music: Ballad of the Silent Majority," in Denisoff and Peterson, *Sounds of Social Change*, 206; Jens Lund, "Country Music Goes to War: Song for the Red-Blooded American," *Popular Music and Society* 1 (1972): 224.

33. Anderberg, "Pompadour-and-Guitar Bloc."

34. Ibid.

35. John Carter Cash, *Anchored in Love: An Intimate Portrait of June Carter Cash* (Nashville: Thomas Nelson, 2007), 190.

36. Siegal, "No Cash for the Rich!"

37. Erin Siegal, e-mail to author, 29 August 2004.

38. Ibid., 1 September 2004.

39. Anderberg, "Pompadour-and-Guitar Bloc."

40. "Defending the Legacy of Johnny Cash?" *Infoshop.org*, 23 August 2004, available at http://www.infoshop.org/inews/stories.php?story=04/08/23/7909012.

41. "Row over 'Political' Cash Tribute," *BBC.com*, 28 August 2004, available at http://news.bbc.co.uk/2/hi/entertainment/3608956.stm.

42. "GOP Fete for Johnny Cash Stirs Debate," *New York Times on the Web*, 28 August 2004, available at http://www.nytimes.com/aponline/arts/AP-CVN-Johnny-Cash-Protest.html?ex=1094794172&ei=1&en=dd565ac202433305.

43. Joe Cook, online posting, *Infoshop.org*, 26 August 2004 (accessed 28 August 2004), available at http://www.infoshop.org/inews/stories.php?story=04/08/23/7909012.

44. Willman, *Rednecks & Bluenecks*, 252–253.

45. Bill Miller, *The Official JohnnyCash.com Member Newsletter*, 12 June 2007.

46. "Cash Supports POW/MIA Cause," *Veterans of Foreign Wars Magazine*, April 1989. "Strikers CASH in on Solidarity," *Teamster*, July/August 1993; reprinted in *The Johnny Cash & June Carter Cash International Fan Club Newsletter* (summer 1993): 25. The article recounts Cash wearing a Local 331 button and meeting with 140 strikers as he expressed support for their cause (in their eighteen-month strike) and denounced management's use of scabs.

47. Adam Sweeting, "Southern Comfort," reprinted in *The Johnny Cash & June Carter Cash International Fan Club Newsletter* (June 1989): 28.

48. Johnny Cash letter to Waylon Jennings, 1 June 1987, Country Music Foundation.

49. Bill Miller, *Cash: An American Man* (New York: Pocket Books, 2004), 8, 10.

50. Ching, *Wrong's What I Do Best*, 41.

51. Mackay, "Populist Ideology and Country Music," 295; Lewis, *All That Glitters*, 209.

52. Eric Lott, *Love and Theft: Blackface Minstrelsy and the American Working Class* (New York: Oxford University Press, 1993); W. T. Lhamon Jr., *Raising Cain: Blackface Performance from Jim Crow to Hip Hop* (Cambridge, Mass.: Harvard University Press, 1998); Michael Rogin, "The Two Declarations of American Independence," *Representations* 55 (summer 1996): 13–30.

53. Willman, *Rednecks & Bluenecks*, 251.

54. Colin Escott, *Lost Highway: The True Story of Country Music* (Washington, D.C.: Smithsonian Books, 2003), 118.

55. Benedict Anderson, *Imagined Communities: Reflections on the Origins and Spread of Nationalism* (London: Verso, 2006 [1983]).

56. For an examination of the ways that women's bodies have been used to signify abstract virtues, see Marina Warner, *Monuments and Maidens: The Allegory of the Female Form* (London: Weidenfeld and Nicolson, 1985).

57. Lewis, *All That Glitters*, 209; Buckley, "Country Music and American Values," 201.

58. Aaron A. Fox, "'Alternative' to What? *O Brother*, September 11, and the Politics of Country Music," in *Country Music Goes to War*, ed. Charles K. Wolfe and James E. Akenson (Lexington: University Press of Kentucky, 2005), 164–191; Anthony DeCurtis, "An American Original Returns," *New York Times*, 24 February 2002, available at http//query.nytimes.com/search/article-page.html?res=9B05E1D7163EF937A15751C0A9649C8B63.

59. Fox, "'Alternative' to What?" 173.

60. Ibid., 175.

61. Ibid., 175.

62. *Lost Highway*, part 3, Country Music Television, 8 March 2003.

6. The Gospel Road

1. Larry Linderman, "Penthouse Interview: Johnny Cash," *Penthouse*, August 1975, reprinted in *Ring of Fire: The Johnny Cash Reader*, ed. Michael Streissguth (Cambridge, Mass.: Da Capo, 2002), 152.

2. Anthony DeCurtis, "Johnny Cash Won't Back Down," *Rolling Stone*, 26 October 2000, 60.

3. *All-Star Tribute to Johnny Cash*, TNT, 1999.

4. Bill C. Malone, *Don't Get above Your Raisin': Country Music and the Southern Working Class* (Urbana: University of Chicago Press, 2002), 89–90.

5. Malone, *Don't Get above Your Raisin'*, 105. See also Roger Williams, *Sing a Sad Song: The Life of Hank Williams*, 2nd ed. (Urbana: University of Illinois Press, 1981 [1970]); Chet Flippo, *Your Cheatin' Heart: A Biography of Hank Williams* (New York: Simon and Schuster, 1981).

6. Malone, *Don't Get above Your Raisin'*, 89–116.

7. Jimmie N. Rogers and Stephen A. Smith, "Country Music and Organized Religion," in *All That Glitters: Country Music in America*, ed. George H. Lewis (Bowling Green, Ohio: Bowling Green State University Popular Press, 1993), 270–284.

8. Jens Lund, "Fundamentalism, Racism, and Political Reaction in Country Music," in *The Sounds of Social Change*, ed. R. Serge Denisoff and Richard A. Peterson (Chicago: Rand McNally, 1972), 79–91; Ellen K. Coughlin, "Religion Scholars Mine Popular Music for Intimations of the Divine," *Chronicle of Higher Education*, 19 April 1989, A4, A9; John Michael Spencer, "Overview of American Popular Music in a Theological Perspective," *Black Sacred Music* 8, no. 1 (spring 1994): 205–217.

9. Rogers and Smith, "Country Music and Organized Religion," 276. See also idem, "Political Culture and the Rhetoric of Country Music: A Revisionist Interpretation," in *Politics in Familiar Contexts: Projecting Politics through Popular Media*, ed. Robert L. Savage and Dan Nimmo (Norwood, N.J.: Ablex, 1990), 185–198.

10. Donald G. Matthews, *Religion in the Old South* (Chicago: University of Chicago Press, 1977), 240.

11. John Lee Eighmy, *Churches in Cultural Captivity: A History of Social Attitudes of Southern Baptists* (Knoxville: University of Tennessee Press, 1987), 201.

12. Rogers and Smith, "Country Music and Organized Religion," 278.

13. Don Cusic, *The Sound of Light: A History of Gospel Music* (Bowling Green, Ohio: Bowling Green State University Popular Press, 1990), ii. See also Paul Oliver, *Songsters and Saints* (Cambridge: Cambridge University Press, 1984).

14. Tex Sample, *White Soul: Country Music, the Church, and Working Americans* (Nashville: Abingdon, 1996).

15. David Fillingim, *Redneck Liberation: Country Music as Theology* (Macon, Ga.: Mercer University Press, 2003), 41–42.

16. Mary A. Bufwack and Robert K. Oermann, *Finding Her Voice: The Illustrated History of Women in Country Music* (New York: Henry Holt, 1993), 198.

17. Malone, *Don't Get above Your Raisin'*, 89–116.

18. Bufwack and Oermann, *Finding Her Voice*, 203.

19. Malone, *Don't Get above Your Raisin'*, 89.

20. *Unearthed* liner notes, 31; *American IV* liner notes.

21. *American IV* liner notes.

22. *Unearthed* liner notes, 31.

23. Luke Torn, "Still Keeping His Eyes Wide Open," *Wall Street Journal*, 15 November 2002), W11.

24. Johnny Cash, *Man in Black* (Grand Rapids, Mich.: Zondervan, 1975), 48.

25. *Unearthed* liner notes, 83, 89.

26. Rosanne Cash, interview with Larry King, *Larry King Live*, CNN, 10 June 2005; cited in Gayle F. Wald, *Shout, Sister, Shout! The Untold Story of Rock-and-Roll Trailblazer Sister Rosetta Tharpe* (Boston: Beacon, 2007), 70.

27. *Unchained* liner notes.

28. Charles Paul Conn, *The New Johnny Cash* (Old Tappan, N.J.: Fleming H. Revell, 1973), 21.

29. Malone, *Don't Get above Your Raisin'*, 110.

30. Cash, *Man in Black*, 13.

31. Ibid., 25, 27; Dolly Parton, *My Life and Other Unfinished Business* (New York: HarperCollins, 1994); Alanna Nash, *Dolly: The Biography* (New York: Rowman and Littlefield, 2002 [1994]).

32. Cash, *Man in Black*, 26.

33. Ibid., 33.

34. Stephen Tucker argues for the ongoing impact of Pentecostalism on Cash's music as well as on other country singers such as Tammy Wynette. See Stephen Tucker, "Pentecostalism and Popular Culture in the South: A Study of Four Musicians," *Journal of Popular Culture* 16, no. 3 (1982): 68–80.

35. Conn, *The New Johnny Cash*, 21.

36. Jack E. Weller, *Yesterday's People: Life in Contemporary Appalachia* (Lexington: University Press of Kentucky, 1965), 121.

37. Cash, *Man in Black*, 47–48.

38. Johnny Cash, with Patrick Carr, *Cash: The Autobiography* (New York: HarperCollins, 1997), 39.

39. Jan Hoffman, "Rosanne Cash Walks Her Own Line," in Lewis, *All That Glitters*, 332.

40. Cash, *Cash: The Autobiography*, 147.

41. Mark Zwonitzer with Charles Hirshberg, *Will You Miss Me When I'm Gone? The Carter Family and Their Legacy in American Music* (New York: Simon and Schuster, 2002), 358.

42. Cash, *Man in Black*, 147.

43. Cash, *Cash: The Autobiography*, 230–232.

44. Ibid., 174.

45. Marshall Grant, *I Was There When It Happened: My Life with Johnny Cash* (Nashville: Cumberland House, 2006); Michael Streissguth, *Johnny Cash: The Biography* (New York: Da Capo, 2006), 139, 87.

46. John Carter Cash, *Anchored in Love: An Intimate Portrait of June Carter Cash* (Nashville: Thomas Nelson, 2007), 130–131.

47. Kurt Loder, "The Final Interview," in *Cash: An American Man*, ed. Bill Miller (New York: CMT and Pocket Books, 2004), 76–79.

48. Cash, *Man in Black*, 197–199.

49. Johnny Cash, with Billy Zeoli and Al Hartley, *Hello, I'm Johnny Cash* (Old Tappan, N.J.: Fleming H. Revell, 1976), 25. The comic book is a Spire Christian Comic book.

50. "El Viaje Misterioso De Nuestro Jomer," *The Simpsons*, Fox, 5 January 1997.

51. Nick Tosches, *Country: The Twisted Roots of Rock 'n' Roll* (New York: Da Capo, 1996 [1977]), 135–136.

52. Conn, *The New Johnny Cash*, 40.

53. Kris Kristofferson, concert, Tallahassee, Fla., 24 February 2007.

54. Cash, *Cash: The Autobiography*, 281.

55. Cornel West, *Democracy Matters: Winning the Fight against Imperialism* (New York: Penguin, 2004).

56. Larry Eskridge, "'One Way': Billy Graham, the Jesus Generation, and the Idea of an Evangelical Youth Culture," *Church History* 67, no. 1 (March 1998): 83–106; Billy Graham, *Just as I Am: The Autobiography of Billy Graham* (New York: HarperCollins, 1997 [1971]).

57. Peter McCabe and Jack Killion, "Interview with Johnny Cash," *Country Music* (May 1973): 24–31.

58. Dave Urbanski, *The Man Comes Around: The Spiritual Journey of Johnny Cash* (Lake Mary, Fla.: Relevant Books, 2003), xxii.

59. Laura Sessions Stepp, "A Family at Cross-Purposes: Billy Graham's Sons Argue over a Final Resting Place," *Washington Post*, 13 December 2006 (accessed 14 December 2006), available at http://www.washingtonpost.com/wp- dyn/content/article/2006/12/12/AR2006121201338_pf.html.

60. Heather Hendershot, *Shaking the World for Jesus: Media and Conservative Evangelical Culture* (Chicago: University of Chicago Press, 2004). On the state of religion in America during this period, see Amanda Porterfield, *The Transformation of American Religion: The Story of a Late-Twentieth-Century Awakening* (Oxford: Oxford University Press, 2001).

61. *Unearthed* liner notes, 90.

62. Patrick Carr, "Johnny Cash's Freedom," *Journal of Country Music* (April 1979): 24–28.

63. Johnny Cash, interview with Larry King, *Larry King Live*, CNN, 26 November 2002.

64. Cash, *Cash: The Autobiography*, 402.

65. *Inside Fame: Johnny Cash*, Country Music Television, 28 March 2003.

66. Urbanski, *The Man Comes Around*, xxi.

67. *The Gospel Road*, directed by Robert Elfstrom, performed by Johnny Cash and June Carter Cash, Luther Corporation 1972, Twentieth Century Fox 1971, DVD, Twentieth Century Fox Home Entertainment 2005.

68. "The New Rebel Cry: Jesus Is Coming!" *Time*, 21 June 1971.

69. *The Gospel Road*.

70. Rogers and Smith, "Country Music and Organized Religion," 274.

71. John R. Cash, *The Man in White* (New York: HarperCollins, 1986), 6.

72. Ibid., 8.

73. Ibid.

74. Ibid., 5.

75. Rogers and Smith, "Country Music and Organized Religion."

76. Cash, *The Man in White*, 2–3. Hereafter, page numbers in Cash's novel are given parenthetically in the text.

Conclusion

1. Rick Rubin, liner notes, *American V: A Hundred Highways*, American Recordings, 2006.

2. Rick Rubin, liner notes, *Unearthed*, American Recordings, 2003, 50.

3. Sut Jhally, "Image-Based Culture: Advertising and Popular Culture," in *Gender, Race, and Class in Media: A Text-Reader*, ed. Gail Dines and Jean M. Humez, 2nd ed. (Thousand Oaks, Calif.: Sage, 2003), 249–257.

Works Cited

Adorno, Theodor. "On Popular Music." In *Cultural Theory and Popular Culture: A Reader*, ed. John Storey, 2nd ed., 197–209. Athens: University of Georgia Press, 1998.

Alexie, Sherman. *Reservation Blues*. New York: Warner Books, 1995.

All-Star Tribute to Johnny Cash. TNT, 1999.

Anderberg, Kirsten. "Pompadour-and-Guitar Bloc Celebrates Johnny Cash's Legacy at the RNC!" 23 August 2004, http://santacruz.indymedia.org/newswire/display/11031/index.php.

Anderson, Benedict. *Imagined Communities: Reflections on the Origins and Spread of Nationalism*. London: Verso, 2006 [1983].

Batchelor, Bob, ed. *Literary Cash: Writings Inspired by the Legendary Johnny Cash*. Dallas: Benbella Books, 2006.

Bederman, Gail. *Manliness and Civilization: A Cultural History of Gender and Race in the United States, 1880–1917*. Chicago: University of Chicago Press, 1995.

Bercovitch, Sacvan. *The Office of "The Scarlet Letter."* Baltimore, Md.: Johns Hopkins University Press, 1991.

———. *The Rites of Assent: Transformations in the Symbolic Construction of America*. New York: Routledge, 1993.

Bergland, Renee. *The National Uncanny: Indian Ghosts and American Subjects*. Hanover, N.H.: University Press of New England, 2000.

Bertrand, Michael T. "I Don't Think Hank Done It That Way: Elvis, Country Music, and the Reconstruction of Southern Masculinity." In *A Boy Named Sue: Gender and Country Music*, ed. Kristine M. McCusker and Diane Pecknold, 59–85. Jackson: University Press of Mississippi, 2004.

———. *Race, Rock, and Elvis*. Urbana: University of Illinois Press, 2000.

The Best of Hootenanny. DVD. Shout Factory, 13 October 2006.

Bhabha, Homi. *The Location of Culture.* London: Routledge, 1994.

Bordo, Susan. *The Male Body: A New Look at Men in Public and in Private.* New York: Farrar, Straus and Giroux, 2000.

Brackett, David. *Interpreting Popular Music.* 2nd ed. Berkeley: University of California Press, 2000.

Brennan, Timothy. *At Home in the World: Cosmopolitanism Now.* Cambridge, Mass.: Harvard University Press, 1997.

Bromell, Nick. *Tomorrow Never Knows: Rock and Psychedelics in the 1960s.* Chicago: University of Chicago Press, 2000.

Buckley, John. "Country Music and American Values." *Popular Music and Society* 6, no. 4 (1978): 293–301.

Bufwack, Mary A., and Robert K. Oermann. *Finding Her Voice: The Illustrated History of Women in Country Music.* New York: Crown, 1993.

———. *Finding Her Voice: The Saga of Women in Country Music.* New York: Crown, 1993.

———. *Finding Her Voice: Women in Country Music, 1800–2000.* Nashville: Country Music Foundation/Vanderbilt University Press, 2003.

Caldwell, John. "Prime-Time Fiction Theorizes the Docu-Real." In *Reality Squared: Televisual Discourse on the Real,* ed. James Friedman, 259–292. New Brunswick, N.J.: Rutgers University Press, 2002.

Campbell, Garth. *Johnny Cash: He Walked the Line, 1932–2003.* London: John Blake, 2003.

The Carter Family: Will the Circle Be Unbroken. PBS, 2005.

Carr, Patrick. "Johnny Cash's Freedom." *Journal of Country Music* (April 1979): 24–28.

Cash, John Carter. *Anchored in Love: An Intimate Portrait of June Carter Cash.* Nashville: Thomas Nelson, 2007.

Cash, John R. *The Man in White.* New York: HarperCollins, 1986.

Cash, Johnny. Interview with Larry King. *Larry King Live.* CNN, 26 November 2002.

———. *Man in Black.* Grand Rapids, Mich.: Zondervan, 1975.

Cash, Johnny, with Patrick Carr. *Cash: The Autobiography.* New York: HarperCollins, 1997.

Cash, Johnny, with Billy Zeoli and Al Hartley. *Hello, I'm Johnny Cash.* Old Tappan, N.J.: Fleming H. Revell, 1976.

Cash, June Carter. *Among My Klediments.* Grand Rapids, Mich.: Zondervan, 1979.

———. *From the Heart.* New York: Prentice Hall, 1987.

Cash, Rosanne. Interview with Larry King. *Larry King Live.* CNN, 10 June 2005.

Cash, Vivian, with Ann Sharpsteen. *I Walked the Line: My Life with Johnny.* New York: Scribner's, 2007.

Cash, Wilber J. *The Mind of the South.* New York: Knopf, 1941.

Ching, Barbara. *Wrong's What I Do Best: Hard Country Music and Contemporary Culture.* New York: Oxford University Press, 2001.

Ching, Barbara, and Gerald W. Creeds, eds. *Knowing Your Place: Rural Identity and Cultural Hierarchy.* New York: Routledge, 1997.

Coates, Norma. "(R)evolution Now? Rock and the Political Potential of Gender." In *Sexing the Groove: Popular Music and Gender,* ed. Sheila Whiteley, 50–64. London: Routledge, 1997.

Cobb, James C. "Country Music and the 'Southernization' of America." In *All That Glitters: Country Music in America*, ed. George H. Lewis, 75–86. Bowling Green, Ohio: Bowling Green State University Popular Press, 1993.

Cohen, Ronald D. *Rainbow Quest: The Folk Music Revival & American Society, 1940–1970*. Amherst: University of Massachusetts Press, 2002.

Conn, Charles Paul. *The New Johnny Cash*. Old Tappan, N.J.: Fleming H. Revell, 1973.

Connell, R. W. *Maculinities*. 2nd ed. Berkeley: University of California Press, 2005.

Controversy: Johnny Cash vs. Music Row. Country Music Television, 16 July 2004.

Coontz, Stephanie. *The Way We Never Were: American Families and the Nostalgia Trap*. New York: Basic Books, 1992.

Cott, Nancy F. *Public Vows: A History of Marriage and the Nation*. Cambridge, Mass.: Harvard University Press, 2000.

Coughlin, Ellen K. "Religion Scholars Mine Popular Music for Intimations of the Divine." *Chronicle of Higher Education*, 19 April 1989, A4, A9.

Cowie, Jefferson, and Lauren Boehm. "Dead Man's Town: 'Born in the U.S.A.,' Social History, and Working-Class Identity." *American Quarterly* 58, no. 2 (June 2006): 353–378.

Cullen, Jim. *Born in the U.S.A.: Bruce Springsteen and the American Tradition*. Hanover, N.H.: University Press of New England, 2005.

Cusic, Don. *Johnny Cash: The Songs*. New York: Thunder's Mouth, 2004.

———. *The Sound of Light: A History of Gospel Music*. Bowling Green, Ohio: Bowling Green State University Popular Press, 1990.

D'Acci, Julie. "Gender, Representation and Television." In *Television Studies*, ed. Toby Miller, 91–94. London: British Film Institute, 2002.

Danker, Frederick E. "The Repertory and Style of a Country Singer: Johnny Cash." *Journal of American Folklore* 85, no. 338 (October–December 1971): 309–329.

Dawidoff, Nicholas. *In the Country of Country: A Journey to the Roots of American Music*. New York: Vintage, 1998.

Davidson, Cathy N., and Jessamyn Hatcher, eds. *No More Separate Spheres!* Durham, N.C.: Duke University Press, 2002.

de Certeau, Michel. *The Practice of Everyday Life*. Berkeley: University of California Press, 1984.

DeCurtis, Anthony. "An American Original Returns." *New York Times*, 24 February 2002. Available at http//query.nytimes.com/search/article-page.html?res=9B05E1D7163 EF937A15751C0A9649C8B63.

———. "Johnny Cash Won't Back Down." *Rolling Stone*, 26 October 2000, 60.

"Defending the Legacy of Johnny Cash?" Infoshop.org, 23 August 2004. Available at http://www.infoshop.org/inews/stories.php?story=04/08/23/7909012 and at http://www.kirstenanderberg.com.

Deloria, Vine, Jr. *Custer Died for Your Sins*. New York: Avon, 1969.

———. *God Is Red*. New York: Grosset and Dunlap, 1973.

DiMaggio, Paul, Richard A. Peterson, and Jack Esco Jr. "Country Music: Ballad of the Silent Majority." In *The Sounds of Social Change: Studies in Popular Culture*, ed. R. Serge Denisoff and Richard A. Peterson, 38–55. Chicago: Rand McNally, 1972.

Dimock, Wai-chee. *Empire for Liberty: Melville and the Poetics of Individualism*. Princeton, N.J.: Princeton University Press, 1989.

Dippie, Brian W. *The Vanishing American: White Attitudes and U.S. Indian Policy.* Middletown, Conn.: Wesleyan University Press, 1982.

Doggett, Peter. *Are You Ready for the Country: Elvis, Dylan, Parsons, and the Roots of Country Rock.* New York: Penguin, 2000.

Echard, William. *Neil Young and the Poetics of Energy.* Bloomington: Indiana University Press, 2005.

Eighmy, John Lee. *Churches in Cultural Captivity: A History of Social Attitudes of Southern Baptists.* Knoxville: University of Tennessee Press, 1987.

"El Viaje Misterioso De Nuestro Jomer." *The Simpsons.* Fox, 5 January 1997.

Elfstrom, Robert, dir. *Johnny Cash: The Man, His World, and His Music.* 1969. DVD. Sanctuary Records Group, 2002.

Escott, Colin. *Lost Highway: The True Story of Country Music.* Washington, D.C.: Smithsonian Books, 2003.

Eskridge, Larry. "'One Way': Billy Graham, the Jesus Generation, and the Idea of an Evangelical Youth Culture." *Church History* 67, no. 1 (March 1998): 83–106.

Eyerman, Ron, and Andrew Jamison, eds. *Music and Social Movements: Mobilizing Traditions in the Twentieth Century.* Cambridge: Cambridge University Press, 1998.

Fiedler, Leslie A. *The Return of the Vanishing American.* New York: Stein and Day, 1968.

Filene, Benjamin. *Romancing the Folk: Public Memory & American Roots Music.* Chapel Hill, N.C.: University of North Carolina Press, 2000.

Fillingim, David. *Redneck Liberation: Country Music as Theology.* Macon, Ga.: Mercer University Press, 2003.

Fine, Jason, ed. *Cash: By the Editors of Rolling Stone.* New York: Crown, 2004.

Flippo, Chet. *Your Cheatin' Heart: A Biography of Hank Williams.* New York: Simon and Schuster, 1981.

Fox, Aaron A. "'Alternative' to What? O *Brother,* September 11, and the Politics of Country Music." In *Country Music Goes to War,* ed. Charles K. Wolfe and James E. Akenson, 164–191. Lexington: University Press of Kentucky, 2005.

———. "The Jukebox of History: Narratives of Loss and Desire in the Discourse of Country Music." *Popular Music* 11 (1992): 53–72.

———. *Real Country: Music and Language in Working-Class Culture.* Durham, N.C.: Duke University Press, 2004.

Fox, Pamela. "Recycled Trash: Gender and Authenticity in Country Music Autobiography." *American Quarterly* 50, no. 2 (June 1998): 234–266.

Frey, William H., Bill Abresch, and Jonathan Yeasting. *America by the Numbers: A Field Guide to the U.S. Population.* New York: New Press, 2001.

Frith, Simon. *Performing Rites: On the Value of Popular Music.* Cambridge, Mass.: Harvard University Press, 1996.

———. *Sound Effects: Youth, Leisure and the Politics of Rock.* London: Constable, 1983.

Garman, Bryan K. *Race of Singers: Whitman's Working Class Hero from Guthrie to Springsteen.* Chapel Hill: University of North Carolina Press, 2000.

Garofalo, Reebee, ed. *Rockin' the Boat: Mass Music and Mass Movements.* Cambridge, Mass.: South End, 1992.

Geertz, Clifford. *The Interpretation of Cultures.* New York: Basic Books, 1973.

Goddu, Teresa A. *Gothic America: Narrative, History, and Nation*. New York: Columbia University Press, 1997.

"GOP Fete for Johnny Cash Stirs Debate." *New York Times on the Web*, 28 August 2004. Available at http://www.nytimes.com/aponline/arts/AP-CVN-Johnny-Cash-Protest. html?ex=1094794172&ei=1&en=dd565ac202433305.

The Gospel Road. Directed by Robert Elfstrom. Performed by Johnny Cash and June Carter Cash. DVD. Twentieth Century Fox Home Entertainment, 2005 [1972].

Graham, Billy. *Just as I Am: The Autobiography of Billy Graham*. 2nd ed. New York: HarperCollins, 1997.

Gramsci, Antonio. *Selections from Prison Notebooks*. Edited and translated by Quintin Hoare and Geoffrey Nowell-Smith. London: Lawrence and Wishart, 1971.

Grant, Marshall, with Chris Zar. *I Was There When It Happened: My Life with Johnny Cash*. Nashville: Cumberland House, 2006.

Gray, Madison J. "3-Day Johnny Cash Auction in New York Rakes in Nearly $4 Million." *Associated Press State & Local Wire*, 16 September 2004.

Green, Blake. "Johnny Cash—The Man, the Legend." *The Legend I* (1972): 4–5.

Grossberg, Lawrence. "Reflections of a Disappointed Popular Music Scholar." In *Rock over the Edge: Transformations in Popular Music Culture*, ed. R Beebe, D. Fulbrook, and B. Saunders, 25–59. Durham, N.C.: Duke University Press, 2002.

Hall, Stuart. "Notes on Deconstructing 'the Popular'." In *Cultural Theory and Popular Culture: A Reader*, ed. John Storey, 2nd ed., 442–453. Athens: University of Georgia Press, 1998.

———. *Stuart Hall: Cultural Dialogues in Cultural Studies*. Edited by David Morley and Kuan-Hsing Chen. London: Routledge, 1996.

Hall, Stuart, and Paddy Whannel. *The Popular Arts*. London: Hutchinson, 1964.

Halperin, Shirley. "Music Man." *Entertainment Weekly* 935, 25 May 2007, 16.

Hasty, Katie. "Cash Earns First No. 1 Album since 1969." Billboard.com, 12 July 2006. Available at http://www.billboard.com/bbcom/news/article_display.jsp?vnu_content _id=1002837777.

Hendershot, Heather. *Shaking the World for Jesus: Media and Conservative Evangelical Culture*. Chicago: University of Chicago Press, 2004.

Hietala, Thomas R. *Manifest Design: Anxious Aggrandizement in Late Jacksonian America*. Ithaca, N.Y.: Cornell University Press, 1985.

Hoffman, Jan. "Rosanne Cash Walks Her Own Line." In *All That Glitters: Country Music in America*, ed. George H. Lewis, 329–338. Bowling Green, Ohio: Bowling Green State University Popular Press, 1993.

Huyssen, Andreas. *After the Great Divide: Modernism, Mass Culture, Postmodernism*. Bloomington: Indiana University Press, 1986.

Inside Fame: Johnny Cash. Country Music Television, 28 March 2003.

Jensen, Joli. *The Nashville Sound: Authenticity, Commercialization, and Country Music*. Nashville: Country Music Foundation/Vanderbilt University Press, 1998.

———. "Patsy Cline's Crossovers." In *A Boy Named Sue: Gender and Country Music*, ed. Kristine M. McCusker and Diane Pecknold, 107–131. Jackson: University Press of Mississippi, 2004.

Jhally, Sut. "Image-Based Culture: Advertising and Popular Culture." In *Gender, Race, and Class in Media: A Text-Reader*, ed. Gail Dines and Jean M. Humez, 2nd ed., 249–257. Thousand Oaks, Calif.: Sage, 2003.

"Johnny Cash Album Sales Soar." *Launch Radio Networks*, 18 November 2003. Available at http://launch.yahoo.com/read/news.asp?contentID=214647.

"Johnny Cash: Fire at Cash's Former Home Still under Investigation." CMT.com, 17 April 2007. Available at http://www.cmt.com/artists/news/1556874/20070411/cash_johnny.jhtml.

"Johnny Cash: Original Gangsta." MTVNews.com 2 February 2007. Available at http://www.mtv.com/bands/c/cash_johnny/news_vma_feature/.

Kaplan, Amy. "Manifest Domesticity." *American Literature* 70, no. 3 (September 1998): 581–606.

Kimmel, Michael. *The Gendered Society*. New York: Oxford University Press, 2000.

———. *Manhood in America: A Cultural History*. 2nd ed. New York: Oxford University Press, 2006.

Kristofferson, Kris, perf. Concert. Tallahassee, Fla., 24 February 2007.

Kun, Josh. *Audiotopia: Music, Race, and America*. Berkeley: University of California Press, 2005.

Lankford, Ronald D., Jr. *Folk Music USA: The Changing Voice of Protest*. New York: Schirmer Trade Books, 2005.

Leppert, Richard, and George Lipsitz. "Age, the Boy, and Experience in the Music of Hank Williams." In *All That Glitters: Country Music in America*, ed. George H. Lewis, 22–37. Bowling Green, Ohio: Bowling Green State University Press, 1993.

Leverenz, David. *Manhood and the American Renaissance*. Ithaca, N.Y.: Cornell University Press, 1989.

———. "Manhood, Class, and the American Renaissance." In *Background Readings for Teachers of American Literature*, ed. Venetria Patton, 261–269. Boston: Bedford/St. Martin's, 2006.

Levine, Robert. "Cash Film's Missing Ingredient: Religion." *New York Times*, 4 March 2006. Available at http://www.nytimes.com/2006/03/04/movies/MoviesFeatures/04cash.html.

Lewis, George. "Tension, Conflict, and Contradiction in Country Music." In *All That Glitters: Country Music in America*, ed. George H. Lewis, 208–220. Bowling Green, Ohio: Bowling Green State University Popular Press, 1993.

Lewry, Peter. *A Johnny Cash Chronicle: I've Been Everywhere*. London: Helter Skelter, 2001.

Lhamon, W. T., Jr. *Raising Cain: Blackface Performance from Jim Crow to Hip Hop*. Cambridge, Mass.: Harvard University Press, 1998.

Lipsitz, George. *Dangerous Crossroads: Popular Music, Postmodernism, and the Poetics of Place*. New York: Verso, 1994.

———. *Time Passages: Collective Memory and American Popular Culture*. Minneapolis: University of Minnesota Press, 1990.

Loder, Kurt. "The Final Interview." In *Cash: An American Man*, ed. Bill Miller, 76–79. New York: CMT and Pocket Books, 2004.

Lost Highway: The Story of Country Music. Part 1. Country Music Television, 22 February 2003.

Lost Highway: The Story of Country Music. Part 3. Country Music Television, 8 March 2003.

Lott, Eric. *Love and Theft: Blackface Minstrelsy and the American Working Class*. New York: Oxford University Press, 1993.

Lund, Jens. "Country Music Goes to War: Song for the Red-Blooded American." *Popular Music and Society* 1 (1972): 221–223.

————. "Fundamentalism, Racism, and Political Reaction in Country Music." In *The Sounds of Social Change*, ed. R. Serge Denisoff and Richard A. Peterson, 79–91. Chicago: Rand McNally, 1972.

Mackay, Jock. "Populist Ideology and Country Music." In *All That Glitters: Country Music in America*, ed. George H. Lewis, 285–304. Bowling Green, Ohio: Bowling Green State University Popular Press, 1993.

Malone, Bill C. *Country Music U.S.A.: A Fifty-Year History*. Austin: University of Texas Press, 1968.

————. *Don't Get above Your Raisin': Country Music and the Southern Working Class*. Urbana: University of Illinois Press, 2002.

————. *Singing Cowboys and Musical Mountaineers: Southern Culture and the Roots of Country Music*. 2nd ed. Athens: University of Georgia Press, 2003.

Mansfield, Brian. "Even in Death, Man in Black Looms Large." *USA Today*, 4–6 November 2005, national ed., sec. A: 1ff.

————. *Ring of Fire: A Tribute to Johnny Cash*. Nashville: Rutledge Hill, 2003.

Marcus, Greil. *Mystery Train: Images of America in Rock 'n' Roll Music*. New York: Plume, 1997.

Matthews, Donald G. *Religion in the Old South*. Chicago: University of Chicago Press, 1977.

May, Elaine Tyler. *Homeward Bound: American Families in the Cold War Era*. New York: Basic Books, 1988.

McCabe, Peter, and Jack Killion. "Interview with Johnny Cash." *Country Music*, May 1973, 24–31.

McCusker, Kristine M., and Diane Pecknold, eds. *A Boy Named Sue: Gender and Country Music*. Jackson: University of Mississippi Press, 2004.

McRobbie, Angela. *Postmodernism and Popular Culture*. London: Routledge, 1994.

————. *The Uses of Cultural Studies*. London: Sage, 2005.

Meyer, Melissa. *Thicker Than Water: The Origins of Blood as Symbol . . . And Ritual*. London: Routledge, 2005.

Miller, Bill, ed. *Cash: An American Man*. New York: CMT and Pocket Books, 2004.

————. *The Official JohnnyCash.com Member Newsletter*, 12 June 2007.

Miller, Stephen. *Johnny Cash: The Life of an American Icon*. London: Omnibus, 2003.

Miller, Toby. *Sportsex*. Philadelphia: Temple University Press, 2002.

Morrison, Craig. *Go Cat Go! Rockabilly Music and Its Makers*. Urbana: University of Illinois Press, 1998.

Nash, Alanna. *Dolly: The Biography*. 2nd ed. New York: Rowman and Littlefield, 2002.

Nelson, Dana. *National Manhood: Capitalist Citizenship and the Imagined Fraternity of White Men*. Durham, N.C.: Duke University Press, 1998.

Oliver, Paul. *Songsters and Saints*. Cambridge: Cambridge University Press, 1984.

Ortega, Teresa. "'My Name Is Sue! How Do You Do?': Johnny Cash as Lesbian Icon." *South Atlantic Quarterly* 94 (winter 1995): 259–272.

Palmer, Gareth. "Bruce Springsteen and Masculinity." In *Sexing the Groove: Popular Music and Gender*, ed. Sheila Whiteley, 100–117. London: Routledge, 1997.

Parrish, Timothy. *Walking Blues: Making Americans from Emerson to Elvis.* Amherst: University of Massachusetts Press, 2001.

Parton, Dolly. *My Life and Other Unfinished Business.* New York: HarperCollins, 1994.

Pearce, Roy Harvey. *Savagism and Civilization: A Study of the Indian and the American Mind.* Baltimore, Md.: Johns Hopkins University Press, 1967.

Pease, Donald E., ed. *National Identities and Post-Americanist Narratives.* Durham, N.C.: Duke University Press, 1994.

Pecknold, Diane. "'I Wanna Play House': Configurations of Masculinity in the Nashville Sound Era." In *A Boy Named Sue: Gender and Country Music,* ed. Kristine M. McCusker and Diane Pecknold, 86–106. Jackson: University of Mississippi Press, 2004.

———. *The Selling Sound: The Rise of the Country Music Industry.* Durham, N.C.: Duke University Press, 2007.

Peddie, Ian, ed. *The Resisting Muse: Popular Music and Social Protest.* Aldershot, Hampshire: Ashgate, 2006.

Peterson, Richard. *Creating Country Music: Fabricating Authenticity.* Chicago: University of Chicago Press, 1997.

Poore, Billy. *Rockabilly: A Forty-Year Journey.* Milwaukee, Wis.: Hal Leonard, 1998.

Porterfield, Amanda. *The Transformation of American Religion: The Story of a Late-Twentieth-Century Awakening.* Oxford: Oxford University Press, 2001.

Pratt, Mary Louise. *Imperial Eyes: Travel Writing and Transculturation.* London: Routledge, 1992.

Radway, Janice. "What's in a Name? Presidential Address to the American Studies Association, 20 November 1998." *American Quarterly* 51, no. 1 (March 1999): 1–32.

Ridin' the Rails: The Great American Train Story. Directed by Nicholas Webster. Webster/Rivkin Productions, 1974.

Roediger, David. *The Wages of Whiteness: Race and the Making of the American Working Class.* New York: Verso, 1991.

Rogers, Jimmie N., and Stephen A. Smith. "Country Music and Organized Religion." In *All That Glitters: Country Music in America,* ed. George H. Lewis, 270–284. Bowling Green, Ohio: Bowling Green State University Popular Press, 1993.

Rogin, Michael. *Fathers and Children: Andrew Jackson and the Subjugation of the American Indian.* New York: Vintage, 1976.

———. "The Two Declarations of American Independence." *Representations* 55 (summer 1996): 13–30.

Romero, Lora. "Vanishing Americans: Gender, Empire, and New Historicism." *American Literature* 63 (1991): 386–404.

"Row over 'Political' Cash Tribute." BBC, 28 August 2004. Available at http://news.bbc.co.uk/2/hi/entertainment/3608956.stm.

Rowe, John Carlos. *Post-Nationalist American Studies.* Berkeley: University of California Press, 2000.

Sample, Tex. *White Soul: Country Music, the Church, and Working Americans.* Nashville: Abingdon, 1996.

Samuels, David W. *Putting a Song on Top of It: Expression and Identity on the San Carlos Apache Reservation.* Tucson: University of Arizona Press, 2004.

Sanjek, David. Foreword to *A Boy Named Sue: Gender and Country Music*, ed. Kristine M. McCusker and Diane Pecknold, vii–xv. Jackson: University Press of Mississippi, 2004.

Shank, Barry. *Dissonant Identities: The Rock 'n' Roll Scene in Austin, Texas*. Hanover, N.H.: University Press of New England, 1994.

————. "'That Wild Mercury Sound': Bob Dylan and the Illusion of American Culture." *boundary 2* 29, no. 1 (2002): 97–123.

Shorter, Edward. *The Making of the Modern Family*. New York: Basic Books, 1975.

Siegal, Erin. "No Cash for the Rich! NYC Man/Woman in Black Bloc Prepare for the Republicans." *PR Web*, 23 August 2004 (accessed on 28 August 2004). Available at http://www.prweb.com/releases/2004/8/prwebxm1151658.ph.

Simmons, Sylvie. "The Gunslinger." *Mojo* (November 2004): 70–78, 83–88.

Slotkin, Richard. *Regeneration through Violence: The Mythology of the American Frontier, 1600–1800*. Middletown, Conn.: Wesleyan University Press, 1973.

Smith, John L. *The Johnny Cash Discography*. Westport, Conn.: Greenwood, 1984.

————. *The Johnny Cash Discography, 1984–1993*. Wesport, Conn.: Greenwood, 1994.

————. *The Johnny Cash Record Catalog*. Westport, Conn.: Greenwood, 1994.

Smith, Stephen A., and Jimmie N. Rogers. "Political Culture and the Rhetoric of Country Music: A Revisionist Interpretation." In *Politics in Familiar Contexts: Projecting Politics through Popular Media*, ed. Robert L. Savage and Dan Nimmo, 185–98. Norwood, N.J.: Ablex, 1990.

Spencer, John Michael. "Overview of American Popular Music in a Theological Perspective." *Black Sacred Music* 8, no. 1 (spring 1994): 205–217.

Stacey, Judith. *Brave New Families: Stories of Domestic Upheaval in Late Twentieth Century America*. New York: Basic Books, 1990.

————. *In the Name of the Family: Rethinking Family Values in the Postmodern Age*. Boston: Beacon, 1996.

Stallybrass, Peter, and Allon White. *The Politics and Poetics of Transgression*. Ithaca, N.Y.: Cornell University Press, 1986.

Stepp, Laura Sessions. "A Family at Cross-Purposes: Billy Graham's Sons Argue over a Final Resting Place." *Washington Post*, 13 December 2006 (accessed 14 December 2006). Available at http://www.washingtonpost.com/wp-dyn/content/article/2006/12/12/AR2006121201338_pf.html.

Storey, John. *Inventing Popular Culture*. Oxford: Blackwell, 2003.

————. "Rockin' Hegemony: West Coast Rock and Amerika's War in Vietnam." In *Cultural Theory and Popular Culture: A Reader*, ed. John Storey. 2nd ed, 225–235. Athens: University of Georgia Press, 1998.

Streissguth, Michael. *Johnny Cash at Folsom Prison: The Making of a Masterpiece*. Cambridge, Mass.: Da Capo, 2004.

————. *Johnny Cash: The Biography*. New York: Da Capo, 2006.

————, ed. *Ring of Fire: The Johnny Cash Reader*. Cambridge, Mass.: Da Capo, 2002.

Sundquist, Eric. *To Wake the Nations: Race in the Making of American Literature*. Cambridge, Mass.: Harvard University Press, 1993.

Sweeting, Adam. "Southern Comfort." *The Johnny Cash & June Carter Cash International Fan Club Newsletter*, June 1989, 28.

Thompson, Stephen I. "Forbidden Fruit: Interracial Love Affairs in Country Music." *Popular Music and Society* 13, no. 2 (summer 1989): 23–37.

Tichi, Cecelia. *High Lonesome: The American Culture of Country Music*. Chapel Hill: University of North Carolina Press, 1994.

———, ed. *Reading Country Music: Steel Guitars, Opry Stars, and Honky-Tonk Bars*. Durham, N.C.: Duke University Press, 1998.

Torn, Luke. "Still Keeping His Eyes Wide Open." *Wall Street Journal*, 15 November 2002, W11.

Tosches, Nick. *Country: The Twisted Roots of Rock 'n' Roll*. New York: Da Capo, 1996 (1977).

Tucker, Stephen. "Pentecostalism and Popular Culture in the South: A Study of Four Musicians." *Journal of Popular Culture* 16, no. 3 (1982): 68–80.

Turner, Frederick Jackson. *History, Frontier, and Section: Three Essays*. Albuquerque: University of New Mexico Press, 1993.

Turner, Steve. *The Man Called Cash: The Life, Love, and Faith of an American Legend*. Nashville: Thomas Nelson, 2004.

Urbanski, Dave. *The Man Comes Around: The Spiritual Journey of Johnny Cash*. Lake Mary, Fla.: Relevant Books, 2003.

Wald, Gayle F. *Shout, Sister, Shout! The Untold Story of Rock-and-Roll Trailblazer Sister Rosetta Tharpe*. Boston: Beacon, 2007.

Wald, Priscilla. *Constituting Americans: Cultural Anxiety and Narrative Form*. Durham, N.C.: Duke University Press, 1995.

Walk the Line. Directed by James Mangold. Performed by Joaquin Phoenix and Reese Witherspoon. 20th Century Fox, 2005.

Walser, Rob. *Running with the Devil: Power, Gender, and Madness in Heavy Metal Music*. Hanover, N.H.: University Press of New England, 1993.

Warner, Marina. *Monuments and Maidens: The Allegory of the Female Form*. London: Weidenfeld and Nicolson, 1985.

Weller, Jack E. *Yesterday's People: Life in Contemporary Appalachia*. Lexington: University Press of Kentucky, 1965.

Wenner, Jan. "The New Bob Dylan: A Little Like Johnny Cash?" *Rolling Stone*, 6 April 1968.

West, Cornel. *Democracy Matters: Winning the Fight against Imperialism*. New York: Penguin, 2004.

Whiteley, Sheila. "Little Red Rooster v. The Honky Tonk Woman: Mick Jagger, Sexuality, Style, and Image." In *Sexing the Groove: Popular Music and Gender*, ed. Sheila Whiteley, 67–99. London: Routledge, 1997.

———, ed. *Sexing the Groove: Popular Music and Gender*. London: Routledge, 1997.

———. *Women and Popular Music: Sexuality, Identity and Subjectivity*. London: Routledge, 2000.

Wilentz, Sean. *Chants Democratic: New York City and the Rise of the American Working Class, 1788–1850*. New York: Oxford University Press, 1984.

Williams, Raymond. *The Long Revolution*. Harmondsworth: Penguin, 1965.

Williams, Roger. *Sing a Sad Song: The Life of Hank Williams*. 2nd ed. Urbana: University of Illinois Press, 1981.

Willman, Chris. *Rednecks & Bluenecks: The Politics of Country Music*. New York: New Press, 2005.

Wolfe, Charles. "Postlude." In *A Boy Named Sue: Gender and Country Music*, ed. Kristine M. McCusker and Diane Pecknold, 196–198. Jackson: University Press of Mississippi, 2004.

Wren, Christopher S. *Winners Got Scars, Too: The Life of Johnny Cash*. New York: Ballantine, 1971.

Zak, Albin J., III. *The Poetics of Rock: Cutting Tracks, Making Records*. Berkeley: University of California Press, 2001.

Zwonitzer, Mark, with Charles Hirshberg. *Will You Miss Me When I'm Gone? The Carter Family and Their Legacy in American Music*. New York: Simon & Schuster, 2002.

Index

White, Josh, Jr., 39
"White Girl," 122
Whiteley, Sheila, 66, 69, 91, 202n10
Whiteside, Jonny, 115–116
Whitman, Walt, 7, 55
"Why Me Lord?" 102
Wilco, in alternative country, 43
Williams, Hank, 11–12, 21, 33, 125; challeng-
   ing gender roles, 86–87; dualisms of coun-
   try music and, 9, 158; sound of, 28, 46
Williams, Hank, Jr., 88
Williams, Hank, III, 43, 153–154
Williams, Raymond, 11
Williams, Tennessee, 98
Willman, Chris, 6, 153; on conservatives and
   Cash, 138–139; on politics in country mu-
   sic, 129, 131–132
Wilson, Brian, 187
Wilson, Owen, 187–188
Winston, Nat, 169
Wolfe, Charles, 3, 11, 68
women: as labor partners, 79, 144; as ram-
   blers, 13, 85–86, 88–91
women's movement, 37
Wooley, Sheb, 142

working class, 53, 149; angst of, 89–90,
   127–128; Cash seen as spokesman for,
   132–137, 143–144; in Cash's concept
   albums, 112–113, 140–141, 147; Cash's
   voice appealing to, 44–45; country music
   standing for, 152; frustration of, 30, 86,
   96–97; Jesus as common man, 164, 166;
   labor of, 75–80, 78; masculinity of, 70,
   96–97, 101–102; solidarity of, 112–113,
   142–143. *See also* class; Southern white
   working class
World War II, 86, 130
"The World's Gonna Fall on You," 144
"Worried Man," 151
"Wreck of the Old '97," 76, 78
Wren, Christopher S., 58

"You Remember Me," 105
"You'll Get Yours, I'll Get Mine," 166
"You're My Baby" (or "Little Wooly
   Booger"), 90
"You're the Nearest Thing to Heaven," 84,
   104

Zak, Albin, 45

LEIGH H. EDWARDS is Associate
Professor of English at Florida State
University. Her areas of specialization
include nineteenth- and twentieth-
century U.S. literature and popular
culture with a focus on American
studies and media studies approaches.